DUTCH GENEALOGY

The Reformed Protestant Dutch Church of Bergen [Jersey City], New Jersey, 1666-1788

The Holland Society of New York

HERITAGE BOOKS
2010

HERITAGE BOOKS
AN IMPRINT OF HERITAGE BOOKS, INC.

Books, CDs, and more—Worldwide

For our listing of thousands of titles see our website
at
www.HeritageBooks.com

A Facsimile Reprint
Published 2010 by
HERITAGE BOOKS, INC.
Publishing Division
100 Railroad Ave. #104
Westminster, Maryland 21157

— Publisher's Notice —

This book was originally published in three volumes. In this reprint of 1913, 1914, and 1915 originals, Heritage Books, Inc. has combined the sections specific to the Reformed Protestant Dutch Church into a single collection. The pages are not, therefore, consecutively numbered, and the table of contents and list of illustrations have been modified appropriately.

In reprints such as this, it is often not possible to remove blemishes from the original. We feel the contents of this book warrant its reissue despite these blemishes and hope you will agree and read it with pleasure.

International Standard Book Numbers
Paperbound: 978-0-7884-0635-5
Clothbound: 978-0-7884-8440-7

CONTENTS

BERGEN RECORDS:	PAGE
Introduction	1
Historical Sketch	5
Baptisms	20
Index	109

BERGEN RECORDS (2ND BOOK):	PAGE
Founding of Jersey City [Bergen]	1
Stuyvesant Statue in Bergen	55
Marriages in Bergen	57
Index	81

BERGEN RECORDS (3RD BOOK):	PAGE
The First Settlers of Bergen	1
Burials in Bergen	21
Church Members in Bergen	57
Minutes of the Consistory	79
Index	83

ILLUSTRATIONS

1913 PAGE

Henry L. Bogert, President—Portrait ... Frontispiece
Bergen—The First Church and Stockade....... 1
Half Moon—Initial Letter.................... 1
Seal—Amsterdam in New Netherland......... 3
Rev. Cornelius Brett—Portrait................ 4
Bergen—The Second Church; Pryors Mill at foot of Hill.................................. 5
The First Parsonage—Initial Letter............ 5
The First Church of Bergen.................. 6
The Door Stone of the First Church............ 6
The Second Church of Bergen................. 8
The Door Stone of the Second Church......... 8
The Present Church of Bergen................ 9
The Door Stone of Present Church............ 9
Seal—The Bergen church.................... 11
Seal—The Reformed church.................. 12
Coat of Arms—Van Winkle.................. 15
Bergen Petition for a Clergyman.............. 16-19

1914

William L. Brower, President—Portrait ... Frontispiece
Communipaw—Heading Cut.................. 1
Map of Bergen 1660......................... 3
Arms of Jacob Walingsen Van Winkle........... 25
Arms of Hartman-Vreeland.................... 52
The First Stone Church at Bergen............. 53
Peter Stuyvesant Statue...................... 54
Bergen Village 1680......................... 55
John Grier Hibben, LL.D.—Portrait........... 86

1915

William L. Brower, President—Portrait ... Frontispiece
Communipaw—Heading Cut.................. 1
The First Schoolhouse in Bergen—Initial Letter.. 1
Register of Members—First Page.............. 56
Town of Bergen—Heading Cut................ 57
Edward Van Winkle, Recording Secretary—Portrait.................................... 78
Bergen Hill—Heading Cut.................... 79
Seward G. Spoor, Corresponding Secretary—Portrait.................................... 82
Arthur H. Van Brunt, Treasurer—Portrait....... 92

YEAR BOOK

OF

The Holland Society

OF

New York

1913

BERGEN BOOK

PREPARED BY THE RECORDING SECRETARY

Executive Office
90 West Street
NEW YORK CITY

A

PRESIDENT 1912

OF

THE HOLLAND SOCIETY OF NEW YORK

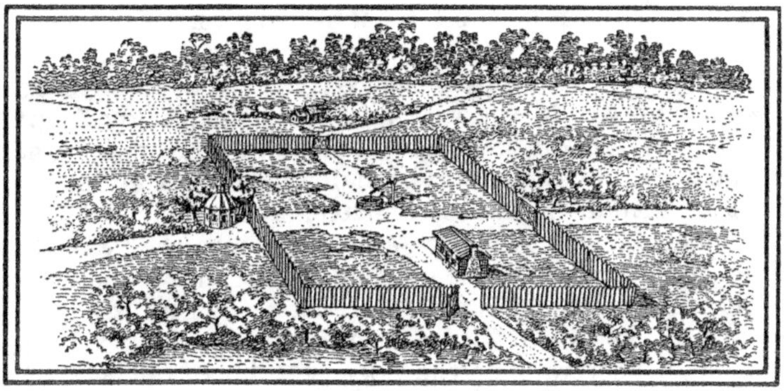

THE BERGEN CHURCH RECORDS

Mijne Heeren,

THE genealogical records of The Reformed Protestant Dutch Church of Bergen, now Jersey City, N. J., will appear in the Year Books for 1913, 1914 and 1915. The present book contains the Register of Baptisms from 1666 to 1788. The Year Book for 1914 will contain the Marriages and the Register of Members; while the Burials, Minutes of the Consistory, etc., will appear in the Year Book for 1915.

The records, as they are here presented, have had unusual care in preparation and have withstood the criticism of reviewers, many years, without showing any flaw. As early as 1880 Theodore Melvin Banta obtained permission from the Consistory of the Bergen Church to copy the "Church book" and in 1888, Thomas Edward Vermilye, Jr., as a member of a special committee of the Society on Records of the Ancient Dutch Churches of America, made a literal translation on loose leaves which is now in the library, marked for identification, Copy A, page 1–215, and which contains the "Register of Members and Baptisms". In the same year Dingman Versteeg, our present library clerk, copied

copied and translated the Marriages, Burial Records, and Minutes of the Consistory, marked Copy A, page 217–314. Both of these translations were made under the direction and supervision of Theodore Melvin Banta as chairman of the committee, above referred to, of which Mr. Vermilye was a member. In the years 1899 to 1903 a tabular transcript of the above-mentioned records was made in a bound volume by Sterling Potter, and marked Copy B, under Mr. Banta's personal direction as Secretary of the Society. This book was then taken over to Jersey City, carefully compared with and corrected from the original by Dingman Versteeg, covering a period of many days. The Reverend Cornelius Brett, D. D., present pastor of the Bergen Church, has spoken with full appreciation of the "patient, painstaking work" of Mr. Versteeg and is on record as to the accuracy of this contribution to the colonial history of the church and New Jersey.

The Register of Baptisms, printed in this volume, is complete, commencing January 1, 1666, continuing to December 18, 1788. There appears to be a break, from 1669 to 1673, of four years, during which time the children may have been entered upon the records of New York or other churches. In after years it frequently occurs that children, born at Bergen, were baptized in New York, the record appearing "baptized in New York".

In presenting this Register of Baptisms in tabular form, all notes given in the original record of a genealogical value have been printed as foot notes at the bottom of each page. Items such as:—"born at 2 P. M." and "Born on Thursday at midnight" have been purposely omitted. In two instances where children were born "out of wedlock" wherein the surname assumed by the child is not given, the entries have also been omitted because of no genealogical value.

All names have been faithfully copied as they appear with all the variations in spellings and errors of the voorlesers; and where omissions occur, even though possible to supply, no inserts have been made. The record is thought to be truly represented. All entries

have

have been arranged in the order of their dates of baptism and consecutively numbered for convenience in indexing.

This work is published in the most likely form which it would have assumed if printed at the time the original entries were made by Bonaventure and Abraham Elzevier, who were the most famous printers of that time. The Elzeviers or Elseviers were a family of famous printers and booksellers of Leyden and afterward Amsterdam; no fewer than fifteen of whom carried on the business in succession from 1580 to 1712. Their *Pliny* (1635), *Virgil* (1636) and *Cicero* (1642) are the masterpieces of their press, and in elegance of design, neatness, clearness and regularity of type, and beauty of paper cannot be surpassed. As far as practicable their typography and all of the peculiar characteristics of their works have been carefully followed. The use of catch-words, signature lettering and half measure foot notes have been imitated exactly. The paper used in this book has been made to imitate the old paper of that day and the button of the Society is reproduced as a watermark. All of the illustrations have been made and engraved after the style of wood cuts then so popular. These cuts were engraved from photographs and descriptions and are historically correct as to detail and ensemble.

The index was carefully prepared by William B. Van Alstyne, M.D., a member of our society who makes a specialty in statistical and genealogical work.

The

EYNDE

Cornelius Brett

PRESENT DOMINE

OF THE

REFORMED PROTESTANT DUTCH CHURCH

JERSEY CITY, NEW JERSEY

THE REFORMED PROTESTANT DUTCH CHURCH
of
BERGEN IN NEW JERSEY
FOUNDED 1660

Historical Note

THE second Indian War in 1655 resulted in the destruction of every bouwerij on the west of the North River. The inhabitants fled to the shelter of New Amsterdam and only the Aborigines were left in possession. As this was the second incident of this character in the early history of New Netherland, Peter Stuyvesant wisely ordered that no settlement should be allowed on the west side of the river except in concentrated villages, which could be easily protected and defended. This decree opened the way for a petition presented to the Council at New Amsterdam during the summer of 1660 praying for permission to found a village on the highlands about two miles from the North River. The petition was granted and between August and October of that year the village of Bergen was founded. The lines of the village are still marked by the streets of Jersey City which surround and pass through it. An open square was reserved with two streets running nearly north and south and east and west meeting in the center. The village was protected by by a rectangular palisade, with a gate at the center of each side. Later a well was dug in the middle of the open square and a corner lot was reserved for a school. With the village came also the church and the school:

in fact a condition made by each pioneer in accepting a grant of village lot or outlying farm was, that ministers of the Reformed faith should be provided and the education of the children secured.

In 1661 the first municipality was created in the form of an inferior court whose decisions were subject to appeal in the general court in New Amsterdam.

In 1662 Englebert Steenhuysen was engaged as voorleser and schoolmaster. His contract required him to teach the children in his own house and to conduct a service on each Lord's day, reading from a printed sermon in Dutch, furnished by The Classis of Amsterdam. There is also on file

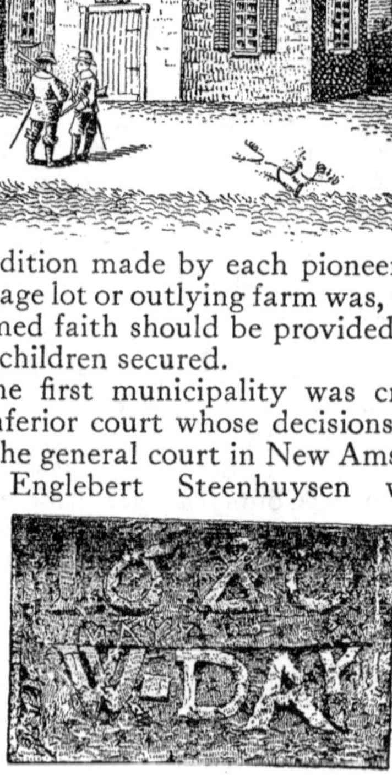

file in Albany a subscription list dated 1662[1]. In 1664 the record of members of the church in full communion begins. The earliest records are in the handwriting of D^om. Henricus Selyns, a minister of the church of Breuckelen, Long Island, and later, after 1682, of the church of New York. In this original list we find the names of eighteen women and nine men. The record is evidently a copy from some earlier document and the break from the beautiful handwriting of the dominie to current entries is plainly discerned. The earliest services were probably conducted, like the school, in a private house: but tradition says there was built, within a few years, a log house, which served the double purpose of school and church. The first stone church was octagonal.[2] It stood south of the village just outside the palisade. One side of the interior was occupied by the pulpit opposite the door: three sides on the right and left of the door were provided with plain wooden seats, while the open space was filled with straight back chairs. The bell[3] hung in the peak of the roof and was rung by a rope which hung in the center.

A succession of voorlesers followed Steenhuysen who left no records. In 1665 Reynier Bastiaense Van Giesen was installed and for forty-two years continued in office. He was succeeded in 1708 by Adriaen Vermeule who served for twenty-eight years and who formerly occupied the same position and that of town clerk at Niew Haarlem. In 1726 P. Van Benthuyzen began his work. After twenty-five years the last voorleser, Abraham Sickels, was installed. During his term of office the first pastor arrived and thereafter the name of "clerk" was substituted for the old title "voorleser". The first clerk was John Collard who received a salary of £2, 15 shillings per annum.

During

[1]Ed. Note: This list is reproduced on pages 16, 17 and 18. A translation of it can be found on pages 13 and 14.

[2]Ed. Note: Built in 1680; octagonal, size—about 20 feet in diameter. Illustrated on page 6.

Door stone set May 20, 1680. Illustrated on page 6.

R^ev. Casparus Van Zuuren, of Long Island, preached the dedicatory sermon May 23, 1681.

Collection at dedication—97 guilders, 10 stivers ($39.20).

Built by William Day, Steven Cortland, Johannis Van Giesen, Cornelis Hopper and Claas Arense. (Toers)—at a cost of 2612 guilders ($1,044.80).

[3]Ed. Note: The first bell was installed in 1683.

During the period of voorlesers the sacraments were administered by ministers from the church of New York; they also seemed to have supervised the records which are preserved with remarkable fidelity.

In 1750 Peter DeWint arrived from the Netherlands and was recognized as pastor, but an irregularity in his ordination was discovered and he was compelled to retire. The first pastor was William Jackson. In 1753 a call was made on this young man by the churches of Bergen and Staten Island.

The condition of the call was that he was to study in a university of Holland and receive ordination from the Classis of Amsterdam. He returned in 1757 and assumed his duties as pastor. He resided in a stone parsonage which stood on the site of the porch of the present church. After a service of thirty-two years, Mr. Jackson was compelled to retire on account of a nervous strain. The consistory secured him the use

use of the parsonage during his life, and he remained twenty-four years as the ward of his old friends.

On the twenty-sixth day of May, 1793, the Rev.

John Cornelison was ordained and installed. A house[1] was purchased for him near Bergen Square where he lived until his death on the twentieth of March, 1828. Two months after the death of Mr. Cornelison, the Rev. Benjamin C. Taylor was called and remained an active pastor for forty-four years, when he was made Pastor Emeritus and resided with his people ten years longer[2].

During the ministry of William Jackson a new church

was

[1]Ed. Note: The Cornelius Sip house on the North-west corner of the square. Costing £605. in 1793.

[2]Ed. Note: Do. Taylor particularly distinguished himself by writing the annals of the classis and township of Bergen.

was built[1], on the old Dutch models, in 1773, and in 1841 it was found that this edifice was too small to accommodate the growing congregation. As the building stood in the cemetery, surrounded by graves, it could not be enlarged without disturbing the remains of the departed. The old building was torn down and its successor erected on a portion of the old "Glebe". The old stones from the first two churches were used in the new walls. It was dedicated in 1842[2] and still remains as the house of worship of the modern congregation.

When Dr. Taylor retired in 1871, Rev. James L. Amerman was installed as pastor. He remained only five years, when he listened to a call from Japan and went out to be professor of theology in the theological seminary at Tokio.

In August, 1876, the Rev. Cornelius Brett, D.D., was installed as pastor and still remains at his post. The Rev. William Van Duzen Strong was assistant pastor for two and a half years, and the same office is now held by Rev. Abram Duryee. Rev. John J. Moment also served as associate pastor for three years.

The

[1]Built in 1773; Size (45 x 60 feet). Illustrated on page 8.

Rev. William Jackson preached the dedicatory sermon.

Building Committee: Daniel Van Winkel, William Jackson, and Johanus Van Houten.

Hendrick Van Winkel surveyed the church land.

Exact cost appears to be missing. From May 17 to October 17, 1773, £362 was laid out for material and labor.

The door stone of this church is shown on page 8.

[2]Ed. Note: Built in 1841; Size (64 x 84 feet). Illustrated on page 9.

Corner Stone laid August 26, 1841.

Reverend Benjamin C. Taylor preached the dedicatory sermon, July 14, 1842.

Building Committee: Jacob D. Van Winkel, Garrit Sip, Abraham Vreeland.

Builders, William H. Kirk & Company and Clark & Van Nest of Newark, New Jersey, at a cost of approximately $9,905.00, which was amount received from sale of pews to highest bidders.

The door stone illustrated on page 9 is over the south door to basement, assembled with the door stones of the two previous churches. These can be seen to-day. The engravings were made from photographs.

"THE RECORD OF 1662"

A Translation and Reproduction of the Original

DOCTOR Cornelius Brett, the present pastor of the Dutch Reformed Church, in Jersey City, in his historical sketch, refers to an early subscription list now on file in Albany. Through the courtesy of A. J. F. van Laer, archivist in charge of the manuscripts section of the New York State Library in Albany, New York, the document was located and photographed. This record has never been photographically reproduced before but a translation appears in the Documents Relative to the Colonial History of New York, Vol. 13, page 232–233. In that translation the name of the well-known notary Tielman van Vleeck is printed, unfortunately, both in the signature to the petition and in the list of subscribers, as Tielman van Neeck.

The original document went through the recent Albany fire and was fortunately not destroyed. After the letter from Mr. van Laer of June 22, 1912, explaining this fact follows a translation of the petition which is photographically reproduced on pages 16, 17 and 18.

New York State Educational Department
NEW YORK STATE LIBRARY,
JAMES I. WYER, JR., Director.

MANUSCRIPTS SECTION,
A. J. F. VAN LAER,
Archivist.

ALBANY, N. Y., June 22, 1912.

MR. EDWARD VAN WINKLE,
90 West Street,
New York City.

DEAR SIR:—

At Mr. Huyck's[1] request we have had photographs made of the "List of those at Bergen who subscribed for a clergyman," of 1662, which is found on pages 279 and 280 of volume 10 of our New York

[1]Edmund N. Huyck, Esq., Vice President of the Holland Society, Albany County.

New York Colonial Manuscripts. I understand that the photographs have been sent to Mr. Huyck, so that you will doubtless receive them soon. Mr. Huyck has also asked me to give you a statement regarding the manner in which this particular document was saved from the flames on March 29, 1911. Inasmuch as this document was mounted in a volume which was carried out after the fire, together with hundreds of other volumes which were more or less damaged by the fire, there is nothing to be said that applies especially to this document. As you will notice from the photographs, the document is badly burned at the top. All the documents that were bound with it present the same appearance and the damage is accounted for by the fact that the volume, together with five other volumes of Council Minutes, stood on a high shelf, immediately under a wooden gallery, which was swept by the flames and completely destroyed. The fire apparently worked its way down, leaving a sort of a mound in the center of the wall case, of which the shelf just mentioned formed the highest point. Other volumes of manuscripts, which stood on lower shelves, near the center of the case, suffered comparatively little; they were evidently covered by debris, or had fallen in a heap, before the flames could reach them. On the other hand, many volumes, which were placed on lower shelves near the ends of the room, and in a double-faced case in the middle of the room, were completely destroyed. All that was left of the manuscript collection was after the fire carefully dug out of the ashes and debris and removed to the old armory, now occupied by the Catholic Union, on Eagle Street and Hudson Avenue, where the water-soaked documents were taken from their mounts and dried between blotting paper. At present we are busy repairing, remounting and arranging the thousands of colonial and state documents that were saved. Many will look neater and fresher than I have ever known them before; on the other hand, thousands of documents, among them the manuscript reproduced for you, will forever bear the marks of the terrible ordeal they went through.

Very truly yours,
(Signed)
A. J. F. van Laer, Archivist.

Petition

PETITION OF THE MAGISTRATES OF BERGEN, ASKING TO BE PROVIDED WITH A CLERGYMAN

To the Noble, Very Worshipful, his Honor, the Director-General and the Honorable Council of New Netherland

Show with due reverence the Schepens of the village of Bergen, that whereas your petitioners have observed and considered the fatherly direction and care of your Hon[ble] Worships regarding the erection of churches and school-houses, more especially that a God fearing man and preacher be secured to promote and teach the fear of the Lord in the community of Bergen and its jurisdiction; Therefore, the Schepens have thought it advisable, each for himself, to propose it, to learn what every man would be willing to pay yearly of his free will, affection and love for God's holy and blessed word, to have a good teacher, till such a time, when the Noble Lords-Directors of the Incorporated West-India Company shall begin, according to the custom of the country, to levy tithes. After the Schepens had made these propositions, the below named persons have voluntarily declared, that they will give a yearly contribution; the sum to be paid by such voluntary offerings may be calculated at 417 guilders in wampum, but there are among these people some, who have expressed themselves willing to do more according to their abilities if God our Lord would bless them and increase their prosperity; among the others, opposite whose names no sums are mentioned, there are some very willing, some very unwise, those, who are willing, are the majority and declare, that when a preacher comes, they too would do their best according to their circumstances, like the others. Whereas the petitioners do not know, whether the people of Haersimons* come under this jurisdiction; therefore the petitioners cannot report, what they would do, but the Schepens find it advisable and

*Ahasimus.

and very necessary, that the village be provided with a preacher and submit to the mature consideration and decision of your Hon[ble] Worships, that it might be notified to the Noble Lords-Directors, our Patroons, by the next ships. Your Hon[ble] Worships know, with what courage the village of Bergen has been established by the community and that the same has maintained itself at great expense to the inhabitants, without any outlay to the Lords-Directors. The community is therefore of opinion, that their Noble Honors should take that into consideration and therefore assist the village of Bergen so much readier according to their discretion and to send one over for one or two years at their expense; during that time the land will with God's help have increased in value, so that then that which the good hearted community will liberally give, can be taken for assistance. Awaiting your Hon[ble] Worships' decision hereon the petitioners remain

Your Noble, Honorable Worships' humble servants

TIELMAN VAN VLEECK
MACHGHYEL JANSEN[1]
HERMAN SMEDMAN
CASPER STEINMETZ.

List of the voluntary contributors, with the sum promised by each.

Tielman van Vleeck	50	Douwe Harmens	6
Michielsen Jansen[1]	25	Jacob Sergiant	8
Harmen Smedeman	25	Arent Louwerens	10
Casper Steinmetz	25	Jan Cornelis	3
Jan Schulten	25	Jan Cornelis the rich	10
Michiele Teunissen	6	Thomas the cooper	3
Jan Lubbersen	6	Cornelis Abrahams	6
Dirck Gerritsen	20	Claes Pietersen Cos of Gemenepa	50
Jacob Leendersen	25	Evert Coertsen	13
Jan the Englishman	6	Dirck Classen	10
Paulus Pietersen	25	Jan Loserecht	6
Willem Jansen	10	Gerrit Gerritsen	6
Joost van Linden	10	Claes Arentsen	8
Adrian Post	20		f 417

List

[1]Ed. Note: Michiel Jansen Vreeland, also Machghyel Jansz Van Schrabbekerke: Vreeland is one of the polders under the authority of Schrabbekerke.

List of those, who are willing, but give no specified sum, keeping it at their discretion.

Jan Swaen
Hendrick Teunissen
Dirck Teunissen
Engelbert Steenhuisen
Widow Pieter Rudolpsen
Harmen Edwarts
Nicolas Verlet

Louerens Andries
Claessie Teuniss, the widow of Romein Teuniss

Refused have

Tyes Lubbersen, Henrich Jansen Spyer, Frerick the cobbler.

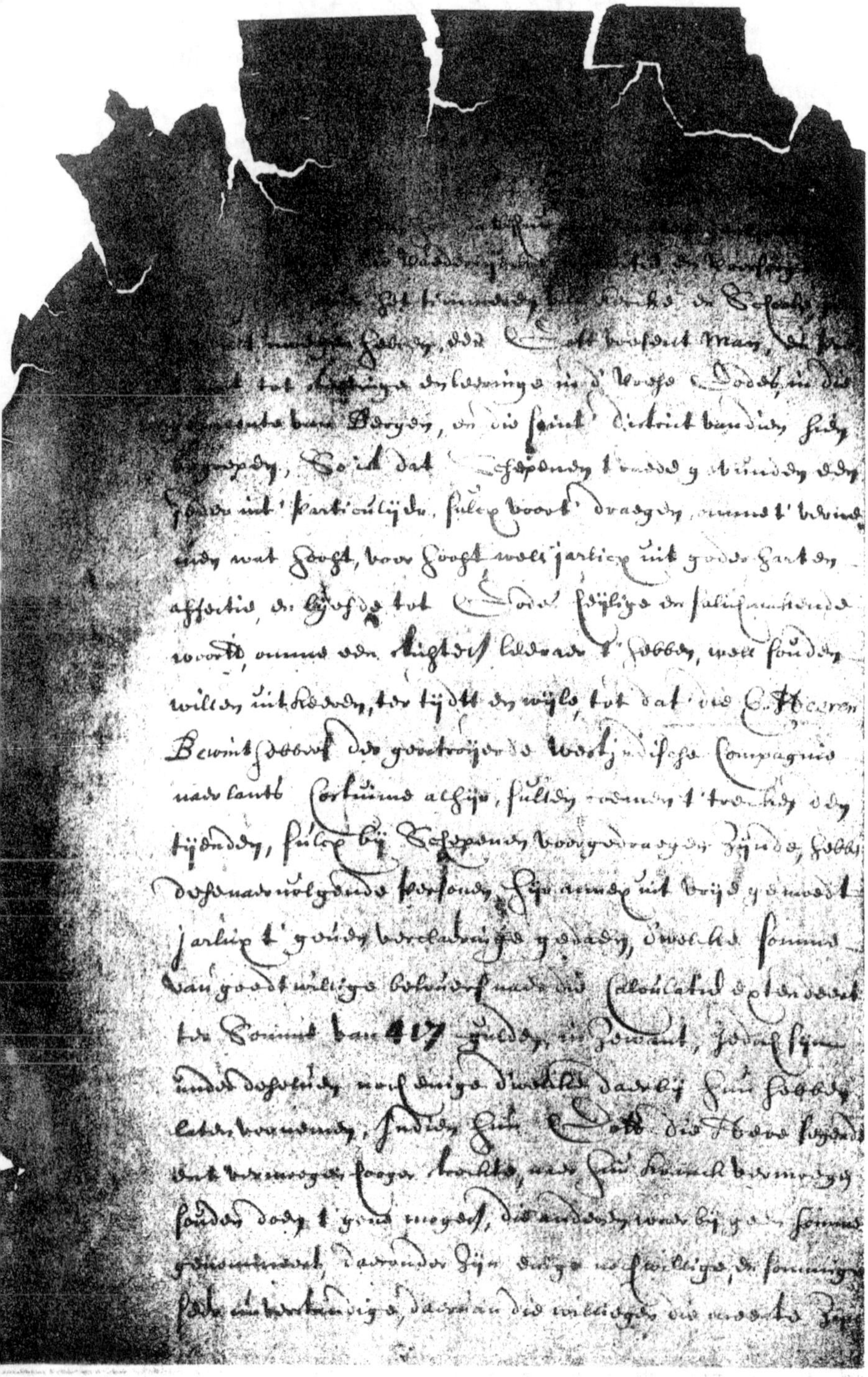

[illegible]
[illegible] met [illegible]
Compagnie van [illegible]
met een Predicant [illegible]
in rijpe deliberatie van d' E. gr. [illegible]
sie, t'gene bij t' Vertrek van [illegible]
E. Heeren Bewint hebbers [illegible]
notificeert worden, u E. gr. A. [illegible]
Couragie hebt Dorp Bergen bij die gemeente [illegible]
en dat met heure Costen van d' inwoonders, [illegible]
[illegible] van d' E. Heeren Bewint hebbers
daerom die gemeente, dat sulcx bij die E. [illegible]
worden geconsidereert, omme t' mede den [illegible]
daerome nae haer hooge discretie [illegible] de
grijpen, en op die sake of [illegible] tot heure [illegible]
oversenden, tegens welcken tijdt t' Landt [illegible]
vermogen, mit Godeshulpe salt hun [illegible]
tot dat t'gene so die goedthartige gemeente [illegible]
te geven willen tot suffisantie kan worden
Verwachtende hier over die supplianten u E. [illegible]
resolutie, dit doende
Verblijvende u E. gr. [illegible]
dienaers
[illegible]
[illegible]
[illegible]
[illegible]

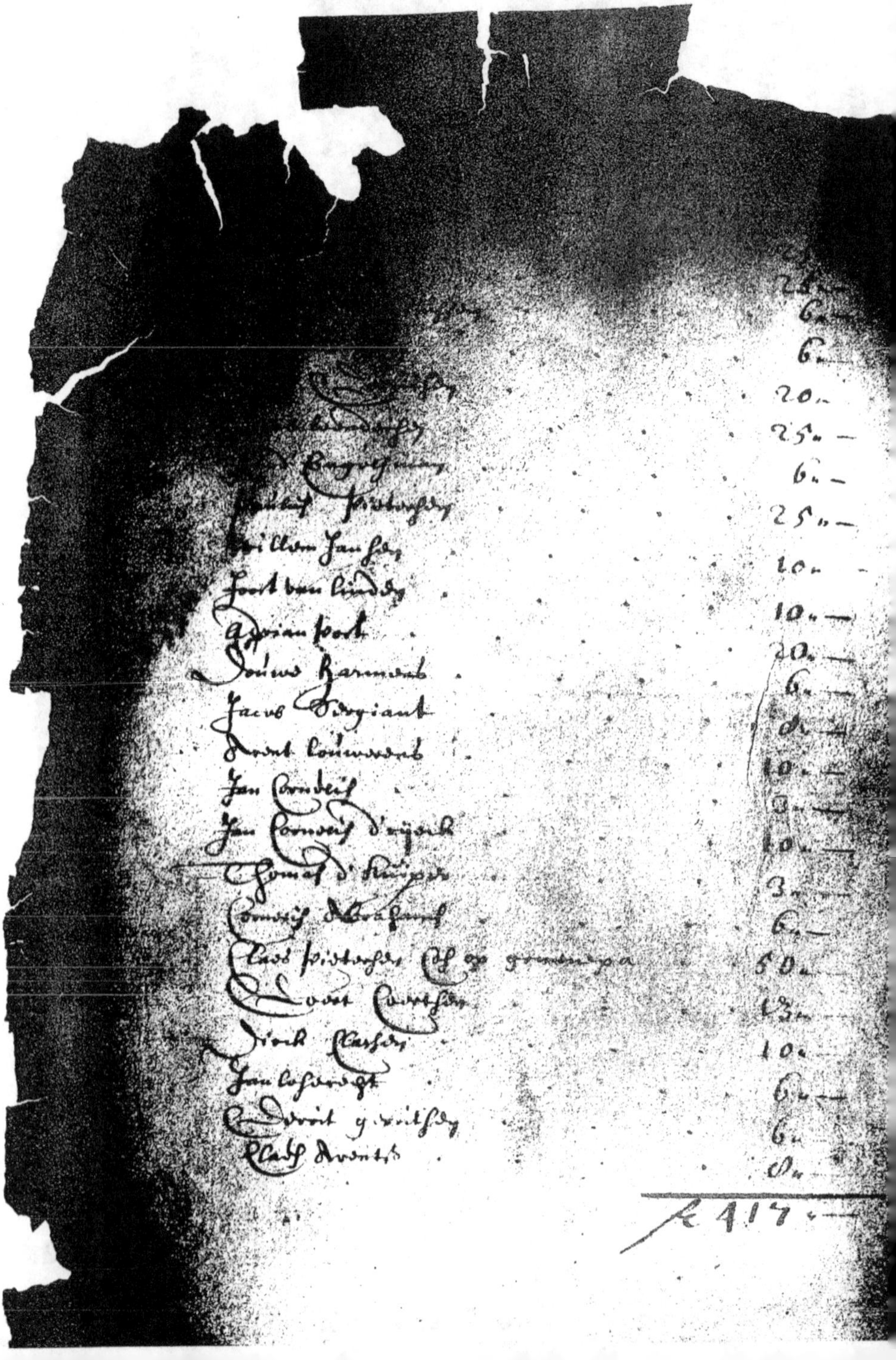

[illegible]	2[illegible]
[illegible]	25
[illegible]sen	6
[illegible]	6
[illegible]sen	20
[illegible]ndersen	25
[illegible] Burgersen	6
[illegible] Pietersen	25
Willem Jansen	10
Joost van Linden	10
Adriaen Post	20
Jonas Harmans	6
Jacob Sergiant	[illegible]
Aert Louwerens	10
Jan Cornelis	[illegible]
Jan Cornelis de Rijck	10
Thomas de Kuyper	3
Cornelis de Brasser	6
Claes Pietersen Cos op Gemoenepa	50
Joost Carstsen	13
Dirck Claesen	10
Jan [illegible]	6
Hendrick Gerritsen	6
Claes Arentsen	[illegible]
	f 417

BAPTISMS IN THE VILLAGE OF BERGEN IN NEW JERSEY BEGINNING 1666

1666 NO.	PARENTS	CHILD	WITNESSES & SPONSORS
1	Pieter Jansen Slot Merritje Jacobs	Jan (Son) bp. Jan. 1	Elyas Michielse Styntie Jacobs
2	Lourus Andriense Jannetje Jans	Pieter bp. Jan. 1	Aennetje Lucas, wife of Lucas Dirckse Merritje Lucas
3	Jde van voorst Hellitje Jans	Joanna bp. Apr. 16	Sr. N. Varlet Cornel Klopper Jannetje Steynmets
4	Sjoert Olfertse Jittje Roels	Annetje bp. June 10	Pieter Merse with his wife
5	Cristiaen Pieterse Treyntje Cornelis	Metje bp. Aug. 19	Jde van voorst Merritje Cornelis
6	Ritsert Eerle Elysabet Eerle	Andree bp. Nov. 4	Merritje Loockermans Aeltje van Kouwenhoven Mr. Sam. Edsal B. Bayard Christiaen Pieterse
7	Ritsert Eerle Elysabet Eerle	Elysabet bp. Nov. 4	Merritje Loockermans Aeltje van Kouwenhoven Mr. Sam. Edsal B. Bayard Christiaen Pieterse

NO.	PARENTS	CHILD	WITNESSES & SPONSORS
			1666
8	Jan Straetmaker Geesje Gerrits	Jannetje bp. Dec. 26	Casperus Steynmets with his wife
9	Reynier Van Giesen Dirckje Cornelis	Abraham bp. Dec. 26	Sr. N. Varlet Hermen Smee Elyas Magielse Miss Anna Stuyvesant
10	Reynier Van Giesen Dirckje Cornelis	Isaack bp. Dec. 26	Jde van voorst Hans Didericks Janneke Edsall
		1667	
11	Claes Jansen Annetje Cornelis	Lysbet bp. Mar. 10	Pieter Jansen Geertje Dircks
12	Gerrit Gerritse Annetje Hermans	Hermanus	Casparus Steynmets Hellitje Jans
13	Lourus Duyts Grietje Jans	Catreyn	Pieter Mercelis and his wife
14	Paulus Pieters Treyntje Maertens	Cristina bp. Apr. 14	Hermen Eduwaertse Jenneke Edsall
15	Hendrick Tonise Grietje Samuels	Treyntje bp. Aug. 15	Guert Gerritse Treyntje Symons
16	Samuel Edsall Jenneke Edsall	Joanna bp. Sept. 4	Sr. N. Bayard Hendrickje Wessels
17	Jan Evertse Kerseboom Grietje Jaspers	Aennetje bp. Oct. 19	Paulus Cornelis Merritje Jacobs
18	Hendrick vandewater Grietje Vermeulen	Marey bp. Nov. 3	Mr. Hans Kiersteede, Jr. Mareya Vermeulen Young woman
19	Jan Lubbertse Maddeleentje Jans	Johannes bp. Nov. 3	Pieter Janse Steenhalder with his wife
20	Gerrit Tysen Hermptje Hermans	Pieter	Symon Carelss, Y. M. Carel Carelse, Y. M. Dickje Meyers, Y. D.
21	Arien van Laer Abigel verplanck	Zara	Abraham van Laer Mayritje Wernaers
22	Casper Steynmets Jannetje Gerrits	Joanna bp. Dec. 29	Jan Straetmaker Aennetje Corneliss

1668 NO.	PARENTS	CHILD	WITNESSES & SPONSORS
23	Hendrick Reycken Eytje Jacobs	Dirck bp. July 8	Hans Didericke Janneke Edsall
24	Thomas Fredrickse Merreytje Ariaens	Jannetje	Jan Loserecht Aennetje Hermens
25	Tys Lubberts Treyntje Jans	Aennetje Oct. 4	Hendrick Reycken Maddaleentje Jans
		1669	
26	Jan Straetmaker Geesje Gerrits	Annetje bp. Feb. 17	Guert Gerrits Janneke Edsall
27	Pieter Janse Slot Merritje Jacobs	Jacob	Magiel Tades Grietje Jacobs
28	Jan Evertse Kerseboom Grietje Jaspers	Annetje bp. Feb. 17	Cornelis Abrahamse Merritje Jacobs
		1673	
29	Dirck Janse van vogsten Elysabet Cornelis	Beelitje bp. Mar. 24	Pieter Mersilise with his wife
30	Matheus Cornelise Anna Lubi	Gerritje bp. June 23	Gerrit Gerritse Gerritje Cornelis
31	Jan Evertse Kerseboom Grietje Jaspers	Annetje bp. Oct. 9	Gerrit Gerritse Merritje Jacobz
32	Mr. Samuel Edsall Jenneke Edsall	Zara bp. Oct. 9	Warnaer Wessels Elyas Magielse Jannetje Magielse
		1674	
33	Tomas Steegh Margritje Steeghs	Jan bp. Mar. 27	Claes Arentse Toers Hertman Magielse Grietje Jacobs
34	Mr. Samuel Edsall	Banjamin bp. Oct. 22	Elyas Magielse Hillitje Jans
		1675	
35	Hertman Magielse Merritje Dirckse	Claes bp. Apr. 6	Dirck Claesen Braack Feytje Hertmans

NO.	PARENTS	CHILD	WITNESSES & SPONSORS
			1675
36	Gerrit Gerritse Annetje Hermans	Hendrick bp. Oct. 25	Engelbert Steen-Huys Jurien Thomase Annet Edsall, Y. D.
		1676	
37	Elyas Magielse Grietje Jacobs	Ragel bo. Mar. 8	
38	Pieter Cornelise Hendrickje Aerts	Cornelis Bo. Apr. 18	
39	Claes Janse Annetje Cornelis	Hendrick bo. Apr. 22	
40	Tonis Elisen Gerritje Gerrits	Hendrickje bp. May 22	Gerrit Tysen Pieter Hesselse Hermptje Hermens
41	Jan Straetmaker Geesje Gerrits	Gerrit bp. Oct. 2	Jacob Cornelis Annetje Steynmets, Y.W.
42	Jacob Jacobse Aeltje Daniels	Jacob bo. Sept. 19	
43	Symon Jacobs Annetje Ariaense	Margrietje ——[1]	
		1677	
44	Cornelis Barentse Cornelia Hendrickse	Barent bp. Apr. 17	R. van Giesen Johannes van Giesen, Y. M. Maddaleena van Giesen, Y. D.
45	Willem Janse Loserecht Beelitje Tysen	Hendrick bp. Apr. 17	Tys Barentse Annetje Hendrickse
46	Walingh Jacobse Catreyna Magielse	Magiel bo. Apr. 27	
47	Helmigh Roelof Jannetje Pieters	Roelof bo. June 11	
48	Hertman Magielse Merritje Dirckse	Aeltje bp. Oct. 8	Dirck Claese Braack Metje Dirckse, Y. W.

[1] Date entirely obliterated.

1677 NO.	PARENTS	CHILD	WITNESSES & SPONSORS
49	Pieter Hesselse Elysabet Gerrits	Merritje bp. Oct. 8	Guert Koerten Reyckje Hermens
		1678	
50	Gerrit Gerritse Annetje Hermens	Johannes bo. Jan. 11	
51	Arien Pieterse Buys Treyntje Hendrickse	Geertruyt bo. Jan. 15	Jan Cornelisse Buys Maddaleentje Jans
52	Adriaen Post Catreyna Gerrits	Adriaen bo. Jan. 24	
53	Matheus Cornelise Anna Lubi	Jacomeyntje bp. Apr. 2	Cornelis Roelofse Jannetje Pieters
54	Staets de Groot Berber Caspers	Metje bp. June 24	Dirck Gerrits and wife
55	Claes Janse Annetje Cornels	Geertje[1] bo. July 21	
56	Simon Jacobse Annetje Ariaense Sips	Jacob[1] bo. Aug. 9	
57	Elyas Magielse Grietje Jacobs	Jacob[1] bo. Aug. 9	
58	Cornelis Roelpfse Maddaleentje van Giesen	Gerritje[1] bo. Aug. 10	
59	Pieter Cornelisse Hendrickje Aerts	Arent bp. Oct. 7	Willem Hoppe, Y. M. Merritje Ariaense
60	Gerrit van Reenen Echtje Everts	Evert	Pieter Merselise Geertruyt Gerrits, widow
61	Jacob Jacobse Aeltje Daniels	Maragrietje bo. Oct. 22	
62	Hertman Magielse Merritje Dirckse	Magiel[1] bo. Dec. 31	
		1679	
63	Fredrick Tomasen Catreyna Hoppe	Andries bo. Jan. 1	
64	Tonis Roelofse Treyntje Claes	Gerritje bo. Jan. 10	

[1] Baptized at New York.

NO.	PARENTS	CHILD	WITNESSES & SPONSORS 1679
65	Hendrick Jorisz Claesje Cornelis	Geesje bo. Feb. 20	
66	Jan Lubbertse Maddaleentje Jans	Willem bp. Apr. 7	Gerbrant Claesen and his wife
67	Davit De-maree, the younger Ragel Cerson	Susana bp. Apr. 7	Jan De-mare Susan Cerson
68	Paulus Pieterse Treyntje Martens	Aeltje bp. June 23	Claes Arents Toers, Y.M. Metje Dirckse Braack, Y. W.
69	Jan Cornelise Bongert Angenietje Streyckers	Jacob	Jan Streycker Cornelis Janse Swaentje Jans
70	Gerbrant Claesen Merritje Claes	Herpert[1] bo. Nov. 12	
71	Arien Pieterse Buys Treyntje Hendrickse	Pieter[1] bo. Dec. 12	
72	Cornelis Roelofse Maddaleena van Giesen	Roelof[1] bo. Dec. 31	
		1680	
73	Adriaen Post Catreyna Gerrits	Gerrit[1] bo. Jan. 1	
74	Helmigh Roelofse Jannetje Pieters	Pieter[1] bo. Jan. 23	
75	Matheus Cornelisse Anna Lubi	Cornelis bo. Mar. 11 bp. Mar. 25	Jacob Lubi Catreyna Magielse
76	Pieter Hesselse Elysabet Gerrits	Johannes bp. Mar. 25	Johannes Magielse, Y.M. Metje Derckse Braack, Y. W.
77	Sjarel Huysman Adriaentje Dirckse	Marey	Davit de Maree Angenietje Streyckers
78	Tomas Tecxe Magrietje Tecx	Willem bp. Mar. 25	Jan Davitse Margarietje Krets

[1] **Baptized at New York.**

1680 NO.	PARENTS	CHILD	WITNESSES & SPONSORS
79	Walingh Jacobs Catreyna Magielse	Treyntje	Jacob Jacobse and his wife
80	Jan Cornelise Bongert Angenietje Stryckerz	Jacob bp. June 21	Jan Streycker Cornelis Janse Swaentje Jans
81	Davit de Maree the younger Ragel Cerson	Ragel bp. June 21	Mr. Pieter Cerson Ragel Cerson
82	Sibi Epkese Mareya Ariaense Sips	Annetje bo. Aug. 17 bp. Oct. 11	Hans Diderickse and his wife
83	Tonis Roelofse Treyntje Claes	Roelof[1] bo. Aug. 28	
84	Tades Magielse Annetje Steynmets	Magiel bp. Oct. 11	Johannes Steynmets Catreyna Magielse
85	Nicola Devouw Marey Csi?	Susanna	Davit De Maree and his wife
86	Claes Jansen Annetje Cornelis	Jacob bo. Oct. 10 bp. Oct. 11	Elyas Magielse Treyntje Claes
87	Hendrick Hoppe Marya Jans	Andries[2] bo. Dec. 21	
88	Hertman Magielse Merritje Dircks Braack	Dirck bo. Apr. 3	
		1681	
89	Hendrick Jorise Claesje Cornelis	Margrietje[3] bp. June 13	Jan Cornelis Bongert Angenietje Streyckers
90	Johannes Spier Merreytje Franse	Hendrick[4]	Kersten de Schemaker Hillitje Jans
91	Jacob Jacobse Aeltje Daniels	Daniel bo. July 28 bp. Aug. 21	Walingh Jacobse Annetje Ariaense Sips

[1] Baptized at New York.
[2] Born at Bergen.
[3] The first baptized in the church [illustrated on page 6].
[4] Also the first baptism in the church.

NO.	PARENTS	CHILD	WITNESSES & SPONSORS
			1681
92	Fredrick Tomase Catreyna Hoppe	Cristina bo. Aug. 5 bp. Aug. 21	Cornelis Tomase Barentje Hendrickse
93	Pieter Cornelise Hendrickje Aerts	Andries bp. Aug. 21	Matys Hoppe Minouw Pouluse
94	Samuel De Mare Marey Druwen	Davit bp. Oct. 3	Jan de Mare Marey De Maree, his mother
95	Adriaen Post Catreyna Gerrits	Claertje bo. Dec. 4	
96	Cornelis Roelofse Maddaleena van Giesen	Reynier bo. Dec. 9	
		1682	
97	Gerrit Gerritse Junior Niesje Pieters	Elysabet bo. Mar. 3 bp. Apr. 18	Pieter Merselisen Annetje Hermens
98	Helmigh Roelofse Jannetje Pieters	Cornelis bo. Mar. 21 bp. Apr. 18	Cornelis Roelofse Pietertje van de voorst
99	Hendrick Epkese Mareya Lubberse	Angenietje bp. Apr. 18	Sibi Epkese and his wife
100	Merselis Pieterse Pietertje van de voorst	Elysabet bp. Apr. 18	Pieter Merselis Hillitje Jans
101	Jan de Maree Jacomeyn Druwen	Lea	Nicola der Pree Reychje Hermens
102	Laurus Ackerman Geertje Egberts	Jannetje bp. Apr. 18	Gerrit Tysen Annetje Ackermans
103	Jacob Leroe Weybrecht Hendrickse	Jannetje	Josias Marse and his wife
104	Lubbert Lubbertse, the younger Hillitje Poulus	Pieter	Roelof Lubbertse Mareya Lubbers
105	Sjarel Macleen Catreyna Tomas	Zara	Hertman Magielse Annetje Jacobs

1682 NO.	PARENTS	CHILD	WITNESSES & SPONSORS
106	Cornelis Magielse Metje Dirckse	Achtje bp. Apr. 18	Dirck Claesen Braack Freytje Hertmans
107	Jan Cornelise Bongert Angenietje Streyckers	Ragel bp. Apr. 18	Stoffel Kabasje Weyntje Cornelis
108	Symon Jacobse Annetje Ariaense Sips	Johannis	Jan Ariaense Sips, Y. M. Aeltje Daniels
109	Ariaen Pieterse Buys Treyntje Hendrickse	Geertruyt bo. between Apr. 23 & 24	
110	Jan Lubbersen Maddaleentje Jans	Geysbert bp. May 21	Jacob Janse van de Bilt Catreyna Hoppe
111	Sibe Epkese Mareyte Ariaense Sips	Margrietje bo. between June 7 & 8 bp. June 26	Hendrick Epkese Aeltje Danniels
112	Hendrick Hoppe Mareytje Jans	Jan bp. June 26	Jan Lubberse and wife
113	Sjarel Huysman Ariaentje Dirckse	Cristeyn	Nicola de vouw and wife
114	Tonis Roelofse Treyntje Claes	Annetje bo. Aug. 13	
115	Pieter Hesselse Eleysabet Gerrits	Ragel bo. Sept. 14 bp. Oct. 2	Claes Arents Toers, Y.M. Claesje Dirckse Braack
116	Walingh Jacobse Catreyna Magielse	Johannes bp. Oct. 2	Johannes Steynmets Merritje Jacobs
117	Tades Magielse Anna Steynmets	Jannetje bo. Oct. 12	
118	Matheus Cornelise Anna Lubi	Jacob bo. Nov. 21	
119	Claes Jansen Annetje Cornelis	Hellegontje bo. Dec. 4	
		1683	
120	Hertman Magielse Merritje Dirckse Braack	Feytje bo. Feb. 21	

NO.	PARENTS	CHILD	WITNESSES & SPONSORS 1683
121	Johannis Spier Mareytje Franse	Frans bp. Apr. 2	Jan Aertsen van de Bilt Annetje Ariaense Sips
122	Gerrit van Reenen Achtje Everts	Jan	Hessel Wiggertse Ariaentje Magielse, Y.W.
123	Mr. Samuel Edsall Rutje Edsall[1]	Rutje	Mr. Hans Kiersteede Hertman Magielse Catreyna Crigers Hendrickje Wessels, wife of Mr. Aldert Anton
124	Mr. Samuel Edsall Rutje Edsall	Ridsert	Same witnesses as above
125	Hendrick Epkese Mareya Lubberse	Roelof bp. Aug. 25	Lubbert Lubberse, the younger with his wife
126	Cornelis Roelofsen Maddaleentje van Giesen	Hendrick bo. Nov. 8	
		1684	
127	Mateys Adolf Hoppe Annetje Poulus	Adries bp. Apr. 2	Poulus Tjurckse Geertje Hoppe
128	Gerrit Steynmets Vroutje Claes	Jannetje[2] bo. Apr. 15	
129	Arien Pieterse Buys Treyntje Hendrickse	Hendrick bp. Apr. 2	Baltus Barentse Machteltje Roelofse
130	Hendrick Hoppe Mareytje Jans	Willem	Willem Hoppe Hendrickje Aerts
131	Sibe Epkese Mareytje Ariaense Sips	Aeltje	Jan Ariaense Sips Hester Hansen
132	Cornelis Roelofse Maddaleena van Giesen	Hendrick	Bastaiensen van Giesen Jannetje Pieters
133	Jurien Tomasen Reyckje Hermens	Aeltje bp. Apr. 2	Johannis Steynmets Aeltje Daniels
134	Adriaen Post Catreyna Gerrits	(a son) bo. Apr. 2 (died unbaptised)	

[1] The wife of Samuel Edsal was baptized and named Rutje.
[2] Their first child. Born at the Hasymus.

1684 NO.	PARENTS	CHILD	WITNESSES & SPONSORS
135	Jan Hendrickse Oosteroom Machteltje Roelofs	Treyntje bo. June 20 bp. June 30	Hendrick Janse oosteroom Willempje Tysen
136	Pieter Cornelise Hendrickje Aertse	Adries bp. June 30	Matys Hoppe Mynouw Pouluse
137	Tades Magielse Anna Steynmets	Annetje bo. Aug. 6	
138	Merselis Pieterse Pietertje van de Voorst	Hillegontje bo. Sept. 27 bp. Oct. 6	Cornelis van de Voorst Annetje van de Voorst
139	Gerrit Gerritse, Jr. Niesje Pieters	Pieter bo. Oct. 4 bp. Oct. 6	Gerrit Gerritse Jannetje Pieters
140	Fredrick Tomasen Catreyna Hoppe	Merreytje bo. Nov. 11	
		1685	
141	Helmigh Roelofse Jannetje Pieters	Cateleyntje bo. Feb. 17	
142	Lubbert Lubbertse, the younger Hillitje Pouluse	Aeltje bp. Apr. 6	Lubbert Lubbertse and his wife
143	Lowrus Arents Toers Franseyntje Thomas	Johannes bp. Apr. 6	Enoch Magielse Vreelant Jacomeyntje van Neste
144	Johannes Spier Mareya Franse	Geertruyt	Abraham Cornelis Treyntje Pieters
145	Pieter Hesselse Eleysabet Gerrits	Ariaentje	Hertman Magielse and his wife
146	Roelof Vanderlinden Susanna Hendrickse	Claesje bp. June 22	Hertman Magielse Vreelant Cornelia Hendricks, Y.M.
147	Claes Arentse Toers Jacomeyntje van Neste	Annetje bo. June 27	
148	Cornelis Verwey Hendrickje Jans	Dieuwer bp. Oct. 5	Jan Lubberse Catreyna Gerrits wife of Adriaen Post

NO.	PARENTS	CHILD	WITNESSES & SPONSORS
			1685
149	Hendrick Hoppe Marytje Jans	Treyntje	Pieter Jansen and his wife
150	Sibe Eppekese Mareytje Ariaense Sips	Sieske	Symon Jacobse Mareya Lubberse
151	Baltus Barentse van Kleeck Freyntje Janse Buys	Pieter	Jan Herperingh Jannetje Barents
152	Hans Spier Treyntje Pieters	Hendrick	Jan Aerts van de Bilt Catreyna Spier, Y. W.
153	Hertman Magielse Merritje Dirckse Braack	Echtje bo. June 19	
		1686	
154	Cornelis Roelofse Maddaleena van Giesen	Dierckje bo. Nov. 7 bp. Apr. 6	Tonis Roelof Dirckje Cornelis
155	Jan Hermense Neeltje Jans	Aertje bp. Apr. 6	Jan Cornelise Buys Reyckje Hermenz
156	Abraham Dutoiet Jannetje Bokee	Ragel bp. Apr. 6	Jacob Jacobse Grietje Jacobs
157	Tonis Janse Spier Catreyna Thomas	Mareytje bp. Apr. 6	Willem Jansen and his wife
158	Casper Cornelise Pruis Neeltje Jans	Susanna	Johannes Spier Maddaleentje Jans Catreyna Magielse
159	Reynier Josiassen van Roen Constantina van de Swalme	Josias	Gerbrant Claese and his wife
160	Gielam Bertolf Marteyntje Hendrickse	Hendrick bp. Apr. 6	Eleyas Magielse Catreyna Magielse
161	Anthoni Lacomba Steyntje Jans	Catreyn	Lourus Ackerman Hillitje Jans
162	Fransoys de Smidt Cateleyntje Coetens	Preyntje	Abraham Bokee Ariaentje Magielse
163	Symon Jacobse Annetje Ariaense Sips	Symon	Johannes Steynmets Joanna vandevoorst

1686 NO.	PARENTS	CHILD	WITNESSES & SPONSORS
164	Gerrit Steynmets Vroutje Claes	Annetje[1] bo. June 25 bp.[2]	
165	Jacob Jacobse van Winkel Aeltje Daniels	Johannas bo. June 25 bp.[2]	
166	Cristoffel Steynmets Jannetje Gerrits	Casperus bp. Oct. 11	Johannes Steynmets Annetje Hermens
167	Arien Pieterse Buys Treyntje Hendrickse	Jacob	Jan Hermensen Grietje Jacobs
168	Johannes Magielse Vreelant Claesje Dirckse Braack	Dirck	Metje Dirckse Elyas Magielse Vreelant

1687

NO.	PARENTS	CHILD	WITNESSES & SPONSORS
169	Johannes Spier Marya Fransen	Maddeleen bp. Apr. 11	Johannes Michielse Vreelant Catreyna Hendrickse Spier, Y. W.
170	Cornelis Doremus Janetje Joris van Elslant	Tomas	Mr. Gilam Bertolf Maeyke Jacobusen wife of Arien Tomasen
171	Claes Arentse Toers Jacomeyntje van Neste	Judicht bo. Apr. 11 bp. Apr. 11	Jan Arentse Toers Franseyntje Thomas wife of Lourus Arentse Toers
172	Lourus Arentse Toers Franseyntje Thomas	Tomas bo. Apr. 4 bp. Apr. 11	Enoch Michielsen Vreelant Jacomeyntje van Neste, wife of Claes Arentse Toers
173	Theunis Roelofse Treyntje Claes	Jannetje bp. May 23	Cornelis Roelofsen Aeltje Bogerts
174	Walingh Jacobse Catreyna Migielse	Treyntje bp. June 27	Jacob Jacobsen Aeltje Daniels, his wife
175	Matheus Cornelise Catreyna Poulus	Metje? bo. July 8	

[1] Born 3 A.M. at the Hasymus.
[2] Baptized at New York.

1687

NO.	PARENTS	CHILD	WITNESSES & SPONSORS
176	Cornelis van Vorst Feytje Gerrits	jde=(Ide)[1] bo. July 9	
177	Hans Spier Freyntje Pieters	Herrempje bp. Oct. 3	Johannes Spier with his wife
178	Pieter Hesselse Elysabet Gerrits	Jannetje bp. Oct. 3	Johannes Steynmets Preyntje Magielse, wife of Adries Claesen
179	Cornelis Roelofse Magdalena van Giesen	Johannes[2] bo. Oct. 6	
180	Helmigh Roelofse Jannetje Pieters	Jacob & Dirck[3] bo. Dec. 11	
		1688	
181	Cornelis Verwey Hendrickje Jans	Cornelis bp. Apr. 2	Baltus Barentse van Kleeck, and Treyntje Jans, his wife
182	Styntje Jans, widow of the late Anthoni De Lacombe	Magdalena	Elyas Magielse Vreelant Mareya Franse wife of Johannes Spier
183	Symon Jacobse van Winkel Annetje Ariens Sips	Treyntje bo. Feb. 7 bp. Apr. 2	Hans Didericx Margrietje Wernaers, his wife
184	Arien Tomase Maeyke Cobase	Merreytje bp. Apr. 2	Fredrick Tomase Fransyntje Tomas, wife of Lourus Arentse Toers
185	Adriaen Post Cathareyna Gerrits	Pieter bp. Apr. 2	Cornelis van Voorst Aeltje Gerrits, Y. W.
186	Abraham Bockque Tanneke Jacobse	Tanneke	Elysabet Gerrits, wife of Pieter Hesselse
187	Claes Hendrickse Willemyntje Hendrickse	Hendrick bp. June 25	Tonis Jansen Spier Catreyna Spier
188	Abraham Dutout Jannetje Boke	Madeleena bp. Oct. 4	Adam Corle Marya Dortusee, his wife

[1] First child.
[2] Born at Achqechgenonck.
[3] Jacob oldest, Dirck youngest.

1688

NO.	PARENTS	CHILD	WITNESSES & SPONSORS
189	Tonis Jansen Spier Catreyna Tomas	Jan bo. Aug. 17 bp. Oct. 4	Tomas Fredrickse Fransyntje Tomas wife of Lourus Arentse Toers
190	Cristoffel Steynmets Jannetje Gerrits	Annetje	Gerrit Gerritse Annetje Jacobs wife of Jo. Stynmets
191	Gerrit Steynmets Vroutje Claes	Annetje	Jo. Steynmets Annetje Cornelis wife of Claes Jansen
192	Pieter Pouluse Treyntje Hans Jacobs	Treyntje bp. Oct. 4	Poulus Pieterse Treyntje Martens, his wife
193	Baltus Barentse van Kleeck Treyntje Jans	Pieter	Jan Berberno Jannetje Barents wife of Jan Pieterse Bos
194	Matheus Cornelise Catreyna Poulus	Treyntje bp. Dec. 17	
		1689	
195	Jacob Jacobse Aeltje Daniels	Symeon bo. between Jan. 21 & 22	
196	Claes Gerbrantse Merritje Claes	Cornelis [1] bo. Jan. 23 or 24	
197	Arien Pieterse Buys Treyntje Hendrickse Oosterum	Johannis bp. Apr. 2	Jan Lubberse Treyntje Jans wife of Baltus Barentse van Kleeck
198	Johannes Spier Mareya Franse	Jannetje bp. Apr. 2	Adriaen Post Catreyna Michielse
199	Cornelis Clasen Aeltje Tonissen Boogert	Claes	Jan Clasen and Treyntje Claes wife of Tonis Roelofsen
200	Tade Michielse Anna Steynmets	Johannes	Gerrit Steynmets Anna Jacobs wife of Johannes Steynmets

[1] Born at Gamonepa.

NO.	PARENTS	CHILD	WITNESSES & SPONSORS 1689
201	Jacob Jacobse van Winckel Aeltje Daniels	Simeon bp. Apr. 2	Symon Jacobsen van Winckel Marya Ariaens Sips wife of Sibe Epkese
202	Tonis Roelofse Treyntje Claes	Vrowtje bp. June 24	Jan Claesen, Y. M. Pietertje Claes, Y. W.
203	Lourus Arentse Toers Fransyntje Tomas	Mareytje bp. Sept. 30	Helmigh Roelofse and his wife
		1690	
204	Walingh Jacobse Catreyna Magielse	Abraham. bp. Apr. 22	Jan Pieter Slot, Y. M. Annetje Steynmets
205	Matheus Cornelise Catreyna Poulus	Jan	Pieter Pouluse Hillitje Poulus wife of Lubbert Lubbertse, Jr.
206	Eduart Erle Elsje Vreelant	Eduart	Enoch Michielse Vreeland Preyntje Michielse Vreelant wife of Adries Claesen
207	Cornelis Roelofse Magdaleena van Giesen	Cornelis	Abraham van Giesen, Y. M. Treyntje Claes
208	Johannes Michielse Vreelant Claesje Dirckx	Achtje	Hertman Michielse Vreelant Ariaentje Michielse Vreelant Y. W.
209	Albert Albertse Terheun Hendrickje Stevens	Rachel	Albert Stevens Jellitje Reyniers
210	Albert Stevensen Jelitje Reyniers	Jannetje bp. Apr. 22	Albert Albertse Terheun Hendrickje Stevens
211	Abraham Boke Tanneke Cin	Jacob bp. Apr. 22	Hessel Pieterse, Y. M. Merritje Claes wife of Gerbrant Claesen
212	Catryna Gerrits widow of Adriaen Post	Johannes bp. June 10	Hermanus Gerritse Cristoffel Steynmets Catryna Michielse the wife of Walingh Jacobs

1690 NO.	PARENTS	CHILD	WITNESSES & SPONSORS
213	Bastiaen van Giesen Aeltje Hendrickse	Hendrick bo. July 3 bp. Oct. 7	Hendrick Jorise Dierckje van Giesen
214	Tonis Roelofse Treyntje Claes	Johannes	Jan Claesen, Y. M. Pietertje Claes, Y. W.
215	Hans Spier Treyntje Pieters	Johannes	Tonis Jansen Merritje Tonis
216	SymonJacobse vanWinckel Annetje Ariaens Sips	Ragel bp. Oct.	
		1691	
217	Helmigh Roelofse Annetje Pieters	Gerritje bo. Jan. 7	
218	Arien Pietersen Buys Treyntje Hendricks	Jannetje bp. Apr. 14	Jan Ariaensen Sip Joanna van der Voorst his wife
219	Pieter Pouluse Treyntje Hans Jacobs	Geertje bp. June 4	Marten Pouluse, Y. M. Cristina Poulus, Y. W.
220	Cornelis Doremus Jannetje Joris	Jannetje	Johannes Vreelant Catryna Gerrits widow of Adriaen Post.
221	Willem Day Annetje Jacobs	Hester bp. June 4	Jo. Steynmets Annetje Jacobs his wife
222	Gerbrant Claese Merritje Claes	Meyndert[1] bo. June 12	
223	Thomas Fransen Treyntje Brestee	Merritje[2] bo. June 14	
224	Johannes Jansen van Tilburg Anna Mary van Giese	(a daughter) bo. July 6 [3]	
225	Abraham Misier Eleysabet Kouwenhoven	Zara[2] bo. between Aug. 28 & 29 bp. [4]	

[1] Born at Gamonepa in the jurisdiction of Bergen, East New Jersey.
[2] Born at Bergen in East New Jersey.
[3] Born on Monday afternoon at Achquechgenouck.
[4] Baptized in New York.

NO.	PARENTS	CHILD	WITNESSES & SPONSORS	1691
226	Adries Claesen Preyntje Michielse Vreelant	Zara bo. Sept. 16 bp. Oct.	Hertman Michielse Vreelant Annetje Jacobs wife of Jo. Steynmets	
227	Juriaen Tomasen Reyckje Hermans	Guert bp. Oct. 5	Helmigh Roelofse Jannetje Pieters his wife	
228	Hessel Pieterse Elysabet Claes	Vrouwtje bo. Aug. 28 bp. Oct. 5	Elysabet Gerrits widow of Pieter Hesselse Cornelis Claes	
		1692		
229	.... Hermans	...... bp. Mar. 29	Gerrit Gerritse & his wife An.... Hermens	
230	Gilam Bertolf Merteyntje Hendricks	Martays	Jo. Michielse Vreelant Jannetje Gerrits wife of Cristoffel Steynmets	
231	Tomas Juriaense Jannetje Straetmaker	Gerrit	Guert Koerten Geesje Gerrits wife of Jan Straetmaker	
232	Frans Post Maeyke Kobus	Adriaen bp. Mar. 29	Helmigh Roelofse his wife Jannetje Pieters	
233	Fredrick Thomasen Catryna Hoppe	Dierck bp. Apr. 4	Gerrit van Dien Hendrickje Aert widow of Pieter Cornelise van Steenwyck	
234	Cornelis van Voorst Feytje Gerrits	Hillegont bo. Mar. 11[1] bp. Apr. 4	Gerrit Gerritse Hilletje Jans widow of Ide van Voorst	
235	Jan Hermensen Neeltje Jans	Aertje	Hessel Pieterse & Elizabeth Eleysbeth	
236	Johannes Spier Merritje Frans	Rachel	Willem Merry	
237	Claes Hendrickse Volck Willemeyntje Hendrickse Spier	Frans	Gerrit Gerrits Jr. his wife Niesje Pieters	

[1] Born at Ahasymus.

1692 NO.	PARENTS	CHILD	WITNESSES & SPONSORS
238	Cristoffel Steynmets Jannetje Gerrits	Annetje	Gerrit Gerritse Annetje Jacobs
239	Sjarel Macheleyn Catreyna Tomas	Daniel bo. Oct. 21, 1690 bp. Apr. 4, 1692	Gerbrant Claesse & Merritje Claes his wife
240	Jan Cristyn Heelena Been	Margrietje	Sjarel Macheleyn & his wife Catreyna Tomas
241	Thomas Creeven Emmetje Eysbrants	Anna	Claes Arentse Toers & his wife Jacomeyntje van Neste
242	Jacob Jacobse van Winckel Aeltje Daniels	Son[1] bo. Apr. 10	
243	Matheus Cornelisen Catreyna Paulus	Jannetje bp. May 17	Marten Pouluse, Y. M. Gerritje Gerrits widow of Barent Vochst?
244	Abraham van Giesen Feytje Andries	Peyntje or Treyntje bo. July 26	
245	Robbert Sichels Geetringt Redde...rs	Son[2]	
246	Abraham Mesier Elysabet van Kouwon Hore	Merreytje bo. Oct. 7	
247	Isaacq van Giesen Cornelia Hendrickx	Reynier bo. Dec. 10 [3]	
248	Mateys Bos? Boir? Catreyna Barwey	Nikola[4] bo. Jan. 7 bp. Apr. 18	Gerbrant Claesen Elysabet van Kouwenhoven
249	Note [5]	Lambert	Gerrit van Reene Annetje Josephs, Y. W.
		1693	
250	Edward Erle Jr. Elsje Vreelant	(A son)[6] bo. May 28	

[1] Sixth son; name not given; died in infancy.
[2] Fourth child and second son.
[3] Born at Gamonepa, in the jurisdiction of Bergen. Second son.
[4] Born at Stone Bridge or Pond, in the jurisdiction of Bergen.
[5] Parents' names obliterated.
[6] Name not given. Born at Sikakis, in the jurisdiction of Bergen.

NO.	PARENTS	CHILD	WITNESSES & SPONSORS 1693
251	Sander Egbertse Elsje Pieters	Herpje bp. June	Jan Willemse van Deventer and his wife Cornelia
252	Cristoffel Steynmets Jannetje Gerrits	Jannetje bp. October	Gerrit Steynmets Ariaentje Steynmets the wife of Casper Steynmets
253	Bastiaen van Giesen Aeltje Hendrick	Reynier bo. July 22 bp. Oct.	Reynier van Giesen Claesje Cornelis. wife of Hendrick Jorisen
254	Thomas Juriaense Jannetje Straetmaker	Juriaen bp. Oct.	Juriaen Tomasen wife Reyckje Hermens.
255	Hertman Michielse Vreelant Merritje Dirckx Braeck	Jannetje bo. Sept. 14 bp. Oct.	Jan Ariaense Sip Claesje Dierckx Braeck, wife of Johannes Michielse Vreelant
256	Helmigh Roelofse Jannetje Pieters	Leysbeth bo. Oct. 16	
257	Fredrick Tomase Catareyna Hoppe	Arien bo. between Nov. 13 & 14	
		1694	
258	Cornelis van Voorst Feytje Gerrits	Annetje [1] bo. Jan. 5	
259	Claes Arentse Toers Jacomeyntje Van neste	daughter[2] bo. between Feb. 3 & 4	
260	Jo. Janse van Tilburge Marey van Giesen	Pieter[3] bo. Jan. 18	
261	Wander Diderickx Aeltje Gerrits	Johannes[4] bp. Feb. 24	Hans Diderickx Annetje Hermens wife of Gerrit Gerritse

[1] Baptized at New York. This Annetje was married to a young man named Marten Wennen. They were married months and got a son, who was named Levinus. Annetje died and was buried at Bergen. After her burial this son also died and has been buried near or about his mother.

[2] Is their fourth child and third daughter.

[3] Sixth child and fourth son.

[4] Baptized at Bergen by Gielam (Berthozf?)

1694 NO.	PARENTS	CHILD	WITNESSES & SPONSORS
262	Sjarel Mackeleyn Catreyna Tomassen	Rachel bo. Oct. 8–93 bp. Feb. 14	Jan Ariaensen Sip and wife, Joanna van Voorst (Bertholf?)
263	Andries Preyer Johanna Steynmets	Seelitje or Heelitje bp. Feb. 24[1]	Jo Steynmets Ariaentje Steynmets wife of Casper Steynmets
264	Isaac van Giesen Cornelia Hendrickx	Reynier bo. Mar. 22[2]	R. van Giesen Dirckje Cornelis his wife
265	Merselis Pieterse Pietertje van Voorst	Annetje[3] bo. Mar. 25 bp. Apr. 10	Jan Ariaense Sips & the wife of Helmigh Roelofse Joanna Pieters
266	Lourus Arentse Toers[4] Franseyntje Tomas	Ariaen bp. May 29	Johannes Tomansse Y. M. Jannetje Tomas, Y. W.
267	Gerrit Juriaense Beelitje Dirckx	Elysabet bp. May 29 bo. May 14	Juriaen Thomasen & wife Reyckje Hermens
268	Abraham van Giesen Feytje Andriesze	Reynier[5] bo. between Aug. 6 & 7 bp. Oct. 1	Johannes van Giesen Andries Claesen Neeltje Dirkcx widow of Jan van de Linden
269	Matheus Cornelisse Catreyna Poulus	Pieter[6] bo. between Aug. 25 & 26 bp. Oct. 10	Lubbert Lubbertse Treyntje Maertens
270	Cornelis Michielse Vreelant Metje Dirck	Son[7] bo. Sept. 18	
271	Tomas Fransen Treyntje Breeste	Jan[8]	

[1] Baptized at Bergen by Gielam (Berthozf?).
[2] Born at Gamonepa. Is their third son and third child.
[3] Fifth child and third daughter.
[4] The wife of Lourus Arentse Toers was baptized and named Franseyntje.
[5] Second child and first son. Born at Minkachque.
[6] First son.
[7] The fourth child and first son.
[8] The second son.

NO.	PARENTS	CHILD	WITNESSES & SPONSORS
			1694
272	Robbert Sicgels Geertruyt Reddehars	Zacherius[1] bo. Nov.	
273	Jan Tamsen Feytje Vreelant	Elyas[2] bo. Dec.	
		1695	
274	Gerrit Gerritse Jr. Neesje Pieters	Abraham[3] bo. Feb. 22	
275	Gerrit Steynmets Catreyna Gerrits	Ariaentje[4] bo. between Mar. 14 & 15	
276	Abraham Ackerman Aeltje van Laer	Adriaen bp. Mar. 26	Lodewyck Ackerman Hilgont Verplanck wife of Davidt Ackerman
277	Jan Bertingh Hilgont Jacobs	Annetje bp. Mar. 26	Jacob Hendrickse Bartol Jacobse Catreyna Bevois
278	Jan Claesen Treyntje Straetmaker	Geesje bo. between Mar. 26 & 27	
279	Eduwert Eerle Jr. Elsje Vreelant	Hanna[5] bo. Mar. 26	
280	Willem Day Annetje Jacobs	Jacob[6] bo. May 11	
281	Jan Claesen Treyntje Straet	Geesje bp. May 14	Jan Straetmaker Annetje Cornelis widow of Claes Janse
282	Willem Pereu Leysbet Sickels	Josias bo. July 21	
283	Jan Ariaensen Sip Joanna van Vorst	Jde[7] bo. Sept. 3	

[1] Fifth child and third son.
[2] Second child and second son.
[3] Sixth child and fourth son. Born at Minnhachquee.
[4] Second daughter and second child.
[5] Fourth child and second daughter. Born at Sicakis.
[6] Third child and second son.
[7] Third son.

1695 NO.	PARENTS	CHILD	WITNESSES & SPONSORS
284	Bertel Jacobsen Elinor Douglas	.... bo. Aug. 27	
285	Wander Diderickx Aeltje Gerrits	Gerrit bo. Sept. 19 bp. Oct. 7	Gerrit Gerritsen Margrietje Wande wife of Jan Didericx
286	Jan Ariens Sips Johanna van Voorst	Jde bp. Oct. 7	Merselis Pieterse Feytje Gerrit, wife of Cornelis van de Voorst
287	Cornelis van de Voorst Fytje Gerrits	Jde[1] bo. Dec. 24	
288	Hertman Michielsen Merritje Diercks Braack	A son bo. Dec. 26	
		1696	
289	Jacob Jacobse (Van Winckel) Grietje Hendrickx	Hendrick[2] bo. between Jan. 19 & 20	
290	Cornelis van de Voorst Fytje Gerrits	Jde[3] bp. Apr. 14	Gerrit Gerritse Jr. Annetje Cornelis van de Voorst widow of Claesen Jansen.
291	Jacob Jacobse van Winckel Grietje Hendrickx	Hendrick bp. Apr. 14	Hendrick Tonisen & his wife Grietje Samuels
292	Gerbrant Claesen Merritje Claes	Gerbrant[4] bo. Apr. 16	
293	Aert Jurijaensen Gerritje Matheus	Annetje[5] bo. May 1 bp. June 2	Matheus Cornelise Reyckje Hermens widow of Jurien Tomasen.
294	Willem Merrit Catreyna Hendricx	Leena bp. May 13	Echtje Everts Barent Hendrickse
295	Andrus Preyers Johanna Steynmets	Johannes[6] bo. May 18	

[1] Born at Hasymus and is the third son and fifth child.
[2] First child, a son, by his second wife.
[3] At the Hasymus.
[4] Their seventh son and tenth child. Born at Gamonepa. Baptized at New York.
[5] First child.
[6] Fourth child, third son.

NO.	PARENTS	CHILD	WITNESSES & SPONSORS 1696
296	Charel Mackleyn Catreyna Tomas	Salomon bo. May 27 bp. June 2	Mersilis Pieterse & his wife Pietertje van de Voorst
297	Davidt Natanielse Annetje Straetmaker	son[1] bo. June 1	
298	Gerrit Steynmets Catreyna Gerrits	Casper[2] bo. June 12	
299	Claes A. Tours Jacomeyntje van Neste	Pietertje[3] bo. Sept. 6 bp. Oct. 5	Enoch Vreelant. & his wife Grietje Wessels
300	Abraham van Giesen Feytje Andriese	Dierckje[4] bo. Sept. 19	
301	Lourus Arentsen Toers Fransyntje Tomas	son[5] bo. between Sept. 19 & 20	
302	Isaacq van Giesen Cornelia Hendricks	Joris[6] bo. Sept. 22 bp. Oct. 5	Johannes van Giesen Claesje Cornelis, wife of Hendrick Jorisen. Neeltje van Vechten widow of Jan vande Linden.
303	Eduwert Erle Jr., Elsje Vrelant	Marmeduck[7] bo. Oct. 6	
304	Tomas Fransen Treyntje Brestee	son[8] bo. between Oct. 25 & 26	
305	Helmigh Roelofse Jannetje Pieters	Johannes[9] bo. between Oct. 27 & 28	

[1] No name. Third child and third son. Born at Wiehaken.
[2] Born at Hasymus. Their first son.
[3] Fifth child and fourth daughter.
[4] Second daughter and third child. Born at Achqechgenonck.
[5] Eighth son and twelfth child. No name; died unbaptized.
[6] Born at Gamonepa. Fourth child and son.
[7] Fifth child and third son. Born at Secakis, jurisdiction of Bergen.
[8] Fifth child and third son.
[9] Sixth son and ninth child.

1696 NO.	PARENTS	CHILD	WITNESSES & SPONSORS
306	Wesselse Pieters Pietertje van Voorst	Catreyna[1] bo. between Nov. 17 & 18	
307	Matheus Cornelisen Catreyna Poulus	Gerrit[2] bo. Nov. 17	
308	Jan Claesen Treyntje Straetmaker	Claes[3] bo. Nov. 30	
		1697	
309	Jacob Jacobse Grietje Hendrickx	Treytje[4] bo. Jan. 4	Jos. Steynmets Mettitje Jacobs the wife of Jan Damarees.
310	Gerrit Gerritse Jr., Nisje Pieters	Lea[5] bo. Apr. 14	
311	Robbert Sichgels Geertruyt Reddenhoers	Marey[6] bo. Apr. 14 bp. May 25	R. van Giesen Marya Sichgels Y. W.
312	Cornelis van Voorst Feytje Gerrits	Johannes[7] bo. May 17 bp. May 25	Hermanus Gerritse Pietertje van de Voorst wife of Merselis Pieterse
313	Johannes vander Oeven Doreta Jans	Hendrick[8] bo. May 22 bp. May 25	Gerrit Juriaensen Catreyna Gerrits, wife of Gerrit Steynmets
314	Barent Cristiaense Geertje Dierckx	Jannetje bo. Apr. 18 bp. May 25	Tomas Louerse Treyntje Hansen the wife of Pieter Louersen
315	Johannes Vreelant Claesje Dierckx	A son[9] bo. June 28	

[1] Fourth daughter and sixth child.
[2] Third son and sixth child.
[3] Second child and first son. Born at Ahasimus.
[4] Second child and first daughter.
[5] Seventh child and third daughter. Born at Minkachgee.
[6] Sixth child and third daughter.
[7] Sixth child and fourth son. Born at Ahasymus.
[8] Sixth son and seventh child.
[9] Born at Gamonepa.

NO.	PARENTS	CHILD	WITNESSES & SPONSORS 1697
316	Bertel Jacobse Elinor Douglas	daughter [1] bo. July 21	
317	Wander Diderickx Aeltje Gerrits	Anentje[2] bo. between July 20 & 21	
318	Gerrit Jurijaensen Beelitje Dirckx	Lea[3] bo. Sept. 11 bp. Oct. 4	Guert Koerten Niessi Pieters, wife of Gerrit Gerritsen Jr.
319	Jacob Ralemont Pietertje Claes	Johannes[4] bo. Sept. 19 bp. Oct. 4	Cornelis Claesen Annetje Cornelis widow of the late Claes Janse
320	William Day Annetje Jacobs	Johannes[5] bo. Nov. 3	
		1698	
321	Claes Hertmanse Vreelant Annetje Hermens	Hertman[6] bo. Mar. 10	
322	Abel Reddenhoers Catrayna Jans	Sofia[7] bo. Jan. 15	
323	Claes Hertmansen Vreelant Annetje Hansen	Hertman bp. Apr. 4	Hertman Michgielse Vreelant Merritje Dierckx Braack his wife
324	Jan Sip Joanna vande Voorst	Johannes[8] bo. May 10 bp. June 27	Jan Claesen Aeltje Gerrits wife of Wander Diderick
325	Gerrit Steynmets Catryna Gerrits[10]	Hermanus[9] bo. May 11 bp. June 5	Johannes Gerritsen Y. M. Ursuleena Steynmets wife of Roelof Westervelt

[1] First daughter and second child. Born at Pemmerepoch.
[2] Third child and second daughter.
[3] Second daughter and second child.
[4] First child.
[5] Fourth child and third son.
[6] First child and son. Born at Gamonepa.
[7] First child and daughter.
[8] Fourth son and seventh child. Baptized by Do. Luperdus.
[9] Second son and fourth child. Baptized at Hackinsack.
[10] Second wife.

1698 NO.	PARENTS	CHILD	WITNESSES & SPONSORS
326	Jan Claesen Treyntje Straetmaker	Annetje[1] bo. between June 29 & 30	
327	Hertman Michielse Vreelant Merritje Dierckx	Ariaentje[2] bo. July 19 bp. Sept. 25	
328	Eduwert Eerle Jr Elsje Vreelant	Johannes[3] bo. Sept. 8	
329	Cornelis M. Vreelant Metje Dierckx Braack	Metje[4] bo. Oct. 3 bp. Oct. 11	Johannes M. Vreelant Claesje Braack his wife
330	Jacob Jacobsen Grietje Hendrickx	son[5] bo. Dec. 21	
		1699	
331	Cornelis van Voorst Feytje Gerrits	Hendrick[6] bo. Jan. 29	
332	Andries Preyer Johanna Steynmets	Jenneke[7] bo. Feb. 24	
333	Jacob Jacobse Grietje Hendrickx	Teunis bp. Apr. 17	Hendrick Epkese and Dieuwer Hendrickx y. d.
334	Claes Arentse Toers Jacomeyntje van Neste	Arent[8] bo. June 10 bp. June 26	Mr. B. Baeyert Merritje Baeyert his wife
335	Merselis Pietersen Pietertje van de Voorst	Leena[9] bo. Aug. 11 bp. Aug. 27	

[1] Third child and second daughter. Born at Ahasymus.

[2] Thirteenth child and sixth daughter. Born at Gemonepa and baptized at Achqueachgenonch.

[3] Sixth child and fourth son. Born at Sikakas.

[4] Fifth child and fourth daughter.

[5] Third child and second son.

[6] Seventh child and fifth son. Born at Ahasymus.

[7] Fifth child and second daughter. Born one quarter of a year and eight days after father's death at Aharsymus.

[8] Sixth child and second son.

[9] Seventh child and fifth daughter. Baptized at Achquechgenonch.

NO.	PARENTS	CHILD	WITNESSES & SPONSORS 1699
336	Isaack van Giesen[10] Cornelia Hendrickx	Dierckje[1] bo. Aug. 15 bp. Sept. 17	
337	Gerrit Jurijaense Beelitje Dierckx	Jurijaen[2] bo. Aug. 15 bp. Sept. 6	
338	Matheus Cornelisen Catryna Poulus	Poulus[3] bo. between Aug. 20 & 21	
339	Abel Reddenhars Catreyna Jans	Jan[4] bo. Sept. 6 bp. Oct. 15	
340	Robbert Sichgelse Geertruyt Reddenhars	Geertruyt[5] bo. Sept. 10 bp. Oct. 8	
341	Jacob Ralemont Pietertje Claes	son [6] bo. Sept. 25 bp. Oct. 15	
342	William Day Annetje Jacobs	Johannes[7] bo. Sept. 26 bp. Nov. 20	
343	Gerrit Gerritse Jr., Niese Pieters	son [8] bo. Oct. 14	
344	Helmigh Roelofsen Jannetje Pieters	Jannetje[9] bo. between Nov. 1 & 2 bp. Nov. 8	

[1] Fifth child and first daughter. Born at Ganonepa; baptized at Hackensack.
[2] Third child and first son. Baptized at New York.
[3] Fourth son and seventh child. Baptized at Hackensack.
[4] Second child and first son. Born at Bergen and baptized at Hackensack.
[5] Seventh child and fourth daughter. Born at Bergen and baptized at Midwout on the Island Nassau.
[6] Second son and second child. Born at Bergen and baptized at New York.
[7] Fifth child and fourth son. Born at Bergen and baptized at Hackensack.
[8] Fifth son and eighth child. Born at Minkachopiee.
[9] Tenth child and fourth daughter. Baptized at New York.
[10] Ed. Note: See page 81, Vol. 1, Part 1, Holland Society Collection Hackensack Reformed Dutch Church Records.

1700 NO.	PARENTS	CHILD	WITNESSES & SPONSORS
345	Jan Oeven Dorete Jans	son [1] bo. Jan. 7	
346	Ulrick Brouwer Hester Devou	son [2] bo. Jan. 23	
347	Rutgert van Hooren Neelt Dierckx	son [3] bo. Feb. 18	
348	Cornelis van Voorst Feytje Gerrits	Cornelis[4] bo. Mar. 8 bp. Apr. 2	Aeltje Gerrits Jo. Gerritse, y. m.
349	Abraham Vreelant Mergrietje van Winckel	Enoch[5] bo. Mar. 14 bp. Apr. 2	Enoch Vreelant Grietje Hendrickx the wife of Jacob Jacobsen van Winckel
350	Jan van der Oeven Dorete Jans	Abraham bp. Apr. 2	Gerrit Gerritse Jr. Neisje Pieters, his wife
351	Rutger van Hooren Neeltje Dierckx	Joris[6] bp. Apr. 2	Cornelis Vreelant Mereytje Rutger, wife of Jan Andresen
352	Cornelis Claesen Aeltje Toenis Boogert	Hillegont bp. June 16	Cornelis van Voorst Geertje Claes, Y. W.
353	Eduward Erle Elsje Vreelant	...... bo. August	
354	Jan Sip Jannetje van Voorst	Cornelis[7] bo. between Sept. 27 & 28 bp. Oct. 6	Hertman M. Vreelant Jannetje Cornelis widow of Claes Jansen
355	Wander Diderickx Aeltje Gerrits	daughter [8] bo. Oct. 27	
		1701	
356	Abel Reddenhars Catreyna Jans	daughter [9] bo. Mar. 3	

[1] Sixth son and eighth child.
[2] First child and first son.
[3] Second child and first son. Born at Gamonepa.
[4] Eighth child and sixth son. Born at Ahasymus.
[5] First son.
[6] These four children are the first baptized by Do. DuBois.
[7] Fifth son and eighth child.
[8] Fourth child and second daughter. Baptized at New York.
[9] Third child and second daughter.

NO.	PARENTS	CHILD	WITNESSES & SPONSORS 1701
357	Uldrick Brouwer Hester de Vouw	Abraham[1] bo. Mar. 9 bp. Mar. 30	Tyme Jansen Valentyn Susanna de Vouw
358	Abel Reddenhars Catreyna Jans	Geertruyt bp. Apr. 3	Gysbert Jansen Hester Jans
359	Lourus van Galen Treyntje Vreelant	Joanna[2] bo. Aug. 21 bp. Oct. 6	Jacob Elyassen Vreelant, Y. M. Zara Bartolfs wife of Davit De Maree, Jr.
360	Gerrit Juriaense Beelitje Dirckx	Son[3] bo. Dec. 4	
		1702	
361	William Day Annetje Jacobs	Daughter[4] bo. Jan. 1	
362	Rutger van Hoorn Neeltje Dirckx	Jan[5] bo. Feb. 3 bp. Apr. 7	Jan van Hooreren Effe van Hooren, Y. W.
363	Isaack van Giesen Cornelia Hendrickx	Claesje[6] bo. between Apr. 12 & 13	
364	Cornelis van Voorst Feytje Gerrits	Son[7] bo. May 7	
365	Robbert Sickels Geertruyt Reddenhars	Johannes[8] bo. June 2 bp. July 6	Abel Reddenhars Hendrickje Buys, wife of Reynier van Giesen, Voorleser?
366	Cornelis van Vorst Fytje Gerrits	Jacob bp. July 7	Wander Diederickx Neesje Pieters, wife of Gerrit Gerritsen, Jr.

[1] Second child and second son. Baptized by Do. Bertollof.
[2] First child and first daughter. Born at Gamonepa.
[3] Fourth child and second son. Born at Bergen.
[4] Sixth child and second daughter. Born at Bergen.
[5] Third child and second son. Baptized by Do. DuBois. Born at Gamonepa.
[6] Second daughter and sixth child. Born at Gamonepa. Baptized at New York.
[7] Sixth son and eighth child.
[8] Eighth child and fourth son.

1702 NO.	PARENTS	CHILD	WITNESSES & SPONSORS
367	Bertel Jacobs Leena Doggelis	Willem bp. July 7	Gerrit Gerritsen, Jr. Aeltje Gerrits, wife of Wander Diderickx
368	Bastiaen van Giesen Aeltje Hendrickx	Son[1] bo. July 23	
369	Thomas Tomasen Zaertje van Dueselen	Jannetje[2] bo. Aug. 27	
370	Abraham van Giesen Feytje Andries	Abraham[3] bo. Nov. 13	
371	Wander Didericks Aeltje Gerrits	Cornelis[4] bo. Dec. 8	
		1703	
372	Abel Reddenhars Cathreyna Jans	Son[5] bo. Jan. 14	
373	Uldrick Brouwer Hester du Vouw	Isaack[6] bo. between Jan. 29 & 30 bp. Apr. 5	Thomas Fredrickse, Y. M. Jannetje Stynmets, Y.W.
374	Gerrit Steynmets Catreyna Gerrits	Heleina[7] bo. Feb. 25 bp. Mar. 10	
375	Abel Reddenhars Catreyna Jans	Hendrick bp. Apr. 5	Hendrick Hoppe Geertruyt Reddenhars, wife of Robbert Sickels
376	Mr. Eduwert Erle, Jr. Elsje Vreelant	Son[8] bo. May 1	
377	Claes Arentse Toers Jacomeyntje van Neste	Nicolaes[9] bo. between May 10 & 11 bp. June 21	Davidt Willense Merritje van Neste his wife

[1] Fifth son. Born at Achquechgenonck.
[2] First daughter and first child. Born in jurisdiction of Nuerck.
[3] Fourth son and sixth child. Born at Achquechgenonck.
[4] Third son and fifth child.
[5] Fourth child and second son.
[6] Third child and third son.
[7] Fifth child and third daughter. Born at Ahasymus. Baptized at New York.
[8] A son at Sikakis.
[9] Seventh child and third son.

NO.	PARENTS	CHILD	WITNESSES & SPONSORS 1703
378	Matheus Cornelise Catarina Poulus	Cornelis[1] bo. Sept. 3 bp. Oct. 30	Gerrit Juriaense Reycke Hermens, his mother, widow of Juriaen Tomasen
379	Lourus van Galen Treyntje Vreelant	Son[2] bo. Oct. 12	
		1704	
380	Gerrit Jurijaense Beelitje Dierckx	Son[3] bo. Jan. 17	
381	William Day Annetje Jacobs	Son[4] bo. Feb. 20	
382	Pieter Helmighse Claertje Post	Jannetje[5] bo. Feb. 16 bp. Feb. 27	Adriaen Post and his wife Lysbet Merselis
383	Cornelis van Voorst Feytje Gerrits	Daughter[6] bo. between Mar. 7 & 8	
384	Roelof Helmighse Achtje Cornelis Vreelant	Helmigh[7] bo. Mar. 11 bp. Apr. 11	Cornelis Beling, Y. M. Feytje Cornelis Vreelant, Y. W.
385	Cornelis van Voorst Feytje Gerrits	Jenneke bp. Apr. 11	Jan van Hooren Annetje Walingh, wife of Hermanus Gerritse
386	Jan Sip Johanna van de Voorst	Abraham bo. Apr. 11 bp. Apr. 11	Jan van Hooren Pietertje van Voorst wife of Merselis Pieterse
387	William Day Annetje Jacobs	Hendricus bp. Apr. 11	Hendrick Claesse, Y. M. Geertje Claes
388	Rutger van Hooren Neeltje Dierckx	Merreytje bo. Mar. 21 bp. Apr. 11	William Bogert Hilgont Joris, his wife

[1] Fifth son and eighth child.
[2] Second child and first son. Born at Gamonepa.
[3] Third son and fifth child. Died right away.
[4] Seventh child and fifth son.
[5] First child and first daughter.
[6] Tenth child and third daughter. Born at Ahasymus.
[7] First child and son.

1704 NO.	PARENTS	CHILD	WITNESSES & SPONSORS
389	Andries Fredericksen Persilla Homs	Leena[1] bo. Sept. 21 bp. Oct. 3	Tomas Frederickse, Y.M Jannetje Tomas, Y. W.
390	Barent Spier Cateleyntje Jacobs	Jacob[2] bo. Sept. 25 bp. Oct. 5	Roelof Helmighse Achtje Cornelis, his wife
391	Dierck Barentse Elisabeth Gerritse	Barent[3] bo. Oct. 8 bp. Oct. 3	Jo. Gerritse and his wife Cataleyntje Helmens
392	Eduwaert Erle Elsje Vreelant	Daughter[4] bo. Oct. 29	
393	Robbert Sickels Geertruyt Reddenhaers	Willem[5] bo. Oct. 26 bp. Dec. 25	
394	Isaack van Giesen Cornelia Hendrickx	Reynier[6] bo. Nov. 17	
		1705	
395	Jacob Jacobse Grietje Hendrickx	Samuel[7] bo. Jan. 5 bp. Feb. 18	
396	Claes Gerbrantse Merritje Juriaens	Gerbrant[8] bo. Jan. 7 bp. Feb. 11	
397	Enoch Michielse Vreelant Achtje van Hooren	Son[9] bo. Mar. 6	
398	Gerrit Juriaensen Beelitje Dirckx	Aeltje[10] bo. Mar. 29 bp. Apr. 16	Hermen Juriaensen, Y.M. Aeltje Juriaensen, Y. D.
399	Abraham van Giese Feytje Andriese	daughter[11] bo. Apr. 21	

[1] First child and daughter.
[2] Second son and first child.
[3] First son and first child.
[4] Tenth child and fourth daughter. Born at Sikakis.
[5] Ninth child and fifth son. Born at Bergen.
[6] Seventh child and fifth son. Born at Gamonepa.
[7] Third son and fourth child, born at Bergen, baptized at Achquechgenonck.
[8] First child and first son. Born at Gamonepa.
[9] A son. Born at Munkachque.
[10] Third daughter and sixth child.
[11] Seventh child and third daughter.

NO.	PARENTS	CHILD	WITNESSES & SPONSORS 1705
400	Jo. M. Vreelant Claesje Diercks	Son[1] bo. July 1	
401	Jan van der Oeven Dorete Jans	Gerrit[2] bo. July 12 bp. Oct. 8	Beeltje Dirckx Merselis Pieterse
402	Bastiaen van Giesen Aeltje Hendricks	Dierck[3] bo. Aug. 3 bp. Aug. 19	
403	Jo. Gerritse Cateleynt Helmigh	Daughter[4] bo. Sept. 6	
404	Uldrick Brouwer Hester Du vouw	Jacob[5] bo. Sept. 11 bp. Oct. 8	Jacob Swaan Annetje Jacobs, wife of William Day
405	Abel Reddenhars Catreyna Jan	Hendrick[6] bo. Oct. 5 bp. Oct. 8	Cornelis van Voorst Feytje Gerrits, his wife
406	Jo. Mechgielse Vreelant Claesje Dirckx	Johannes bp. Oct. 8	Roelof Helmighse Feytje Cornelis, Y. W.
407	Wander Diderickx Aeltje Gerrits	Mergaet[7] bo. Oct. 7 bp. Oct. 8	Gerrit Juriaense Hillegont Sip
408	Jo. Gerritse Cateleyntje Heelmigh	Antte bp. Oct. 8	Cornelis Helmighse, Y. M. Catreyna Gerrits, the wife of Gerrit Steynmets
409	Tomas Fraensen Treyntje Brestede	Daughter[8] bo. Oct. 9	
		1706	
410	Lourus van Galen Treyntje Vreelant	Merytje[9] bo. Feb. 4 bp. Apr. 1	Hendr. Bertollof, Y. M. Rachel Vreelant

1 Fifth son and tenth child. Born at Gamonepa.
2 Seventh son and ninth child.
3 Seventh child and sixth son. Born at Achquechgenonk.
4 First child and daughter.
5 Fourth child and fourth son.
6 Fifth child and third son.
7 Sixth child and second daughter.
8 Eighth child and third daughter. Born at Monachgye.
9 Third child and second daughter. Born at Gamonepa.

1706 NO.	PARENTS	CHILD	WITNESSES & SPONSORS
411	Mateys de Mot Magrietje Hendrickx	daughter [1] bo. May 14	
412	Cornelis van Voorst Feytje Gerrits	Merreytje[2] bo. May 22 bp. July 1	Arien Sip, Y. M. Cateleyntje Helmigh the wife of Jo. Gerritse
413	William Day Annetje Jacobs	Janneke[3] bo. Sept. 17 bp. Oct. 7	Robbert Sickels Jannetje Stynmets, Y. D.
414	Jan Sip Johanna van Voorst	Hendrick[4] bo. Sept. 30 bp. Oct. 7	Hendrick Claesen, Y. M. Hilligont Merselis, Y. W.
415	Barent Spier Cateleyntje Jacobs	Benjamin[5] bo. July 28 bp. Oct. 7	Carel Jacobse, Y. M. Hellegont Jacobs
		1707	
416	Enoch Michielse Vreelant Achtje van Horne	Feytje[6] bo. Feb. 2 bp. Mar. 13	Cornelis Michielse Vreelant Metje Dierckx Braack his wife
417	Rutger van Hooren Neeltje Dierckx van Vechten	Annetje[7] bo. Feb. 6 bp. Mar. 13	Davidt Coesaerdt
418	Jo. Tomasen Merreytje van Deusen	Thomas[8] bo. May 7 bp. May 15	Frederick Thomasse Catreyna Hoppe, his wife
419	Claes Arentse Toers Jacomyntje van Neste	Jooris[9] bo. May 16 bp. June 3	Cristoffel Stynmets Saartje van Neste, his wife
420	Gerrit Jurjanse Belitje Dirckx	Cornelis bo. Oct. 6 bp. Oct. 14	Roelof Helmighse Hillegont Merselisse

[1] First child and first daughter.
[2] Eleventh child and fourth daughter.
[3] Eighth child and third daughter.
[4] Tenth child and seventh son.
[5] Fifth child and third son.
[6] First daughter and second child. Born at Minkachquee.
[7] Fifth child and third daughter.
[8] First son and child. Baptized by Do. Giljam at the time when Do. Vincentius Antonides preached at Bergen.
[9] Eighth child and fourth son.

NO.	PARENTS	CHILD	WITNESSES & SPONSORS	1708
421	Johannes Gerritsen Catrina Helmigs	Helmig[1] bo. Feb. 18 bp. Apr. 6	Roelof Helmigsen Aagtje Vreeland, his wife	
422	Evert Evertsen Hillegont Jacobsen	Evert bo. Feb. 12 bp. Apr. 6	Gerret Gerretsen Catlyntje Jacobs	
423	Abel Reddenhars Catarina Lubberts	Johannes bo. Feb. 5 bp. Apr. 6	Jan Sip, and his wife	
424	Andries Hoppe Abigail Hoppe	Hendrik[2] bo. May 21 bp. June 27	Hendrik Hoppe Marrytje Hoppe, his wife	
425	Louwrens van Gaalen Tryntje Vreeland	Maria[3] bo. May 31 bp. July 26	Cornelis Blinkerhoft Marreytje Vreeland the younger	
426	Harpert Gerbrants Hillegont Merselis	Maritje[4] bo. May 12 bp. July 26	Merselis Pieterse Marrytje Gerbrants	
427	Matthys de Mott Margrietie Blinkerhoff	Machiel[5] bo. Aug. 7 bp. Sept. 5	Anthony de Moth Antje Haargjes	
428	Roelof Helmigsen Aagtje Vreelant (deceased)	Aagtje[6] bp. Oct. 18	Cornelis Vreelant and his wife	
429	Enoch Michielsen Vreelant Aagtje van Hoorn	Joris bp. Oct. 18	Ruth van Hoorn Neeltje van Vechten, his wife	
430	....	Jan Man[7] bp. Oct.		
431	Johannes Tomassen Marytje van Deusen	Abraham[8] bo. Sept. 29	Gerrit Jureaansen Grietje van Deusen	

[1] Second child of above. This is the first child that is born after Mr. Adr. Vermeule came as voorleser.
[2] First child and son. Baptized at Hakkingsak.
[3] Third daughter and fourth child.
[4] First child and daughter.
[5] A son being the second child. Baptized at Flat Bush by Do. Bernardus Freeman.
[6] Second child being a daughter.
[7] An aged person, the same being examined by the Reverend Consitory here, his name was (Janman).
[8] Second child being a son. Baptized at New York.

1708 NO.	PARENTS	CHILD	WITNESSES & SPONSORS
432	Benjamin Herrisnut Antje Herrisnut	Benjamin	Gerrit Gerritsen Printje Smits
433	Wander Diderikx Aaltje Gerrits	Jacob[1] bp. Sept. 3	Gerrit Stynmets Catlyntje Helmigs
434	Jan Ariaansen Sippe Jannetje van Vorst	Helena[1] bo. Nov. 7 bp. Dec. 3	Evert Duyke Antje Seboy
		1709	
435	Cornelis Blinkerhoff Aagtje Vreelant	Marritje[2] bo. Feb. 27 bp. Apr. 4	Dirk Hendricksen Blinkerhoff Marretje Harmanssen Vreeland
436	Adrian Vermeule Christina Fredrikx his second wife	Fredrik[3] bo. May 20 bp. June 14	Thomas Fredriksen, Y. M. Geertruy Fredrikx, Y.D.
		1710	
437	Hendrick Claasen Jannetje Verkerke	Cataryna bp. Apr. 3	Roelof Verkerke Catarina Symmons his wife
438	Andries Hoppe Abigail Akkerman	Son[4] bo. Apr. 28	
439	Abel Reddenhars Cataryna van Blerkum	Sofia bo. Mar. 8 bp. Apr. 3	Cornelis van Vorst Feytje his wife
440	Gerret Roos Judith Arentsen Toers	Johannes bo. in May bp. June	
441	Gerret Jurreaansen Beeltje Dirkx	Johannes bo. June 3 bp. July 3	Geurt Jurreaansen, Y. M. Gerretje Helmigs, Y. W.

[1] Baptized at New York.
[2] First child being a daughter.
[3] First son by second wife.
[4] Second child a son, born at Bergen.

NO.	PARENTS	CHILD	WITNESSES & SPONSORS 1710
442	Johannes Gerretsen van Wagenin Catelyntie Helmigs	Gerret[1] bo. Oct. 7 bp. Oct. 9	Cornelis van Vorst and his wife
443	Enoch Machielsen Vreeland Aafje van Hoorn	Joris[2] bo. Sept. 25 bp. Oct. 9	Cornelis Blinkerhof and his wife
444	DanielvanWinkel Jannetje Cornelis Vreelant	Metje bp. Oct. 9	Cornelis Machielsen Vreelant and his wife
445	Cornelis Blinkerhof Aagtje Hartmans Vreelant	Claasje[3] bo. Dec. 31 bp. Mar. 4, 1711	Claas Hartmansen Vreelant Aaltje Blinkerhof

1711

NO.	PARENTS	CHILD	WITNESSES & SPONSORS
446	Louwrens van Gaalen Tryntje Elyassen Vreelant	Cataryna[4] bo. Mar. 25 bp. Apr. 3	Aagtje Vreelant, the wife of Cornelis Blinkerhof Harpert Gerrebrantsen
447	Evert van Naamen Wyntje van Naamen	Elysabeth bp. Apr. 3	Ruth van Hoorn, and his wife, Neeltje van Hoorn
448	Gerret Roos Judik Tours	Johannes[5] bo. Mar. 25 bp. Apr. 3	Gerret van Gelder Jacomyntje Tours the childs grandmother
449	...... Pieters	Elysabet bo. Oct.	Gerret Jureaansen Tenneke Pieters, Y. W.
450	Robbert Sikkelsen Geertruyt Riddenhars	Abram bo. Nov. 12 bp. Nov. 22	Johannes Gerretsen van Wagenen and his wife
451	Matthys De Moth Margrietje Blinkerhoff	Antje[6] bo. Dec. 24	Cornelis Blinkerhoff Aaltje van Giesen
452	Johannis Tomassen Marytje van Deusen	Arien[7] bo. Dec. 17	Cornelis Tomassen Marytje, his wife

[1] Third child being a son.
[2] Fourth child.
[3] Second child. Born at Gamoenepa and baptized at Akkingsack.
[4] Fifth child. Born at Gamoenepan.
[5] First son and first child.
[6] Fourth child. Baptized at Achkwegnonck.
[7] Third son. Baptized at Achqueghgenonch.

1712 NO.	PARENTS	CHILD	WITNESSES & SPONSORS
453	Adrian Vermeule Christina Fredrikx	Leuntje[1] bo. Apr. 8 bp. Apr. 13	Fredrik Tomasen Catarina Hoppe, his wife
454	Hendrik Klaasen Kuyper Jannetje Verkerke	Annatje bp. Apr. 13	Geertje Klaas Kuyper
455	Daniel van Winkel Jannetje Cornelissen Vreelant	Aaltje bp. Apr. 13	Jacob Jacobsen van Winkel Grietje, his wife
456	Gerret Roos Judith Toers	Antje	
457	...... Paersel	Willem[2]	Helmig and his wife
458	Cornelis Blinkerhoff Aagtje Vreeland	Hendrik[3] bo. Dec. 15 bp. 1713	Jacobus Blinkerhoff and Feytje Hartmans
		1713	
459	Gerret Roos Judith Toers	Niklaas bo. Sept. bp. 1714	
460	Cornelis Blinkerhoff Aagtje Vreelant	Aagtje[4] bo. Mar. 23 bp. 1715	Enog. Vreelant Margrietje De Moth
		1715	
461	Meyndert Gerrebrantsen Treyntje Jacobsen van Winkel	Marritje[5] bo. Mar. 29	Claas Gerrebrantsen Neeltje Jureaansen
462	Casper Preyer Saartje Andriessen	Anna	Abraham Andriessen Selytje Preyer
		1716	
463	Matthys de Moth Margrietie Blinkerhoff	Johannes[6] bo. Aug. 7	Jacobus Blinkerhoff Margrietje Banta

[1] Second child.
[2] This child was baptized in the summer and was about three years old.
[3] Third child. Baptized at Akkingsak.
[4] Fourth child.
[5] First child being a son(?)
[6] Sixth child. Born at Akkingsak.

NO.	PARENTS	CHILD	WITNESSES & SPONSORS 1717
464	Casperus Preyer Saartje Andries	Pryntje bo. Oct. 22	Abraham Braesen Elysabet Brasen
465	Meyndert Gerrebrantsen Treyntje Jacobsen van Winkel	Jacob[1] bo. Nov. 4	Hendrik van Winkel Grietje Banta
466	Cornelis Gerrebrands Jannetje Pier	Marreytje bo. Nov. 9	Tomas Pier Neeltje Gerrebrands
		1718	
467	Hendrik Sickel Geertruy Fredrikse	Robbert bo. May 25	Zacharias Sickelsen Sofia Sickelsen, wife of Roelof Helmigsen
468	Matthys de Moth Margrietje Blinkerhoff	Joris[2] bo. Nov. 3	Dirck Blinkerhoff and his wife
		1719	
469	Meyndert Gerrebrantsen Treyntje Jacobsen van Winkel	Gerrebrand[3] bo. Feb. 19	Daniel Van Winkel, and his wife
		1720	
470	Matthys de Moth Margrietje Blinkerhoff	Jacob[4] bo. Feb. 22	
471	Jacob Gerretsen van Wagening Lea Gerrets	Gerret[5] bo. May	Dirk van Hoorn and his wife
472	Hendrik Sickels Geertruy Fredrikx	Katryna bo. Aug. 26	Dirk Fredricksen Jannetje, his wife
		1721	
473	Johannes Helmigsen Catelyntje Helmigsen	Jannetje[6] bp. Feb. or Jan.	

[1] Second child.
[2] Seventh child being a son.
[3] Third child.
[4] Eight child, a son.
[5] First child.
[6] Sixth child a daughter.

1721	NO.	PARENTS	CHILD	WITNESSES & SPONSORS
	474	Meyndert Gerrebrantsen Tryntje Jacobsen van Winkel	Grietje[1] bo. Feb. 19	Cornelis Gerrebransen and his wife
	475	Cornelis Gerrebrants Jannetje Pier	Catharina[2] bo. Oct. 13	Hendrik Sikkels, and his wife
			1722	
	476	Casperus Preyer Saartje Andriessen	Johannis bo. June 22	Johannis Pietersen, and his wife
	477	Hendrik Sickelsen Geertruy Fredrickx	Geertruy bo. Oct. 26	Dirk Fredricksen Jannetje, his wife
			1723	
	478	Matthys de Mot Margrietje Blinkerhoff	Marreytje[3] bp. Apr. 15	Hendrik Stoothoft, and his wife
	479	Marten Wennem Jannetje Vreelant	Antje[4] bp. Apr. 13	Cornelis van Voorst Tenneke van Vorst
	480	Pieter Merselisen Tenneke Preyers	Pieter[4] bp. Apr. 15	Caspar Preyer Saartje Andries, his wife
	481		Anno Jacob[5] Mar. 4	..... Vreeland, and his wife Marr. .ye
	482	Johannis Johannissen Vreelant Antje Diderickx	Son[6] bo. July 30	
	483	Jde Sip Antje van Wagening	Daughter[7] bo. Aug. 5	
	484	Cornelis Gerrebrants Jannetje Pier	Gerrebrant[8] bo. Sept. 10	
	485	Gerret Mattheeussen Catryntje Kuypers	Catryntje[9] bo. Aug. 9 bp. Sept. 20	Cornelis Mattheeussen, Y. M. Jannetje Mattheeussen, Y. W.

[1] Fourth child.
[2] Second daughter.
[3] Ninth child.
[4] Third child.
[5] Record obliterated.
[6] Second child being a son.
[7] Third child being a daughter.
[8] Third child being a son. Father and mother witnesses.
[9] First child.

1723

NO.	PARENTS	CHILD	WITNESSES & SPONSORS
486	Caspar Preyers Sara Andries	Selytje bp. Sept. 20	Marten Winning, and his wife
487	Jde Sip Antje van Wagening	Catelyntje[1] bp. 20?	Helmeg van Wageneng Catryntje van Winkell
488	Johannes Vreeland Antje Diedrikx	Johannes[2]	Johannes Helmegsen van Houten, and his wife Helena
		1724	
489	Casper Preyer Sara Andries	Casparis	Casparis Stymets Helena Stymets
490	Michiel Hartmansen Vreeland Elysabeth Gerretse	Claesje ? bp. Mar. 30	Jacob Garretsen van Wagening, and his wife
491	Johannes Helmigsen van Houten Helena Johannissen Vreelant	Jannetje	
492	Hendrik van der Hoeven Eva Slot	Johannis bp. Mar. 30	Juriaan Gerritse Aaltje
493	Myndert Gerrebrantsen Tryntje van Winckel	Metje bp. Mar. 30	Hendrik van Winkel Eva Slot
494	Meyndert Gerrebrantsen Treyntje Jacobsen van Winkel	Metje[3] bo. June 10	Hendrik van Winkel Eva Slot
495	Jacob Gerretsen van Wagening Lea Gerrets	Neesje[2] bo. Sept. 2	Gerret Jureaansen, and his wife
		1725	
496	Pieter Marselisse Tenneke Preyer	Andries[1] bo. Feb. 14	Ide Sip Helena Marselissen
497	Hendrick Sikkelsen Geertruy Fredrikx	Frederik bo. Dec. 1	Cornelis Gerrebrantsen and his wife

[1] Third child.
[2] Second child.
[3] Fifth child, a son. [Sic.]

1726 NO.	PARENTS	CHILD	WITNESSES & SPONSORS
498	Meyndert Gerrebrantsen Tryntje	Tryntje[1] bo. Apr. 3	Abraham Vreeland, and his wife
499	Cornelis Gerbrands Jannetje Pier	Teunes[2] bo. Apr. 8	Abraham Pier, and his wife
500	Casperus Preyer Saartje Andriesen	Niklaas bo. June	Rutger van Hoorn, and his wife
		1727	
501	Jacob Gerretsen van Wagening Lea Gerrets	Beeltje[2] bo. Mar. 1(?) bp. 1727	Jureaan Gerretsen, Y. M. Aaltje Jureaansen, Y. W.
502	Jacob Gerretsen van Wagening Lea Gerrets	Johannes[3] bo. July 5(?) bp. 1727	Michiel Hartmansen and his wife
		1728	
503	Hendrik Sickelsen Geertruy Fredrickx	Johannes bo. Sept. 11	Johannes de Groot Elysabet, his wife
504	Cornelis Gerrebrants Jannetje Pier	Cornelis[4] bo. Oct. 27	Davidt Abeel, and his wife
		1729	
505	Zacharias Sikkels Arianntje Hartmansen Vreelant	Geertruy[3] bp. Feb. 14	Michiel Hartmansen, and wife Elysabet Gerritse
506	Poulus Mattheeusen Helena Spier	Cattrina bo. May 10 bp. May 16	Garret Mattheeusen Jannetje Mattheeusen
507	Cornelis Gerretsen Aaltje van Winkel	Gerret[5] bp. May 16	Gerret Juriaensen, and his wife

[1] Sixth child.
[2] Fourth child.
[3] Third child.
[4] Fifth child.
[5] First child and son.

NO.	PARENTS	CHILD	WITNESSES & SPONSORS	1729
508	Johannes Sickels Claasje Blinkerhof	Aactje[1] bp. May 16	Cornelis Blinkerhof and his wife	
509	Juriaen Gerretsen Margrietje Diderickx	Gerret[2] bp. Sept. 14	Michiel Vreelant, and Else his wife	
510	Morgen Smit Catrina Tades	Tades[3] bo. Sept. 13 bp. Sept. 14	Johannis Tades Antje Tades	
511	Hendrik van der Hoeven Eva Slot	A son[4] bo. Sept. 16		
512	Casperis Preyer Saartje Andriessen	......[5] bo. Sept. 23		
		1730		
513	Michiel Cornelissen Vreelant Jenneke Helmigsen van Houten	Helmig[6] bo. Jan. 29 bp. Feb. 26	Johannis Helmigsen van Houten, and his wife	
514	Marten Wennem Jannetje Johanissen Vreeland	Marrytje[7] bo. Mar. 6 bp. Mar. 16	Zacharias Zicgelse Elysabet Gerrets, wife of Michiel Hartmansen Vreelant	
515	Johannes Sikkels Claesje Blinkerhoff	Aaegtje[8] bo. Dec. 26 bp. Jan. 25, 1731	Cornelis Blinkerhof Aaegtje Hartmans Vreelant his wife	
		1731		
516	Harmanis Stymets Elsje Couwenhoof	Antje bo. Jan bp. Jan. 25	Jde Sip Antje, his wife	
517	Jacob Brouwer Lea Slot	Johannis[9] bo. Feb. 6 bp. Apr. 14	Johannis Pietersen, and his wife	

[1] First child and daughter.
[2] First son.
[3] Second son.
[4] Fourth child. Baptized at New York.
[5] Ninth child. Baptized at New York.
[6] Baptized by Do. du Bois. Fifth child.
[7] Fifth child.
[8] Second child.
[9] First child. Baptized in New York by Do. Dubois.

1731 NO.	PARENTS	CHILD	WITNESSES & SPONSORS
518	Arent Toers Annatje Spier	Jacomyntje[1] bo. Apr. 2 bp. May 3	Poulus Matteusse and Judik
		1732	
519	Arent Toers Annatje Spiers	Daughter[2] bo. Mar. 2	
520	Michiel Cornellissen Vreelant Jenneke Helmegsen van Houten	Aaegtje[3] bo. Feb. 14 bp. Mar. 27	Johannes Helmegsen van Houten and wife
521	Pieter Maerle Merrytje Andries	Andries bo. May 31 bp. June 5	Jacob Gerretsen van Wageneng Lea Gerrets, his wife
522	Hendrik van der Hoeven Evaje Slot	Marytje bo. June 30 bp. July 23	Jacob Brouwer Lea, his wife
523	Johannes Cavelier Calyntje	Son and[4] Daughter bo. Aug. 3	
524	Pieter Marselissen Jenneke Preyer	Daughter[5] bo. Oct. 15	Jacob Tomassen Marytje, his wife
525	Jurien Gerretsen Grietje Diederikx	Son[6] bo. Nov. 15 bp. at 1732	Gerret Juriaansen, and his wife
		1733	
526	Jan Hendricksen Annatje Preyer	Son[7] bo. Mar. 19	
527	Michiel Hartmensen Vreeland Elysabet Gerrets	Belitje[8] bo. Mar. 19 bp. Apr. 24	Cornelis Blinkerhoff Aacgtje, his wife

[1] First daughter.
[2] Second child, a daughter.
[3] Sixth child.
[4] A son and daughter. Baptized at New York; living in the Gemoenepahe Road.
[5] Ninth child, a daughter. Baptized at Achknechgenonck.
[6] Second son. Baptized at Achkuegnonck.
[7] First child being a son.
[8] Sixth child.

NO.	PARENTS	CHILD	WITNESSES & SPONSORS 1733
528	Jan Hendriksen Annatje Preyer	Johannis bp. Apr. 24	Pieter Marselissen Jenneke his, wife
529	Arent Toers Annetje Spier	Jacomyntje bp. Apr. 24	Gerrit Roos, and wife?
530	John Diederikz Geertruy van Winkel	Antje bp. Apr. 24	Johannes Johannessen Vreeland Antje Diederikx, his wife
531	Abraham Spier Annatje Spier	Son[1] bo. May	
532	Cornelis Gerbrantsen Jannetje Pier	Neeltje[2] bo. June 6 bp. June 25	Jacob Pier, and his wife
533	Poulus van Nieuw-kerk Helena Spier	Catlyntje[3] bo. May 7 bp. June 25	Barent Spier Catlyntje, his wife
534	Ide Sip Antje van Wagenyng	Arjaantje[4] bo. June 2 bp. June 25	Jan van Hoorn Helena his wife
535	Johannes Sikkels Claesje Blinkerhoff	Son[5] bo. July 5	
536	Joris Enogsen Vreelant Annatje van Winkel	Aafje[6] bo. Sept. 8 bp. Sept. 24	Jan van Hoorn, and his wife
537	Dirck Fredriksen Jannetje van Hoorn	Andries[7] bo. Oct. 28	Jacob and Lea
538	Juriaan Gerritsen Grietje Diedrikx	Son[8] bo. Oct. 7	
539	Johannes Cavelier Catlyntje	Margrieta bo. Sept. 29 bp. Oct. 15	Jacob van Wagening, and his wife

[1] First child a son.
[2] Seventh child.
[3] Second child.
[4] Fourth child.
[5] Third child being a son.
[6] First child being a daughter.
[7] Sixth child.
[8] Third son.

1735

NO.	PARENTS	CHILD	WITNESSES & SPONSORS
540	Arent Toers Annatje Spier	Catelyntje bp. Mar. 4	Barent Spier Catelyntje, his wife
541	Pieter Marselissen Jenneke Preyer	Antje bp. Mar. 4	Johannis Helmegsen van Houten Helena Vreeland, his wife
542	Juriaan Gerretsen Grietje Diderikx	Aaeltje bp. Mar. 4	Johannis Vreeland, and his wife Antje
543	Petrus Stuyvesant Pryntje Preyers	Pieter bp. Mar. 4	Michiel Cornelissen Vreeland Jenneke his wife
544	Hendrik van Winkel Catryntje Waldron	Daniel bp. Mar. 4	Daniel van Winkel Jannetje his wife
545	Morgen Smit Catje Tades	Cornelis bo. Mar. 4	
546	Johannis Helmigsen van Houten Helena Johannissen Vreelant	Johannis bp. June 17	Johannis Johannissen Vreelant Antje his wife
547	Cornelis Diderickx Antje Roos	Altje[1] bo. Sept. 28	
548	Jacob Brouwer Lea Slot	Coobis[2] bo. Sept. 30	
549	Jde Sip Antje Gerrits	Jannetje bp. Sept. 30	Johannis van Houten Lena his wife

1736

550 Apr. 3, 1736, I have taken the position of voorleser for the church of Bergen. P. V. Benthuysen

NO.	PARENTS	CHILD	WITNESSES & SPONSORS
551	Benjamin Spier	Barent bo. Feb. 21 bp. Apr. 3	Barent Spier, and his wife

[1] First child being a daughter.
[2] Second child being a son.

NO.	PARENTS	CHILD	WITNESSES & SPONSORS 1736
552	Jan van Hoorn	Jannetje[1] bo. Feb. 25 bp. Mar. 8	Jde Sip, and his wife
553	Jacob van Wagenin	Jacoobus bp. Mar. 8	Cornelis Gerrits, and his wife
554	Maghiel Vreeland	Marritje bp. Mar. 8	Juryan Gerrits, and his wife
555	Willem Sickels Eliezabet Kuypers	Nicolas[2] bo. Mar. 15 bp. Apr. 13	Hendryck Cuypers Jannetje Verkerck, his wife
556	Pieter Stuyvesant Printje Pryer	Kasper bo. Mar. 1 bp. Apr. 13	Pieter Marselis Jenneke Pryer, his wife
557	Gerret Hennejon Maritje van Vorst	Jede bo. Apr. 3 bp. Apr. 13	Jede Siph Antje van Wagenen, his wife
558	Derck (C or) Kadmus Jannetje Van Horen	Neltje bp. June 23	Joris Vrelant Annatje van Wagenen, his wife
		1737	
559	Arent Toers Annatje Spier	Nicolas[3] bo. Mar. 23 bp. Apr. 26	Poulus Nieuw-kerk Helena Spier, his wife
560	Michiel Cornelis Vreelant Jenneke van Houten	Dirk[4] bo. Mar. 11 bp. Apr. 26	Johannis Gerresse van Wagenen Catlintje van Houte, his wife
561	Michiel Cornelis Vreelant Jenneke van Houten	Jacob[4] bo. Mar. 11 bp. Apr. 26	Johannis Johannisse Vreelant Feytje Vreelant
562	Jurjan Gerresse Grietje Diedriks	Belitje bo. Apr. 24 bp. Apr. 26	Gerret Jurjanje Belitje Dircks, his wife
563	Gerret Nieuwkerk Catrina Kuyper	Jannetje bo. May 5 bp. May 9	Hendryck Kuyper Sara Kuyper

[1] Third daughter.
[2] Second child.
[3] First son.
[4] Twins. Nos. (560 and 561) Dirk is the oldest.

1737 NO.	PARENTS	CHILD	WITNESSES & SPONSORS
564	Pieter Marselis Jenneke Pryer	Johanna bo. June 17 bp. June 27	Jurjan Gerresse Margrietje Diedryck, his wife
565	Hendryck Sikels Sara Ackerman	Hendryck bo. Aug. 5 bp. Sept. 5	Abraham Sikels Martje Gerbrentse
566	Helmech van Wagenen Martje Brinckerhoef	Aaffie[1] bo. Aug. 9 bp. Sept. 5	Cornelis Brinckerhoef Aaggie Vreelant, his wife
567	Zacharias Sikels Rachel van Winkelen	Daniel bo. Aug. 10 bp. Sept. 5	Daniel van Winckelen Jannetje Vrelant, his wife
568	Benjamin Spier Maritje Spier	Sara bo. Aug. 18 bp. Sept. 5	Hendryck Spier Leija Spier
569	Joris Vrelant Annatje van Wagenen	Enoch bo. Sept. 22 bp. Sept. 27	Jde Siph Antje van Wagenen, his wife
570	Pieter Stuyvesant Pryntje Pryjer	Jenneke bo. Nov. 28 bp. Mar. 5	Michiel Vrelent Jenneke van Houten, his wife
		1738	
571	Poulus Nieuw-kerk Helena Spier	Barent bp. Mar. 12	Johannis Spier Gessie Spier
572	Derk Kadmus Jannetje van Horn	Cathariena bo. May 27 bp. June 5	Cornelis Gerbrantse Jannetje Spier, his wife
573	Helmigh van Wagenen Martje Blinkerhoef	Catlintje bo. Dec. 25 bp. Dec. 31	Jde Sip Annatje van Wagenen, his wife
		1739	
574	Jurjan Gerretse Margrietje Diedriks	Gerret bp. Apr. 16	Michiel Hartmanse Vrelant Eliesabet Gerretze, his wife

[1] First child.

NO.	PARENTS	CHILD	WITNESSES & SPONSORS 1739
575	(My fifth son)	Johannis[1] bo. May. 9 bp. June 18	Hendrik van Winckel Catriena Waldron
576	Joris Vrelant Annatje van Wagenen	Gerret bo. May 18 bp. May 18	Jde Sip Antje van Wagenen, his wife
577	Uldrik Brouwer Marya Van de Vorst	Johannes[2] bp. June 18	Jacob Brouwer Leja Slot, his wife
578	Jacob Brouwer Leja Slot	Hesther[3] bo. Sept. 6 bp. Oct. 15	Uldrik Brouwer Marya Van de Vorst, his wife
579	Arent Toers Annatje Spier	Cattrientke[4] bo. Sept. 30 bp. Oct. 15	Hendrik Spier Geesie Spier
580	Petrus Stuyvesant Pryntje Pryer	Pieter[5] bo. Oct. 7 bp. Oct. 15	Cornelis van Vorst Claasie de Moth his wife
581	Hendrik Siggels Sara Ackerman	Altje[4] bo. Oct. 8 bp. Oct. 15	Abraham Ackerman Hendrikje Hoppe his wife
582	Johannis Spier Geertruy Roome	Barent bo. Feb. 18 bp. Apr. 2	Barent Spier Catlyntje Hafte? his wife
583	Abraham Sikkels Aagttje Blinkerhof	Aagttje[6] bo. Feb. 20 bp. Apr. 1	Cornelis Blinkerhof Aagttje Vreland, his wife
584	Joseph Waldrum Aafttje Heylhaaken	Antje bo. Feb. 27 bp. Apr. 1	Derk Kadmus Gezie Spier
585	Poulus Niew-kerk Helena Spier	Jannetje bp. May 26	Gerret Diedrikx Jannetje N-Kerk, his wife

[1] "My fifth son" in the above doubtless refers to the fifth son of P. Van Benthuysen who as "Voorleser" also kept the Church Records.
[2] First son.
[3] First daughter.
[4] Fourth daughter.
[5] Third son.
[6] First daughter.

1739 NO.	PARENTS	CHILD	WITNESSES & SPONSORS
586	Cornelis Gerretze Aaltje van Winckel	Cornelis bp. May 26	Michiel Hartmans Vrelant Elizabeth Gerretze, his wife
587	Hendrik van Winckel Catriena Waldrum	Joseph bo. June 4 bp. June 23	Daniel Waldrum Maria Pels, his wife
588	Jde Ziph Antje van Wagenen	Gerret bo. Aug. 21 bp. Oct. 6	Cornelis Van Wagenen Jannetje Van Wagenen
589	Myndert Gerbrantz Tryntje van Winckel	Myndert bo. Sept. 1 bp. Oct. 6	Zacharias Ziggels Rachel van Winckel his wife
		1740	
590	Abraham Diederickx Gertruy Bon	Antje bo. Sept. 11 bp. Oct. 6	Johannis Vreland Antje Diederickx, his wife
		1741	
591	Joris Vrelant Annatje van Wagenen	Enoch bo. Feb. 18 bp. Apr. 7	Dirk Kadmus Jannetje van Horrn, his wife
592	Gerret van N-Kerk Catrina Cuyper	Hendrik bo. Apr. 4 bp. Apr. 7	Johannes Jurryyansen Zara Cuyper, his wife
593	Helmigs van Wagenen Martje Blinckerhof	Martje[1] bp. Apr. 7	Gerret Kroese Klaase Blinkerhof, his wife
594	Helmigs van Wagenen Martje Blinckerhof	Antje[1] bp. Apr. 7	Hendrik de Moth Jannetje van Wagenen, his wife
595	Johannes Diederick Hester Vreland	Margrietje bp. Apr. 7	Cornelis Diederick Antje Roos, his wife
596	Hendrik vander Hoef Eva Slot	Sara bp. May 19	Thomas Ouwtwaater Sara Slot, his wife

[1] Twins. Martje being oldest. 593 and 594.

NO.	PARENTS	CHILD	WITNESSES & SPONSORS 1741
597	Cornelis Jurrianse Aaltje van Winckel	Belia bo. Oct. 1 bp. Nov. 2	Michiel Hartmanse Vrelant Elizabet Jurrianse, his wife
598	Pieter van Benthuyse Margrietje Olfers	Isaac bo. Oct. 14 bp. Nov. 2	Johannes van Houten Helena Vreland, his wife
599	Pieter Stuyvesant Printie Pryer	Zara bo. Nov. 1 bp. Nov. 2	Arent Toers Anna Spier, his wife
		1742	
600	Joseph Walderon Aafje Heilhaaken	Sara bo. Jan. 14 bp. Apr. 12	Joris Vrelant Annatje van Wagenen
601	Michiel Vreland Jenneke van Houten	Johannes bo. Mar. 12 bp. Apr. 12	Pieter van Benthuyze Margrietje Olphers, his wife
602	Jan van Hoorn Helen Zip	Johannes bp. Aug. 2	Jde Zip Antje van Wagenen, his wife
		1743	
603	Johannes Diederick Hester Vreland	Martje bo. Mar. 26 bp. Mar. 28	Jacob Diedericks Jannetje Van Winckel, his wife
604	Abraham Diederickx Geertruy Bon	Johannes bo. Apr. 9 bp. June 6	Hessel Pieters van Wagenen Catriena Bon, his wife
605	Uldrick Brower Maria van de Vorst	Abraham bo. July 26 bp. Aug. 29	Abraham Brouwer Eliesabet Ackerman, his wife
		1744	
606	Pieter Stuyvesant Printje Preyer	Catriena bo. Apr. 15 bp. Apr. 16	Casparus Preyer Sara Andrise, his wife

	NO.	PARENTS	CHILD	WITNESSES & SPONSORS
1744	607	Abraham Sieggels Aagtje Blinckerhof	Gertruy[1] bo. May 8 bp. June 11	Hendrick Siggels Sara Ackerman, his wife
	608	Jacob van Wagenen, Jr. Jannetje van Houten	Catlyntje[2] bo. July 23 bp. Sept. 17	Jde Sip Antje van Wagenen his wife
	609	Mattheuz Aarsen Sofia van Vorst	Johannis bo. July 28 bp. Sept. 17	Gerret Hennion Maria van Vorst, his wife
			1745	
	610	Abraham van Tuyl Mettje Vreland	Abraham bp. Apr. 16	Johannis van Houten Helena Vreland, his wife
	611	Cornelis Jurrianzen Aaltje van Winckel	Jannetje bp. Apr. 16	Johannis Jurriansen Margrita van Winckel
	612	Jacob Diedericks Jannetje van Winckel	Jannetje bp. Apr. 16	Johannis Vreland Antje Diederiks, his wife
	613	Albertus Spier Osseltje Westervelt	Catlyntje bo. May 13 bp. June 17	Arent Toers Annatje Spier, his wife
	614	Johannis Everse Zeittje Spier	Johannes bo. June 2 bp. June 17	Johannis Spier Geertruyt Romme
	615	Joseph Waldron Aaftje Heijhaken	Benjamin bo. Aug. 31 bp. Sept. 16	Michiel Cornelisse Vreland Jenneke van Houten, his wife
	616	Johannis Diederikx Hester Vreland	Lea bo. Oct. 30 bp. Apr. 21	Abraham Diedrik Geertruy Bon, his wife
			1746	
	617	Pieter Stuyvesant Pryntje Preyer	Johannis bo. Jan. 2 bp. Apr. 21	Jan van Hoorn Helena Sip, his wife
	618	Uldrik Brouwer Maria Vos	Thomas bo. Feb. 3 bp. Apr. 21	Thomas Vos Catharina Buis, his wife

[1] Second daughter and second child.
[2] First child.

NO.	PARENTS	CHILD	WITNESSES & SPONSORS
			1746
619	Johannis Spier Geertruy Romme	Johannis bo. Feb. 11 bp. Apr. 21	Poulus van N-Kerk Helena Spier, his wife
620	Albertus Spier Osseltje Westervelt	Johannis bo. Aug. 28 bp. Sept. 15	Johannis Westervelt Aagtje de Groot, his wife
		1747	
621	Abraham v. Tuyl Mettje Vreland	Jenneke bo. Feb. 4 bp. Apr. 21	Michiel Cornelisse Vreland Jannetje Vreland
622	Abraham Diederikx Geertruy Bon	Aaltje bo. Mar. 20 bp. Apr. 21	Johannis Diederikx Hester Vreland, his wife
623	Johannis Everse Seydke	Barent[1] bo. May 30 bp. June 10	Arent Toers Annatje Spier, his wife
624	Jacob van Wagenen Jannetje van Houten	Helena[1] bo. Apr. 22 bp. June 10	Hartman Blinckerhof Klasie van Houten, his wife
625	Abraham Pryer Martje Sickkels	Aryantje[2] bp. Sept. 28	Zacharias Sickkels Rachel van Winckel, his wife
626	Abraham Sickkels Aagtje Blinckerhof	Cornelius[3] bo. June 12 bp. July 29	Hendrik Blinckerhof Gesie Blinckerhof
627	Cornelius Boskerk Belytje van Wagenen	Cornelius bo. Sept. 15 bp. Sept. 28	Michiel Hartman Vreland Elizabet Jurriansen, his wife
		1748	
628	Cornelius Jurrianse Aaltje van Winckel	Aaltje bo. June 7 bp. June 20	Jacob van Wagenen Leya Jurriansen, his wife
629	Abraham van Tuyl Mettje Vreland	Jenneke bo. July bp. Sept. 12	

[1] Second child.
[2] First child.
[3] First son. Baptized at New York.

1748 NO.	PARENTS	CHILD	WITNESSES & SPONSORS
630	Johannes Pryer Geertruy Siekkels	Geertruy bo. July 11 bp. July 12	Hendrik Sikkels Sara Ackerman, his wife
		1749	
631	Joris Vreland Annatje van Wagenen	Johannis bo. Sept. 21 bp. Sept. 25	Michiel Cor. Vreeland Jenneke van Houten, his wife
632	Harmanus Veder Antje Hennion	Gerrit[1] bo. Oct. 26 bp. Nov. 1	Cornelius van Vorst Claasie de Moth, his wife
633	Johannis Everse Zytje Spier	Jacob bo. Dec. 16 bp. Apr. 2. 1750	Jacob Brouwer Leya Slot, his wife
634	Cornelus van Wagenen Helena Bon	Annatje bo. Dec. 17 bp. Apr. 2, 1750	Abraham Diederikx Geertruy Bon, his wife
		1750	
635	Albertus Spier Osseltje Westervelt	Barent bo. Mar. 4 bp. Apr. 2	Paulus N-Kerk Lena Spier, his wife
636	Johannis Jurrianse Margrietje van Winckel	Gerrit bo. Mar. 6 bp. Apr. 2	Michiel H. Vreland Eliezabet Jurrijansen, his wife
637	Robbert Sickkels Antje Winne	Marten bo. Aug. 13 bp. Oct. 1	Lyvynus Winne Annatje Siph, his wife
638	Cornelius Jurrijansen Aaltje van Winckel	Cornelus[2] bo. Dec. 8 bp. Jan. 27, 1751	Casparus Pryer Sara Andriesen, his wife
		1751	
639	Abraham Pryer Martje Sickkels	Zara bo. Feb. 9 bp. May 6	Anderies Pryer Geertruy Sickkels, his wife

[1] First child.
[2] Baptized at New York.

NO.	PARENTS	CHILD	WITNESSES & SPONSORS 1752
640	Abraham Diederikx Geertruy Bon	Margrietie bo. Apr. 1 bp. May 6	Jacob Gerritsen van Wagenen Margrietie Diederikx
641	Johannis Pryer Geertruy Sickkels	Hendrik bo. Apr. 30 bp. May 6	Hendrik Sickkels Zara Ackerman, his wife
642	Dirk Vreland Neesje Neefje	Feytje bo. Aug. 17 bp. Nov. 5	Albartus Spier Osseltje Westervelt, his wife
643	Johannis van Wagenen Neesje van Wagenen	Jacobus[1] bo. Oct. 7 bp. Nov. 5	Jacob van Wagenen Leya Jurrijanse, his wife
644	Joris Vreland Annatje van Wagenen	Gerrit bo. Nov. 1 bp. Nov. 5	Anderias Pryer Geertruy Sickkels, his wife

1753

NO.	PARENTS	CHILD	WITNESSES & SPONSORS
645	Johannis Diederiks Hester Vreland	Aaltje bp. June 2	Zacharias Sickkels Rachel van Winckel, his wife
646	Anderias Pryer Geertruy Sickkels	Casparus bo. June 14 bp. June 16	Abraham Pryer Martje Sickkels, his wife
647	Joris Kadmus Jannetje Vreland	Jenneke bo. July 17 bp. Sept. 9	Michiel Cornelise Vreland Aagtje Vreland, his daughter
648	(Young) Cornelus van Vorst, Jr. Annatje van Hoorn	Cornelus[2] bo. Sept. 6 bp. Sept. 9	Cornelus van Vorst Klaasje de Moth, his wife

1754

NO.	PARENTS	CHILD	WITNESSES & SPONSORS
649	Johannis Johannisse van Wagenen Neesje van Wagenen	Catlyntje[3] bo. Jan. 2 bp. Mar. 17	Jacob van Wagenen Jannetje van Houten, his wife

[1] First child being a son.
[2] First son.
[3] First daughter.

1754

NO.	PARENTS	CHILD	WITNESSES & SPONSORS
650	Jan York Eliesabeth Ovenmoef	Hendrick bo. Feb. 8 bp. May 19	Joris Vreland Annatje van Wagenen, his wife
651	Livinas Winne Annatje Ziph	Antje[1] bo. May 8 bp. May 19	Robbert Sickkels Antje Winne, his wife
652	Zacharias Sickkels Rachel van Winckel	Abraham bo. Aug. 25 bp. Sept. 29	Abraham Sickkels Aagtje Blinckerhof, his wife
653	Marselis Marselisse Eliesabet Vliereboom	Johan[2] bo. Sept. 13 bp. Sept. 29	Jan Marselisse, Y. M. Jenneje Pryer, Y. W.
654	Derck Vreland Neesje Neefje	Mettje bo. Oct. 31 bp. Mar. 2, 1755	Pieter Adolf Martje Jurrijanse, his wife
655	Harmanis Veeder Antje Hennion	Jacob bo. Dec. 4 bp. Jan. 1, 1755	Hendrik Sobriska Maria Haring, his wife

1755

NO.	PARENTS	CHILD	WITNESSES & SPONSORS
656	Abraham Spier Aagtje Sickkels	Aagtje[3] bo. Mar. 23 bp. June 1	Abraham Kadmus Geertje Bras, his wife
657	Mattheys Everse Helena Spier	Marytje[4] bo. Mar. 27 bp. June 1	Johannis Everse Seytje Spier, his wife
658	Andries Pryer Geertruy Sickkels	Zacharias[5] bo. May 26 bp. June 1	Nicolaas Pryer, Y. M. Selytje Pryer, Y. W.

1756

NO.	PARENTS	CHILD	WITNESSES & SPONSORS
659	Joris Vreland Annatje van Wagenen	Helena bo. May 20 bp. June 20	Joris Cadmus Jannetje Vreland, his wife

[1] First daughter.
[2] First child.
[3] First child and first daughter.
[4] Third child and second daughter.
[5] Second child.

NO.	PARENTS	CHILD	WITNESSES & SPONSORS 1756
660	Hendrik Fielding Aagtje van Winckel	Jannetje bo. May 28 bp. June 21	Gerret Jurriyansen, Y. M. Feytje van Winckel, Y. W.
661	Johannis van Wagenen Neesje van Wagenen	Leya[1] bo. Dec. 17 bp. Jan. 9, 1757	Johannis Van Wagenen Sr. Altje Vreland, his wife
		1757	
662	Helmich van Houten Aagtje Vreland	Jenneke bp. Nov. 13	Joris Kadmus Jannetje Vreland, his wife
663	Andrias Pryer Geertruy Sickels	Johannis bo. Nov. 17 bp. Nov. 27	Johannis Pryer Geertruy Sickels, his wife
664	Cornelis Vreland Catriena Kadmus	Michiel[2] bo. Nov. 24 bp. Dec. 25	Helmich van Houten Aagtje Vreland, his wife
665	Cornelius Gerbrantz Jannetje van Hoorn	Helena[3] bo. Dec. 11 bp. Dec. 25	Cornelus van Vorst Annatje van Hoorn, his wife
666	Jacob van Wagenen, Jr. Aagtje Vreland	Annatje[4] bo. Dec. 31 bp. Jan. 22, 1758	Joris Vreland Annatje van Wagenen, his wife
		1758	
667	Joris Kadmus Jannetje Vreland	Jannetje[5] bo. Jan. 7 bp. Feb. 5	Cornelus Vreland Catriena Kadmus, his wife
668	Harmanis Veeder Antje Hennion	Cornelus bo. Feb. 27 bp. Mar. 5	Theunis Gerbrantz, Y.M. Neeltje Gerbrantze, Y. W.
669	Mattys Everse Helena Spier	Catlyntje bo. May 12 bp. May 14	Paulus Nieuwkerk Helena Spier, his wife

[1] Third child and second daughter.
[2] First son and first child.
[3] First child.
[4] First child and first daughter.
[5] Fifth child and third daughter.

1758 NO.	PARENTS	CHILD	WITNESSES & SPONSORS
670	Jacob van Winckel Rachel Kammegaar	Daniel bo. July 21 bp. July 30	Joseph Waldron AaftjeHeylhaake, his wife
671	Claas Vreland Catlyntje Siph	Michiel[1] bo. July 31 bp. Aug. 13	Gerrit Vreland, Y. M. Belytje Vreland, Y. W.
672	Dominie William Jackson Annatje Vrelenhuysen	William[1] bo. Aug. 14 bp. Aug. 20	Patrik Jackson Annatje vander Spiegel, his wife
673	Robbert Sickels Antje Winne	Ariyantje[2] bo. Aug. 31 bp. Sept. 10	Michiel Demoth Clausie Winnie, his wife
674	Derck Vreland Neesje Neefje	Leya bo. Sept. 17 bp. Nov. 5	Jan York Elisabeth York, his wife
675	Livynus Winne Annatje Siph	Marten bo. Sept. 25 bp. Oct. 8	Johannis Winne, Y. M. Maria Winne, Y. W.
676	Abel De Grauw Maayke Van Eydestyn	Casparus bo. Oct. 15 bp. Nov. 5	Abraham Sickels Aagtje Blinckerhof, his wife
677	Joris Vreland Annatje van Wagenen	Jenneke bo. Dec. 1 bp. Dec. 7	Levynus Winne Annatje Siph, his wife
		1759	
678	Helmich Vreland Neeltje van Hoorn	Michiel bo. Jan. 14 bp. Feb. 11	Helmich van Houten Aagtje Vreland, his wife
679	Jacobus Smith Jannetje Bos	Catriena bo. Feb. 7 bp. Feb. 25	Daniel Salders Annatje Bos, Y. W.
680	Marcelis Marcelisse Elizabet Vlireboom	Aaltje bo. Mar. 19 bp. Mar. 26	
681	Joris Kadmus Jannetje Vreeland	Jannetje bo. Mar. 17 bp. Apr. 22	Dirk Vreeland Martje Vreeland, his wife

[1] First child.
[2] First daughter.

NO.	PARENTS	CHILD	WITNESSES & SPONSORS 1759
682	Jde Marselisse Adriaantje Sip	Peter bo. May 24 bp. June 17	Marselisse Marselisse Elizabet Vliereboom, his wife
683	Pieter de Groot Hester Brouwer	Leya[1] bo. June bp. July 15	Jacob Brouwer Leya Slot, his wife
684	Hendrik Fielding Aagtje van Winckel	Catriena bo. June 24 bp. July 29	Gorge Fielding Debora Fielding, Y. W.
685	Joseph Waldron Antje Diederikx	Gertruy bo. July 31 bp. Aug. 12	James Kalyer Geertruy Diederikx, his wife
686	Johannis Winne Aaltje Diederikx	Antje bo. Nov. 11 bp. Nov. 25	Cornelis Diederikx Antje Roos, his wife.
687	Johannis van Wagenen Aaltje Vreland	Lea bo. Dec. 4 bp. Dec. 25	Johannis Johannisse van Wagenen Neesje van Wagenen, his wife
688	Andreas Pryer Geertruy Sickels	Hartman bo. Dec. 20 bp. Dec. 26	Hartman Sickles, Y. M. Jenneke Pryer, Y. W.
		1760	
689	Margrieta Marten	James bo. Feb. 12 bp. Mar. 12	
690	Johannis Everse Seytje Spier	Catlyntje bo. Mar. 11 bp. Mar. 30	Matthys Everse Helena Spier, his wife
691	Gerbrant Gerbrantze Catriena Spier	Jannetje bo. Mar. 1 bp. Mar. 30	Cornelius Gerbrantze Jannetje van Hoorn, his wife
692	Jacobus Smith Jannetje Bos	Antje bo. Nov. 13 bp. Dec. 7	Michiel Bos Elizabeth Bos

[1] First child.

1760 NO.	PARENTS	CHILD	WITNESSES & SPONSORS
693	Dominie Wilhelmus Jackson Annatje Vrelmighuysen	Theodorus Jacobus bo. Dec. 26 bp. Dec. 28	Hendericus Kuyser Catrina Gerbrantz, his wife
694	Hermanus Veeder Antje Hennion	Marytje bo. Dec. 27 bp. Dec. 28	Johannis van Wagenen Neesje van Wagenen
695	Matthys Everse Helena Spier	Barent bo. Dec. bp. Feb. 1,	Mattheus Nukerck, Y. M. Jannetje Nukerck, Y. W.
696	Cornelus Vreland Catharina Kadmus	Dirck bo. May 25 bp. June 22	Joris Kadmus Jannetje Vreland, his wife
		1761	
697	Daniel van Winckel Aaltje Jurriyansen	Jurrian[1] bo. Feb. 22 bp. Mar. 1	Johannis Jurriansen Jannetje Banta, his wife
698	Helmich van Houten Aagtje Vreland	Michiel bo. Mar. 9 bp. Mar. 15	Joris Cadmus Jannetje Vreland his wife
699	Cornelius van Vorst Annatje van Hoorn	Johannis bo. Mar. 3 bp. Mar. 29	Cornelis Gerbrantze Jannetje van Hoorn, his wife

700 April 3rd. *Have I, Abraham Sickels accepted to serve as Voorleser for the Church at Bergen.*

NO.	PARENTS	CHILD	WITNESSES & SPONSORS
701	Johannis van Wagenen Neesye van Wagenen	Antje bo. Sept. 25 bp. Sept. 27	Jacob van Wagenen Aegye Vreelant, his wife
702	Hendrick Fiylden Aegye van Winkel	Aegye bo. Oct. 19 bp. Oct. 25	Daniel van Rype Beeletye van Rype, his sister
703	Casparis Stuyvesant Saara Kouwenove	Pieter bo. Nov. 6 bp. Nov. 22	Pieter Stuyvesant Jenneke Stuyvesant, his sister

[1] First child.

NO.	PARENTS	CHILD	WITNESSES & SPONSORS	1761
704	Jooris Cadmus Jannitje Vreelant	Joris bo. Oct. 10 bp. Nov. 22	Machiel Vreelant Annatye Vreelant, his wife	
		1762		
705	Corneelus Gerbrantse Jannitje van Hooren	Corneelus bo. Jan. 4 bp. Jan. 24	Cornelus Gerbrantse Jannitje Pier, his wife	
706	William Androw Donen Catherin French	William Androw bp. Jan. 6	Ann Miller, Godmother	
707	Machiel Vreelant Annatie Vreelant	Yoris[1] bo. Jan. 31 bp. Feb. 7	Jooris Cadmus Jannitye Vreelant, his wife	
708	Andries Pryer Geertruy Sickels	Abraham bo. Jan. 31 bp. Feb. 7	Pieter Stuyvesant Pryntie Pryer, his wife	
709	Johannis Winne Aeltie Diederix	Jannitje[2] bo. Feb. 5 bp. Feb. 7	Robbert Sickels Antye Winne, his wife	
710	Nicklaes Pryer Hester Banta	Casparis[1] bo. Feb. 8 bp. Feb. 21	Casparis Pryer Marytye van Rype	
711	Seel Marselisse Elisabet Vlierboom	Pieter bo. Feb. 18 bp. Feb. 21	Johannis Bon Jenneke Marseluse	
712	Claes Vreelant Antye Bessed	Antye bo. Feb. 28 bp. Mar. 7	Martynes Schoonmaker Susanna Bessed	
713	Johannis Brouer Catrina Walderon	Jacop bo. Apr. 13 bp. Apr. 18	Jacop Brouer Eva Slot	
714	Daniel Solder Jackkemeyntie Toers	Johannis bo. Apr. 30 bp. May 2	Mattewes Nieukerk Katlyntie Toers	

[1] First son.
[2] Second daughter.

1762

NO.	PARENTS	CHILD	WITNESSES & SPONSORS
715	Abel de Grau Mayeke Tades	Antye bo. Apr. 2 bp. Apr. 16	Jooris Stek Antye Tades, his wife
716	Cornelus Vreelant Catrina Cadmus	Cornelus bo. Sept. 20 bp. Oct. 17	Machiel Vreelant, Jr. Annatie Vreelant, his wife
717	Helmigh van Houte Aegye Vreelant	Jenneke bo. Oct. 16 bp. Oct. 31	Helmigh Vreelant Jannetye Sip
718	Daniel van Reype Elisabet Terheun	Catrientye[1] bo. Dec. 2 bp. Dec. 12	Joost Sabriske Annatie Terheun, his wife
719	Jacoobes Smit Jannetye Bos	Leeya bo. Nov. 11 bp. Dec. 12	Isack Bos Leeya Brouer, his wife
		1763	
720	Johannis van Houte Aeltie Sickels	Johannis[2] bo. Jan. 22 bp. Jan. 22	Jacop Demot Feytye van Houte, his wife
721	Dominie Willem Jaksen Annatie Vreelinghuyse	Hanna[1] bo. Jan. 27 bp. Feb. 6	Machiel Corneluse Vreelant Anatye Jackson
722	Harmanis Veeder Antie Hennion	Ariaentie[3] bo. May 12 bp. May 29	Do. Willem Jaksen Annatie Vreelinghuysen, his wife
723	Cornelus Sip Beelitye Vreelant	Antye bo. May 20 bp. May 29	Dirrick Vreelant Marritye Vreelant, his wife
724	Lavynis Winne Annatie Sip	Jde bo. May 22 bp. May 29	Gerrit Sip Jenneke Marseelus, his wife
725	Jacop van Winkel Raechel Cammegaer	Catrientie bo. June 1 bp. June 12	Josep van Winkel Treyntie Gerbrantse

[1] First daughter.
[2] First son.
[3] Second daughter.

NO	PARENTS	CHILD	WITNESSES & SPONSORS 1763
726	Henry Fielden Aegye van Winkel	Margrietye bo. Aug. 29 bp. Sept. 18	Daniel Sickels Antie Diderix, his wife
727	Johannis Brouer Catrientie Walderon	Josep[1] bo. Sept. 16 bp. Sept. 18	Josep Walderon Antie Diederix, his wife
728	Matthys Everse Leena Spier	Leena bo. Aug. 29 bp. Oct. 2	Abraham Spier Catleyntie Toers
		1764	
729	Josep Walderon Antie Diderix	Josep bo. Jan. 25 bp. Feb. 19	Johannis Brouer Catrientye Walderon, his wife
730	Cornelis Sip Beeletye Vreelant	Jde[2] bo. May 3 bp. May 27	Lavynus Winne Annati Sip, his wife
731	Cornelis Sip Beeletye Vreelant	Elisabet[2] bo. May 3 bp. May 27	Dirrick Vreelant Marritie Vreelant, his wife
732	Claes Vreeland Antye Bessed	Elisabet bo. May 30 bp. June 10	Hartman Vreelant Marritye Gerbranse, his wife
733	Daniel Solder Jackemyntie Toers	Annatje bo. July 7 bp. July 22	Johannis van Waert Annatie Spier
734	Machiel Vreelant, Jr. Annatie Vreelant	Jannatje bo. July 19 bp. July 22	Jacop van Wagenen Aegye Vreelant, his wife
735	Cornelus Gerbrantse, Jr. Jannitye van Hooren	Jannetye bo. Sept. 3 bp. Sept. 16	Hendricus Cuyper Catrientye Gerbrantse, his wife
736	Gerrit Sip Jenneke Marseluse	Antye[3] bo. Sept. 6 bp. Sept. 16	Lavynes Winne Annatye Sip, his wife

[1] Second son.
[2] Twins (730–731).
[3] First daughter.

1764

NO.	PARENTS	CHILD	WITNESSES & SPONSORS
737	Andries Preyer Geertruy Sickels	Arriaentie[1] bo. Nov. 10 bp. Nov. 11	Daniel Sickels Antje Diderix, his wife
738	Seel Marseeluse Eeliesabet Vliereboom	Yacop bo. Dec. 29 bp. Jan. 27, 1765	
739	Joris Cadmus Jannetye Vreelant	Metye bo. Dec. 22 bp. Dec. (Feb.? 1765)	Johannis Vreelant Femmetye van Tuyl
		1765	
740	Daniel van Winkel Aeltie van Reype	Catrientie[2] bo. Jan. 30 bp. Feb. 10	Jacop van Winkel Rachel Cammegaer, his wife
741	Do. Willem Jaksen Annatye Vreelinghuysen	Hendrikus[3] bo. Feb. 9 bp. Feb. 10	Annatye van der Spiegel, the wife of Petrik Jaksen
742	Johannis van Hooren Beelitye van Reype	Johannis[4] bo. Mar. 30 bp. Apr. 14	Cornelus Gerbrantse, Jr. Jannetye van Hooren
743	Johannis Post Catryntie Retan	Saertye bo. July 3 bp. July 21	Abraham Retan Sara, his wife
744	Cornelus van Vorst Annatie van Hoorn	Klaesye[2] bo. Aug. 31 bp. Sept. 15	Klaesye de Mot, the wife of the late Cornelius Van Vorst
745	Jacobus Calyer Geertye Diderix	Jacobus[5] bo. Oct. 9 bp. Oct. 27	Johannis Diderix Hester Vreelant, his wife
746	Jacobus Smit Jannetye Bos	Cornelus bo. Nov. 8 bp. Nov. 24	Abel de Grau Mayeke Tadese
747	Jacop van Winkel Rachel Cammegaer	(Joseph;)[6] bo. Nov. 26	

[1] First daughter.
[2] Second daughter.
[3] Third son.
[4] First son.
[5] Second son.
[6] Name not given in the original record.

NO.	PARENTS	CHILD	WITNESSES & SPONSORS 1765
748	Johannis Brouer Catrientye Walderon	Leeya bo. Dec. 25 bp. Jan. 19, 1766	Pieter de Groot Hester Brouer, his wife

1766

NO.	PARENTS	CHILD	WITNESSES & SPONSORS
749	Josep Walderon Antye Diderix	Geertruy bo. Feb. 11 bp. Feb. 16	Jeems Collerd Geertruy Diderix, his wife
750	Eckbert Post Saertye Stuyvesant	Adriaen[1] bo. Mar. 30 bp. Apr. 13	Johannis Post Catrientye Retan, his wife
751	Matthewes Nieukerk Catlyntie Toers	Gerrit[1] bo. Apr. 9 bp. Apr. 13	Gerrit Nieukerk Catryntie Nieukerk
752	Tammi Ellen Elisabet Pouelse	Raechel bo. Mar. 3 bp. Apr. 27	Jacop van Winkel Raechel Cammegaer, his wife
753	Gerret Banta Neeltie Gerbrantse	Cornelus bo. Aug. 8 bp. Aug. 31	Cornelus Gerbrantse Yannetye Pier, his wife
754	Hermanis Veder Antie Henneyon	Cornelus bo. Aug. 25 bp. Sept. 28	Johannis Brouer Catrientye Walderon, his wife
755	Claes Vreelant Antye Bessed	Saara bo. Oct. 7 bp. Oct. 26	Pieter Simmensen Leena Bessed
756	Casparis Stuyvesant Sara Kouenove	Samuel bo. Oct. 8 bp. Nov. 23	Eckbert Post Sara Stuyvesant, his wife
757	Johannis Winne Aeltye Diderix	Marte bo. Nov. 24 bp. Dec. 7	Lavynes Winne Annatie Sip, his wife
758	Daniel Solder Jackemeyntie Toers	Sara[2] bo. Feb. 16 bp. Mar. 15	Tewes Nieukerk Geertruy Kog, his wife

[1] First son.
[2] Second daughter.

1766 NO.	PARENTS	CHILD	WITNESSES & SPONSORS
759	Do. Wilyem Jaksen Annatye Vrelinghuyse	Peterick[1] bo. Apr. 17 bp. Apr. 19	Annatie van der Spiegel, widow of Peterick Jaksen
760	Lavynes Winne Annatie Sip	Jde bo. May 3 bp. May 10	Cornelus Sip Beeletye Vreelant, his wife
		1767	
761	Daniel van Reype Elizabeth Terhuen	Cornelus bo. May 23 bp. May 30	Nicklaes Toers Jannetje van Reype, his wife
762	Barnabas Day Mary Berdet	Davit bo. June 5 bp. July 19	
763	Cristiaen Cemmel Dirricke Verveele	Sara bo. July 17 bp. Aug. 2	
764	Daniel Diderix Aegye Sickels	daughter [2] bo. Aug. 24	
765	Gerret Sip Jenneke Marselus	Pieter[3] bo. Aug. 18 bp. Aug. 30	Seel Marselus Elisabet Vliereboom
766	Niclaes Pryer Hester Banta	Jacop[4] bo. Sept. 13 bp. Sept. 13	Jannetye Banta Gerret van Rype
		1768	
767	Johannis Vreelant Keetye Hooglant	Machiel[3] bo. Apr. 18 bp. May 15	Helmig van Houten Aegye Vreelant, his wife
768	Jacop van Winkel Raegel Cammegaer	Josep bo. May 18 bp. May 29	Josep van Winkel Geertruy Sickels, his wife
769	Do. Willem Jaksen Annatye Vreelinghuysen	Johannis bo. June 8 bp. June 12	Annatie van der Spiegel

[1] Fourth son.
[2] First daughter. Died August 31, 1767.
[3] First son.
[4] Second son.

1768

NO.	PARENTS	CHILD	WITNESSES & SPONSORS
770	Mattys Eeverse Helena Spier	Leeya bo. July 5 bp. July 25	Jacop van Wagenen, Jr. Aegye Vreelant, his wife
771	Seel Marselis Elisabet Vliereboom	a daughter bo. Aug. 16	
772	Barent Nieukerk Antie Toers	Arent bo. Sept. 1 bp. Oct. 2	Nickklaes Toers Jannetye van Reype, his wife
773	Cornelus van Vorst Annatie van Hooren	Neeltie bo. Sept. 16 bp. Oct. 2	John van Hooren Beletye van Reype, his wife
774	Helmig van Houte Aegye Vreelant	Machiel bo. Sept. 17 bp. Oct. 30	Johannis Vreelant Knelia Hoaglant
775	Mattewes Nieukerk Catlyntie Toers	Arent bo. Oct. 22 bp. Oct. 30	Daniel Solder Jackemeyntie Toers, his wife
776	Jacop Vreelant Marrytie Banta	Marrytye bo. Dec. 5 bp. Dec. 25	Johannis Vreelant Knelia Hoaglant, his wife
		1769	
777	Joris Cadmus Jenneke Preyer	Dirrik bo. Mar. 16 bp. Apr. 16	Abraham van Tuyl Jenneke Cadmus
778	Jacop Diderix Tietye Verveele	Geertruy bo. May 1 bp. May 14	Jemes Callerd Geertruy Diderix, his wife
779	Abraham Toers Frenkye Santfort	Cornelus bo. June 11 bp. July 9	Johannis van Houten Aeltie Sickels, his wife
780	Daniel Diederix Aegye Sickels	Jannetye[1] bo. June 16 bp. June 26	Josep van Winkel Geertruy Sickels, his wife
781	Eckbert Post Saertje Stuyvesant	Preyntie bo. June 25 bp. July 9	Nicklaes Pryer Hester Banta, his wife

[1] Second daughter.

1769

NO.	PARENTS	CHILD	WITNESSES & SPONSORS
782	Daniel Sickels Antie Diederix	Zacharias[1] bo. June 25 bp. July 9	Robbert Sickels Antie Winne, his wife
783	Gerret van der Hoef Saertie Pryer	Marretye[2] bo. July 3 bp. July 23	Petrus van der Hoef, Y. M. Arriaentie Prier, Y. W.
784	Gerrit van Reype Jannetye Diderix	Jurrie[1] bo. July 20 bp. Aug. 6	Daniel van Winkel Aeltie van Reype, his wife
785	Billi Eerle Catrientie Bos.	Elsye bo. June 22 bp. Sept. 3	Pieter De Groot Hester Brouer, his wife
786	Johannis van Hoorn Beeletye van Reype	Aeltie bo. Sept. 7 bp. Oct. 1	Gerret van Reype Aeltie van Reype, his sister
787	Berney Bisday Polly Berdet	Henne bo. Nov. 12	
788	Josep Walderon Antie Diderix	Johannis bo. Nov. 17 bp. Nov. 26	Jacop Diderix Titye Verveele, his wife
789	Johannis Diderix Antye van Wagenen	Aegye bo. Nov. 23 bp. Nov. 26	Johannis van Wagenen Catlyntie van Wagenen, his sister
790	Cornelus Gerbrantse Jannetye van Hoorn	Neeltie bo. Nov. 28 bp. Dec. 24	Johannis van Hoorn Beeletye van Reype, his wife
791	Seel Marseeluse Elisabet Vliereboom	Aeltie bo. Dec. 16 bp. Jan. 21, 1770	

1770

NO.	PARENTS	CHILD	WITNESSES & SPONSORS
792	Gerrit Sip Jenneke Marseelus	Jenneke bo. Mar. 12 bp. Mar. 18	Cornelus Sip Beeletye Vreelant, his wife
793	Nicklaes Toers Jannetye van Reype	Annatie bo. Apr. 3 bp. Apr. 15	Mattewes Nieukerk Catleyntie Toers, his wife

[1] First son.
[2] First daughter.

NO.	PARENTS	CHILD	WITNESSES & SPONSORS 1770
794	Casparis Stuyvesant Saertie Kouenove	Johannis bo. Apr. 22 bp. May 13	Kobes Brouer Jannetye van Saen, his wife
795	Do. Willem Jaksen Annatie Vreelinghuyse	Patrick bo. Apr. 28 bp. May 13	Annatie van der Spiegel
796	Hendrik Sickels Jenneke Stuyvesant	Raechel[1] bo. May 1 bp. May 13	Pieter Stuyvesant Leena de Marre, his wife
797	Abel de Grau Maycke Eydestyn	Cornelus bo. June 9 bp. July 9	Hendricus Kuyper Catrientie Gerbrans, his wife
798	Jacop Nieukerk Fytie Henneyon	Mareytye[2] bo. July 18 bp. July 22	Mattewes Nieukerk Geertruy Kog, his wife
799	Daniel Solder Jackkemeyntie Toers	Jaccemyntie bo. July 13 bp. Aug. 15	Mattewes Nieukerk Catleyntie Toers, his wife
800	Joris Cadmus Jenneke Pryer	Casparis bo. Aug. 16 bp. Sept. 16	Cornelus Corsen Neeltie Cadmus, his wife
801	Pieter Stuyvesant Lena de Mare	Pieter[3] bo. Sept. 20 bp. Oct. 7	Henderick Sickels Jenneke Stuyvesant, his wife
802	Christiaen Cemmel Dirrickye Verveel	Elisabet bo. Oct. 13 bp. Oct. 28	
803	Peterus Van der Hoef Raegel van Blerkom	Henderick bo. Oct. 22 bp. Oct. 28	Gerrit van der Hoef Sara Pryer, his wife
804	Jacop Vrelant Wyntie der Jee	Machiel bo. Oct. 11 bp. Nov. 11	Dirreck Vreelant Marretye Vreelant, his wife
805	Jacop van Winkel Raeghel Cammegaer	Leeya bo. Nov. 7 bp. Nov. 25	Daniel van Winkel Aeltie van Reype, his wife

[1] First daughter.
[2] First daughter.
[3] First son.

1770 NO.	PARENTS	CHILD	WITNESSES & SPONSORS
806	Cornelies Blinkerhof Jannetye Kip	Hendrick[1] bo. Dec. 31 bp. Jan. 6, 1771	Hendrick Blinkerhof Geesye Blinkerhof
807	Jacop Diderix Tietye Verveele	Daniel bo. Dec. 20 bp. Jan. 20, 1771	Daniel Verveele
808	Jakobes Brouwer Jannetye van Saen	Yannetye bo. Dec. 30 bp. Jan. 20, 1771	Ysack van Saen Jannetye Ackerman
		1771	
809	Corneelus Sip Beeletye Vreelant	Jde bo. Jan. 14 bp. Jan. 20	Gerrit Sip Jenneke Marseelus, his wife
810	Harmanis Veeder Antie Hennion	Jacop bo. Feb. 18 bp. Mar. 17	Jacop Nieukerk Fytye Hennion, his wife
811	Daniel Eerell Marytye Wilyems	Saertie bo. Feb. 26 bp. Apr. 26	Saertie Akkerman
812	Gerret vander Hoef Saara Preyer	Eeva[2] bo. Apr. 25 bp. May 12	Jakobes van der Hoef Marreytye van der Hoef
813	Matteewes Nieukerk Catlyntie Toers	Hendrick[3] bo. June 22 bp. July 7	Hendrick Nieukerk Janetye Nieukerk
814	Johannis Sickels Sara Walderon	Hendrick bo. July 21 bp. Aug. 16	Hendrick Sickels Jenneke Stuyvesant, his wife
815	Eenog Vreelant Keetye Kip	Joris bo. Aug. 16 bp. Sept. 15	Joris Vreelant Annatie van Wagenen, his wife
816	Do. Willem Jaksen Annatie Vreelinghuyse	Ferdinandus Vrelinghuysen bo. Sept. 15 bp. Sept. 29	

[1] First Son.
[2] Second daughter.
[3] Third son.

NO.	PARENTS	CHILD	WITNESSES & SPONSORS 1771
817	Eckbert Post Sara Stuyvesant	Pieter bo. Nov. 4 bp. Dec. 8	
818	Corneelus Eerrell Elisabet Donkim	Marreytye bo. Aug. 9 bp. Jan. 19, 1772	
819	Johannis van Hoorn Belletye van Reype	Neeltie bo. Dec. 28 bp. Jan. 19, 1772	Rut van Bront Leena van Hooren
		1772	
820	Daniel Diderix Aegye Sickels	Aegye[1] bo. Jan. 9 bp. Jan. 20	
821	Hendrick van Winkel Jannetye Brouwer	Catrina bo. Jan. 26 bp. Mar. 1	
822	Pieter Kool Susanna Lattoret	Elisabet bo. Oct. 7, 1771 bp. Feb. 22	
823	Berney Bisday Polley Berdet	Leuwes bo. June 20 bp. Aug. 9	
824	Koobes Makniel Antye Lisk	John bo. Aug. 25 bp. Sept. 6	Johannis van Wagenen Neesje van Wagenen, his wife
825	Daniel van Reype Betye Terhuen	Dirrick bo. Aug. 28 bp. Sept. 6	Albert Terhuen Marrytye Demarre
826	John Jork Arriaentie Smit	Elisabet bo. Oct. 7 bp. Nov. 1	Joris Cadmus Jenneke Pryer, his wife
827	Josep Walderon Antie Diderix	Antie bo. Oct. 13 bp. Nov. 1	Jems Collerd Geertruy Diderix, his wife
828	Pieter Stuyvesant Leena De Marre	Johannes bo. Oct. 19 bp. Nov. 1	Johannes De Marre and his wife

[1] Third daughter.

1772 NO.	PARENTS	CHILD	WITNESSES & SPONSORS
829	Johannis Vreelant Knelia Hoagland	Jannetye bo. Oct. 22 bp. Nov. 1	Cornelus Vreelant Catrientie Cadmus, his wife
830	Hendrick Sickels Jenneke Stuyvesant	Pieter bo. Oct. 24 bp. Nov. 15	Robbert Sickels Antie Winne, his wife
831	Nicklaes Toers Jannetye van Reype	Aeltie bo. Nov. 8 bp. Nov. 15	John van Hooren Belletye van Reype, his wife
832	Jacop Nieukerk Fytye Henneyon	Poulus bo. Nov. 25 bp. Nov. 27	Geertie Kogh, wife of Mattewes Niewkerk
		1773	
833	Isak van Gelder Elisabet Wekken	Wynant bo. Feb. 17 bp. Jan. 17	Kobes van Gelder Bekye Eerrel, his wife
834	Jacop Diderix Tietje Verveele	Yannetye bo. Jan. 25 bp. Feb. 14	Daniel Sickels Antye Diderix, his wife
835	Johannis Buys Leena Marseelus	Petrus[1] bo. Apr. 21 bp. May 23	Catrina Buys
836	Johannis Buys Leena Marseelus	Catrina[1] bo. Apr. 21 bp. May 23	Catrina Buys
837	Peetrus van der Hoef Raagel van der Hoef	Jannetie bo. May 6 bp. May 18	Leujkes? van Blerkum Elisabet van Blerkum, his wife
838	Meyndert Gerbrantse Elisabet	Tryntie bo. May 29 bp. June 6	John van Hooren Beeletye van Reype, his wife
839	John Meyer Elisabet	Elisabet bo. Nov. 7 bp. Dec. 5	
840	Seel Marseelus Elisabet Vliereboom	Annatie bo. Nov. 26 bp. Dec. 5	Jenneke Marseelus

[1] Twins (835 and 836).

NO.	PARENTS	CHILD	WITNESSES & SPONSORS 1773
841	Casparis Stuyvesant Saartie Kouwenhove	Saara bo. Nov. 15 bp. Jan. 1	
842	Eckbert Post Saara Stuyvesant	Johannis bo. Dec. 18 bp. Jan. 1, 1774	Johannis van Reype Elisabet Post, his wife
843	Jacop Gerbrantse Keetye Eerrel	Meyndert bo. Oct. 11 bp. Feb. 30, 1774	Josep van Winkel Geertruy Sickels, his wife
		1774	
844	Nettennel Eerrell Polley	Neeltie bo. Feb. 30	Kasparis Steymets Raagel Banker, his wife
845	Jacop Preyer Selley Eiddwm	Abigel bo. Jan. 24 bp. Feb. 27	
846	Klaes Vreelant Nensei Bessed	Beelitye bo. Apr. 17 bp. May 1	Dirrick Vreelant Beleetye Vreelant, the wife of Corneelus Sip
847	Gerrit vander Hoef Saertie Pryer	Hendrik[1] bo. June 18 bp. July 10	Niklaes Preyer Hester Banta, his wife
848	Isack van Gelder Elisabet Wekken	Isack bo. June 15 bp. July 24	
849	Johannis van Hooren Beeletye van Reype	Gerrit bo. June 28 bp. July 24	Daniel van Reype Elisabet Terhuen, his wife
850	Johannis Vreelant Knelia Hoaglant	Jannetye bo. June 23 bp. July 24	
851	Pieter Kool Susanna Lattoret	Isack bo. July 4 bp. Aug. 7	
852	Do. Willem Jaksen Annatie Vreelinghuyse	Heeva bo. Sept. 17 bp. Sept. 18	Anatie van der Spiegel

[1] First son.

1774 NO.	PARENTS	CHILD	WITNESSES & SPONSORS
853	Daniel van Winkel Aeltie van Reype	Hendrick bo. Nov. 27 bp. Dec. 11	Josep van Winkel Geertruy Sickels, his wife
854	Johannis Diderix Antie van Wagenen	Aegye bo. Dec. 21 bp. 25, 1775	John Bon, Y. M. Catlyntie van Wagenen, Y. W.
		1775	
855	John York Arriyaentie Smith	John bo. Feb. 8 bp. Mar. 5	Jacop van Wagenen Aege Vreelant, his wife
856	Johannis van Houten Aeltie Sickels	Saara bo. Feb. 15 bp. Mar. 5	Hendrick Sickels Annatie Bokkenhoove, his wife
857	Hendrick van Winkel Selley Pier	Raeggel[1] bo. Mar. 29 bp. Apr. 2	Jacop van Winkel Susanna Westervelt, his wife
858	Johannis Mutsker Jannetye Fielden	Jacop[2] bo. Feb. 15 bp. Mar. 27	
859	Nicklaes Lisier Marrytye Kroese	Jacop bo. Mar. 10 bp. Apr. 30	Abraham Sickels Aegye Blinkerhof, his wife
860	Jacop Diderix Titye Verveele	Aeltie bo. May 28 bp. July 9	Eckbert Post Saara Stuyvesant, his wife
861	John Buys Annatie Marseelus	Daniel bo. June 10 bp. July 9	Daniel Fish
862	Isack Jansen Jannetye Boerum	Johannis bo. Aug. 7 bp. Sept. 3	
863	Gerrit van Reype Catleyntie van Wagenen	Margrietye bo. Oct. 10 bp. Oct. 15	Niklaes Toers Jannetye van Reype, his wife

[1] First daughter.
[2] First son.

NO.	PARENTS	CHILD	WITNESSES & SPONSORS	1775
863	Jacop van Hooren Catrientie Stuyvesant	Raeggel bo. Oct. 25 bp. Nov. 12	Eckbert Post Sara Stuyvesant, his wife	
864	Jorg Wels Loos Gilbert	Abigel bo. Oct. 8 bp. Nov. 12	Marreyte van der Hoef	
865	Gileam Ouytwater Antye Vreelant	Johannis bo. Nov. 5 bp. Nov. 26	Johannis van Wagenen Aeltie Vreelant, his wife	
		1776		
867	Johannis Marseelus Aeltie van Reype	Marseelus bo. Jan. 8 bp. Feb. 18	Seel Marseelus Elisabet Vliereboom, his wife	
868	Wiert Banta Leeya de Groot	Pieter de Groot[1] bo. Feb. 16 bp. Mar. 17	Pieter de Groot Hester Brouer, his wife	
869	Pieter Kadmus Blaudina Kip	Elisabet bo. Mar. 3 bp. Mar. 17	Abraham Spier Annatie Spier	
870	Jurrey Callerd Polley Toeder	Anatie[2] bo. Mar. 21 bp. Mar. 31	Jemes Callerd Geertruy Diderix, his wife	
871	Jacop Nieukerk Fytye Hennion	Poulus[1] bo. Apr. 13 bp. Apr. 28	Barent Nieukerk Antie Toers, his wife	
872	Abraham Sickels Polley van Waert	Abraham[3] bo. June 28 bp. July 7	Gerrit van der Hoef Sara Preyer, his wife	
873	John Vreelant Keetie de Marre	Neeltie bo. July 20 bp. Aug. 12	Johannis Vreelant Keetye, his wife	
874	Leevey Raeft Saara Buys	Saara bo. May 25 bp. Aug. 16		

[1] First son.
[2] First daughter.
[3] First son.

1776 NO.	PARENTS	CHILD	WITNESSES & SPONSORS
875	John Wieller Elisabet Bertolf	Wyburg[1] bo. Oct. 28 bp. Feb. 17	
		1777	
876	Hendrick van Winkel Sara Spier	Raeggel bo. Feb. 13 bp. Mar. 16	Josep van Winkel Geertruy Sickels, his wife
877	Richert Broeks Sara Broeks	Jards bo. Apr. 27 bp. Apr. 27	Gergs Maeds Samalli Richard Ann Matkins
878	Johannis Eeverse Styntie Eyderstyn	Elisabet bo. Oct. 9 bp. Nov. 2	Jacop Eeverse Katleyntie Eeverse, his sister
879	Barent van Nieukerk Antie Toers	Jannetye bo. Nov. 15	
		1778	
880	Jacop van Wagene Aegje Blinkerhof	Klaesye bo. Mar. 17 bp. Mar. 22	Klaesje van Houten, the wife of Hartman Blinkerhof Hendrick Blinkerhof
881	Harmanis Gardenier Marya Retan	Leeya bo. Apr. 14, 1777 bp. Apr. 19, 1778	
882	Johannis Vreelant Keetye Hooglant	Jenneke bo. Apr. 1 bp. May 3	
883	Jacop Nieukerk Fytye Henneyon	Jacop bo. Apr. 28 bp. June 11	
884	Klaes Vreelant Nensei Besset	Steeve bo. May 31 bp. June 11	
885	Johannis Diderix Antie van Wagenen	Geertie bo. July 1 bp. July 12	Daniel Sickels Antie Diderix, his wife

[1] Daughter.

NO.	PARENTS	CHILD	WITNESSES & SPONSORS
			1778
886	Kasparus Preyer Katrienie Kleyndinni	Geertie[1] bo. July 5 bp. July 26	Hartman Preyer Geertruy Sickels, his mother
887	Hendrick van Winkel Saara Spier	Johannis bo. Nov. 9 bp. Nov. 29	Abraham van Winkel Susanna Westervelt
888	John Marseelus Aeltie van Reype	Corneelus bo. Oct. 15 bp. Nov. 29	
889	Gerrit van der Hoef Saara Preyer	Araientie bo. Oct. 23 bp. Nov. 29	Jacop Preyer Saara Jddo, his wife
890	John Ackkerman Antie Demsei	John bo. Nov. 20 bp. Jan. 1, 1779	
891	Kobes van Gelder Saara Ackkerman	Jsack bo. Oct. 1 bp. Jan. 1, 1779	
892	Walter Kleyndinni Jenneke Marseelus	Marseelus bo. Nov. 24 bp. Dec. 27	
893	Do. Willem Jaksen Annatie Vreelinghuyse	Robbert bo. Dec. 21 bp. Jan. 1, 1779	Annatie van der Spiegel
894	Casparis Stuyvesant Saertie Kouenove	Ned bo. Dec. 12 bp. Jan. 15, 1779	
		1779	
895	Johannis Vreelant Leena Gerbrantse	Joris[2] bo. Jan. 10 bp. Feb. 7	Joris Kadmus Jenneke Preyer, his wife
896	Abraham Sickels Palley van Waert	Raechel[1] bo. Feb. 24 bp. Mar. 7	Daniel Sickels Antie Diderix, his wife

[1] First daughter.
[2] First son.

1779 NO.	PARENTS	CHILD	WITNESSES & SPONSORS
897	Antibby Earle Elisabet Etsel	Edwart bo. Dec. 23 bp. May 16	
898	Keetye Baelden	Margritie van Winkel bo. May 2 bp. May 24	
899	Corneelus Gerbrantse Jannetye Kip	Pieter bo. Sept. 12 bp. Oct. 3	
900	Johannis van Houte Raeghel de Marre	Helmig bo. Aug. 1 bp. Oct. 17	
901	Jacop Preyer Selli Idoo	Geertie bo. Nov. 10 bp. Dec. 12	Casparis Preyer Geertie Sickels
902	Daniel Diderix Aegye Sickels	Antye bo. Nov. 15 bp. Dec. 26	Jannetye Diderix, the wife of Gerrit van Reype
903	Gerrit van Reype Catrientie van Reype	Grietye bo. Dec. 31 bp. Jan. 23, 1780	
		1780	
904	Kasparis Preyer Katrientie Kleyndini	Nelley bo. Feb. 1 bp. Mar. 5	Nelley Kleyndinni
905	John Smit Nensey de Marre	Nancey bo. Feb. 5 bp. Mar. 5	Johannis van Houte Raeghelde Marre, his wife
906	Jooris Cadmus Aegye Fielden	Jannetye bo. 1780 bp. Mar. 19	Gerrit Vreeland Jannetye Cadmus, his wife
907	John Vreelant Keetye de Marre	Catrientie bo. Mar. 8 bp. Apr. 16	
908	Koobes van Gelder Serrey Ackerman	John bo. Feb. 16 bp. Apr. 30	

NO.	PARENTS	CHILD	WITNESSES & SPONSORS 1780
909	Machiel Vreelant Annatie Vreelant	John bo. May 1 bp. May 28	Johannis Vreelant Leena Gerbrantse, his wife
910	Ep Post Saara Stuyvesant	Corneelus bo. May 26 bp. June 11	Peetrus van der Hoef Raeggel van Blerkum, his wife
911	Jacop van Hooren Catrientie Stuyvesant	Catrientie bo. June 21 bp. June 25	Eckbert Post Saara, his wife
912	Jacop Nieukerk Fytye Henneon	Gerrit bo. July 21 bp. Aug. 6	Mattewes Nieukerk Geertie Kog, his wife
913	Hendrick Ackkerman Rebekke Halenbeek	Johannis bo. Sept. 10 bp. Oct. 15	
914	Johannis Eeverse Steyntie Eydersteyn	Johannis bo. Oct. 14 bp. Oct. 24	
915	Pieter Stuyvesant Leena de Marre	Maria bo. Nov. 22 bp. Nov. 26	Jacop Preyer Selli Ido, his wife
916	Thomas Cubberley Mary Mersaro	Ann bo. Nov. 14 bp. Dec. 16	
917	—— Parsel	Amela[1] bp. Dec. 16	
918	John Marseelus Aeltie van Reype	Aeltie bo. Dec. 29 bp. Feb. 4, 1781	John van Hooren Beeletye van Reype, his wife
		1781	
919	Hendrick Nieukerk Jenneke Vreelant	Gerrit bo. Jan. 8 bp. Jan. 21	Mattewes Nieukerk Catleyntie Toers, his wife
920	Gilyaem Outwater Antye Vreelant	Aeltie bo. Dec. 11 bp. Feb. 18	Jacop van Wagene Aegye Blinkerhof, his wife

[1] A daughter of about seven years old and is named Amela Parsel.

1781 NO.	PARENTS	CHILD	WITNESSES & SPONSORS
921	Hendrick Blinkerhof Leeya van Wagene	Hartman bo. Apr. 15 bp. May 13	Jacop van Wagene Aegye Blinkerhof, his wife
922	Mattewes Nieukerk Geertie Kog	Johannis bo. May 18 bp. June 10	Jacop Nieukerk Fytye Hennion, his wife
923	Gerrit Vreelant Jennetye Kadmus	Jacop bo. June 25 bp. July 22	Jacop Vreelant Jenneke Cadmus, his wife
924	Walter Kleyndinni Jenneke Marseelus	Neeltie bo. July 9 bp. Aug. 5	
925	Machiel Vreelant Geertruy Sickels	Catlyntie[1] bo. Aug. 28 bp. Sept. 15	Cornelius Sip Beeletye Vreelant, his wife
926	Casparis Preyer Catrientie Kleydenni	Saertie bo. Sept. 29 bp. Oct. 28	Gerrit van der Hoef Saertie Preyer, his wife
927	Jooris Vreelant Jannetye Blinkerhof	Machiel bo. Oct. 31 bp. Nov. 25	Hendrik Nieukerk Jenneke Vreelant, his wife
928	Johannis van Houten Raagel de Marre	Catrientie bo. Nov. 14 bp. Dec. 23	
		1782	
929	Jacop Eeverse Catrientie Smit	Janneke bo. Mar. 20 bp. Apr 14.	Mattewes Nieukerk Geertie Kog, his wife
930	John Gerritse Metye Cadmus	Jannetye bo. Mar. 25 bp. Apr. 28	Gerrit Vreelant Jannetye Cadmus,his wife
931	John Vreelant Keetye De Marre	Jannetye bo. June 22 bp. July 21	John van Hooren Beeletye van Reype, his wife
932	Jacop Nieukerk Fytye Hennion	Marrytye bo. July 13 bp. Aug. 18	Niklaers Toers Yannetye van Reype

[1] First daughter.

NO.	PARENTS	CHILD	WITNESSES & SPONSORS 1782
933	Jacop van Wagene Aegye Blinkerhof	Catlyntie bo. Aug. 3 bp. Sept. 18	Hendrick Blinkerhof Leeya van Wagene, his wife
934	Gerrit van der Hoef Sara Preyer	Sara bo. Sept. 9 bp. Nov. 24	Jeems Dad Marrytye van Scheyve, his wife
935	Johannis Vreelant Keetye Hooglant	Keetye bp. Nov. 24	Johannis van Houten Raegel De Marre, his wife
936	Tames Cubberly Pally Misyero	Sofiah bo. Nov. 10 bp. Dec. 8	
937	Gerrit van Reype Catrientie van Reype	Catlyntie bo. Nov. 29 bp. Dec. 21	Casparis Preyer Antye van Wagene, his wife
		1783	
938	Barent Everse Jeinie Mekdannel	Barent bo. Mar. 1 bp. Mar. 17	Jacop Eeverse Catrientie Smit, his wife
939	Abraham Sickels Palli van Wert	Annatie bo. Feb. 27 bp. Mar. 23	Niklaes Toers Jannetye van Reype, his wife
940	Davit Hennion Catleyntie Eeverse	Marreytye bo. Mar. 13 bp. Apr. 20	Johannis Everse Sellei Griffens, his wife
941	Jacop Preyer Selley Ido	Palley bo. May 17 bp. June 15	Johannis van Houte Aeltie Sickels, his wife
942	Hendrick Ackkerman Rebekke Halenbeek	Edwart bo. May 2 bp. Aug. 3	
943	Daniel van Winkel Antie Winne	Cornelus bo. Aug. 6 bp. Sept. 31	Jooris Sipper Catrientie van Winkel, his wife
944	Jacop Brouer Jannetye van Saan	Jacobes bo. Aug. 7 bp. Sept. 31	

1783 NO.	PARENTS	CHILD	WITNESSES & SPONSORS
945	Jeems Dad Marreyti van Schyve	Thomas bo. Aug. 27 bp. Sept. 28	Abraham Preyer Arriaentie Preyer, his sister
946	Johanis van Houte Raegel De Marre	Eegye bo. Aug. 27 bp. Sept. 28	John van Houte Annatie Callerd, his wife
947	Johanis Callerd Geertruy Pryer	Johannis bo. Sept. 9 bp. Oct. 12	Jacop Preyer Sellei Eiddo, his wife
948	Hendrick Nieukerk Jenneke Vreelant	Joris bo. Nov. 25 bp. Dec. 21	Aegye Vreelant
949	Jurri van Winkel Antye Sip	Gerrit bo. Dec. 16 bp. Dec. 21	Daniel van Winkel Aeltie van Reype, his wife
		1784	
950	Jooris Cadmus Aegye Tielden	Aegye bp. Jan. 4	Gerrit van Reype Catrientie van Reype, his wife
951	Nicklaes Toers Jannetye van Reype	Arent[1] bo. Jan. 27 bp. Feb. 1	Daniel van Reype Elisabet Terhuen, his wife
952	John Marseelus Aeltie van Reype	Elisabet bo. Jan. 19 bp. Feb. 15	Jacop Marseelus, Y. M. Heeleena van Horren, Y. W.
953	John van Houte Annatie Callerd	Geertie bo. Feb. 10 bp. Feb. 21	Johannis Callerd Geertie Preyer, his wife
954	Johannis Eevers Saara Kirffens	Steyntie bo. Jan. 4 bp. Feb. 22	Davit Henneyon Catlyntie Evers, his wife
955	Gerrit Vreelant Jannetye Cadmus	Annatie bo. Feb. 15 bp. Mar. 14	Hendrick Nieukerk Jenneke Vreelant, his wife
956	Jooris Vreelant Jannetye Blinkerhof	Hartman bo. Mar. 15 bp. Apr. 11	Jacop van Wagene Aegye Blinkerhof, his wife

[1] First son.

NO.	PARENTS	CHILD	WITNESSES & SPONSORS	1784
957	John Vreelant Keetye De Marre	Nensy bo. Mar. 19 bp. Apr. 25	Nicklaes Toers Jannetye van Reype, his wife	
958	Koobes van Gelder Saara Ackkerman	Samuel bo. Mar. 23 bp. May 9	Samuel Berdet and his wife	
959	Casparis Preyer Keetye Klyndinni	Palley bo. May 10 bp. June 5	Abraham Sickels Palley van Weert, his wife	
960	Jannetye Wilson	Gerrit bo. May 29		
961	John Killi Leeya Diderix	John bo. May 23 bp. June 20	Nickklaes Toers Jannetye van Reype, his wife	
962	Hendrick Blinkerhof Leeya van Wagene	Catleyntie bo. July 13 bp. Aug. 1	Casparis Preyer Antie van Wagenen, his wife	
963	Eckbert Post Saara Stuyvesant	Preyntie bo. July 13 bp. Sept. 12	Pieter Stuyvesant Leena de Marre, his wife	
964	Joris Shipper Catrientie van Winkel	Raeggel bo. Sept. 4 bp. Sept. 26	Hendrick van Winkel Saera Spier, his wife	
965	Hendrick Errel	Hendrick bo. July 17 bp. Oct. 10	Petterick Reyli Elisabet de Vael, his wife	
966	Barent Eeverse Jannetye Mekdannil	Jacop bo. Sept. 5 bp. Oct. 24	Jacop Eeverse Catrientie Smit, his wife	
		1785		
967	Machiel Vreelant Geertie Sickels	Catleyntie bo. Jan. 9 bp. Feb. 13	Marten Winne, Y. M. Elisabet Vreelant, Y. W.	
968	Abraham Sickels Palley van Wert	Elisabet bo. Mar. 15 bp. Apr. 17		

1785 NO.	PARENTS	CHILD	WITNESSES & SPONSORS
969	Johannis Eeverse Sellei Griffens	Seytye bo. Apr. 13 bp. May 16	Mattewes Nieukerk Cateleynt Toers, his wife
970	Abel Smith Rachel Douwe	Catrientie bo. Mar. 18 bp. June 12	
971	Casparis Sebriske Annatie Vreelant	Machiel bo. May 31 bp. July 3	Machiel Vreelant Annatie Vreelant, his his wife
972	John van Hooren Jannetye Gerbrantse	John bo. June 23 bp. July 3	Corneelus Gerbrantse Leena van Hooren, his wife
973	Gerrit van Reype Catrientye van Reype	Elisabet bo. July 13 bp. July 31	Daniel van Reype Elisabet Terhuen, his wife
974	Jacop van Wagene Aegye Blinkerhof	Johannis bo. July 27 bp. July 31	Casparis Preyer Antie van Wagene, his wife
975	John Shipper Keetye Baelden	Marya bo. July 29 bp. Aug. 14	Jooris Sipper Catrientie van Winkel, his wife
976	Abraham van Winkel Antye Klyndinney	Walter bo. Oct. 4 bp. Nov. 6	
977	Zagharis Sickels Ellener Toers	Frenses bo. Oct. 17 bp. Nov. 20	Abraham Sickels Palley van Weert, his wife
978	Hendrick Banta Margriety Diderix	Hendrick bo. Nov. 21 bp. Jan. 15	Gerrit Banta Neeltye Gerbrans, his wife
979	Davit Henneyon Catlyntie Eevers	Seytye bo. Dec. 23 bp. Jan. 15	Gerrit Nieukerk, Y. M. Marytye Hennion, Y. W.
980	Johannis Callerd Geertruy Preyer	Jacobes bo. Dec. 19 bp. Jan. 15, 1786	John van Houte Annatye Callerd, his wife

NO.	PARENTS	CHILD	WITNESSES & SPONSORS
			1786
981	Barent Eeverse Jannetye Makdennel	Barent bo. Mar. 12 bp. May 7	Johannis Eeverse Selley Griffens, his wife
982	Daniel van Winkel Antye Winne	Aeltye bo. Apr. 11 bp. May 7	Gerrit van Reype Jannetye Winne, his wife
983	Benyamen Eth (or Etli) Pekkee Brouyer	Keetye bo. Mar. 1 bp. June 4	
984	Arei Banta Leena Westervelt	Eefye bo. Apr. 2 bp. June 4	
985	Jooris Vreelant Jannetye Blinkerhof	Annatie bo. July 30 bp. Aug. 27	Machiel Vreelant Annatie Vreelant, his wife
986	Jooris Sipper Catrientie van Winkel	Joosep bo. Sept. 20 bp. Sept. 29	Josep van Winkel Geertruy Sickels, his wife
987	Jacop Nieukerk Fytye Hennion	Johannis bo. Oct. 23 bp. Nov. 19	Barent Nieukerk Antie Toers, his wife
988	Ned De Vael Nensei Don	Enney bp. Nov. 19	
989	Machiel Vreelant Geertie Sickels	Antye bo. Dec. 14 bp. Jan. 14	Daniel Sickels Antye Diderix, his wife
		1787	
990	John van Hooren Jannetye Gerbrans	Corneelus bo. Feb. 3 bp. Mar. 11	
991	John Blinkerhof Selli Smith	Saara bo. Feb. 17 bp. Mar. 11	Jacop van Wagene Aegye Blinkerhof, his wife
992	Walter Klyndinni Jenneke Marseelus	Jannetye bo. Mar. 4 bp. Mar. 25	Pieter Marseelus Jannetye Deryie, his wife

1787 NO.	PARENTS	CHILD	WITNESSES & SPONSORS
993	Abraham van Winkel Nensi Kleyndinni	Walter bo. Mar. 26 bp. May 6	
994	Jacop Eeverse Catrientie Smit	Seytye bo. Apr. 17 bp. May 6	
995	Jurrie van Winkel Antye Sip	Daniel bo. May 13 bp. June 3	Pieter Sip Jenneke Sip, his sister
996	Tammes Mekdennil Annatie van Scheyve	John bo. May 23 bp. June 17	
997	Adam Rap Arriaentie Preyer	Geertruy bo. May 28 bp. July 1	Yeems Dad Marreytye van Scheyve, his wife
998	Machiel de Mot Marreytye Manderviel	Jooris bo. June 1 bp. July 1	
999	Gerrit van Reype Leena Vreelant	Jooris bo. June 3 bp. July 1	John Vreelant Aegye Vreelant, his wife
1000	Gerrit Vreelant Jannetye Cadmus	Jooris bo. July 12 bp. Aug. 12	
1001	Abel Smith Raeggel Douwe	Sara bo. July 20 bp. Aug. 12	
1002	Pieter Marseeluse Yannetye Deryee	Elisabet bo. Aug. 13 bp. Aug. 26	Seel Marseelus Elisabet Vliereboom, his wife
1003	Zagharias Sickels Ellener Toers	Raeggel bo. Sept. 13 bp. Sept. 23	John van Houte Annatie Kalyer, his wife
1004	Hartman Preyer Santye Post	Andries bo. Nov. 16 bp. Dec. 2	Adam Rap Arriaentie Preyer, his wife
1005	Adriaen Post Raeggel Sickels	Eckbert bo. Nov. 15 bp. Dec. 2	Eckbert Post Saara Stuyvesant, his wife

NO.	PARENTS	CHILD	WITNESSES & SPONSORS 1788
1006	Casparis Kadmus Catlyntie Dad	Saertie bo. 1788 bp. Feb. 24	
1007	Abraham Sickels Palli van Wert	Geertruy bo. Feb. 10 bp. Mar. 23	John Marseelus Aeltie van Reype, his wife
1008	Jeemes Dad Marreytye van Scheyve	Johannis bo. Feb. 14 bp. Mar. 23	Gerrit vander Hoef Sara Preyer, his wife
1009	Corneelus van Reype Elisabet Vreelant	Daniel bo. Mar. 7 bp. Mar. 23	Daniel van Reype Elisabet Terhuen, his wife
1010	Johannis Eevers Selley Griffens	Johannis bo. Feb. 18 bp. Apr. 6	Arent Nieukerk, Y. M. Leena Eeverse, Y. W.
1011	Cornelus Gerbrants Leena van Hooren	Jannetye bo. Mar. 5 bp. Apr. 20	John van Hooren Jannetye Gerbrants
1012	Hendrick Blinkerhof Leeya van Wagene	Klaesje bo. Apr. 8 bp. May 4	Jooris Vreelant Jannetye Blinkerhof, his wife
1013	Gerrit van Reype Jannetye Winne	Johannis bo. May 10 bp. May 25	Marte Winne, Y. M. Jannetye Diderix, Y. W
1014	Johannis Collerd Geertruy Preyer	Geertruy bo. June 15 bp. July 13	Jeemes Callerd Geertruy, his wife
1015	John Dey Femmetye Creen	Benjamin bo. Sept. 22 bp. Oct. 19	
1016	Gerrit Nieukerk Palley Ackkerman	Catleyntie bo. Oct. 10 bp. Nov. 2	Arent Nieukerk, Y. M. Jakkemeyntie Solders, Y. W.
1017	Daniel van Winkel Antie Winne	Jacop bo. Oct. 28 bp. Nov. 16	Marte Winne Grietye Banta

1788 NO.	PARENTS	CHILD	WITNESSES & SPONSORS
1018	Jooris Sippe Catrientie van Winkel	Marrya bo. Oct. 16 bp. Nov. 16	
1019	Gerrit van Reype Catrientie van Reype	Margrietie bo. Oct. 31 bp. Nov. 16	Corneelus Gerbrantse Leena van Hooren, his wife
1020	Adam Rap Arriaentie Preyer	Johannis bp. Dec. 19	
1021	Barent Eevers Yannetye Mekdennel	Jenneke bo. Dec. 18 bp. Feb. 1 1789	Tammes Mekdennel Annetie van Scheyve

INDEX OF THE BAPTISMAL REGISTER

of the

REFORMED PROTESTANT DUTCH CHURCH OF BERGEN

Prepared and Arranged by

WILLIAM B. VAN ALSTYNE, M. D.

Owing to complications due to varieties in spelling baptismal names and surnames, a peculiar method has been used in the preparation of this index. All variations of the same family name have been embraced under one heading, indexed, as far as practical under the form in most common use and following it, when possible, by a contrasting form. All variations of the same individual name have been grouped under one heading, whenever possible under the form then in general use and include middle names and patronymics in combination with family names. Those entering the names in the church record not only varied the orthography and the use of patronymics but occasionally made wrong entries; for instance, baptism 235 is that of a child of Jan Hermensen and Neeltje Jans, the sponsors being Hessel Pieterse and "Elizabeth Eleysbeth". "Eleysbeth" is not a family name nor a patronymic and the sponsor in this case was probably either Elizabeth Gerrits, mother of Hessel Pieterse, or his wife, Elizabeth Claes. Still another instance is number 516 where a child of Harmanis Stymets and "Elsje Couwenhoof" is baptised. Harmanis married November 2, 1733, at New York City, Elsje Heermans, baptised there November 5, 1701, daughter of Folkert Heermans and Margrita Eckeson. Harmanis Stymets and Elsje Heermans appear as the parents of other later children baptised in New York City and she was not a widow "Couwenhoof" when she married Stymets. Appended is a list of the surnames occurring under more than two variations:

INDEX

Ackerman, Ackermans, Ackkerman, Akkerman.
Aertse, Aarsen, Aert, Aerts.
Andriesen, Andresen, Andriense, Andries, Andriese, Andriessen, Andriesze, Andrise.
Bertolf, Bartolfs, Berthoef, Bertholf, Bertollof.
Bogert, Bogerts, Bongert, Boogert.
Bokee, Bockque, Boke.
Bras, Braesen, Brasen.
Brestede, Breeste, Brestee.
Brinckerhoef, Blinckerhof, Blinkerhoef, Blinkerhof, Blinkerhoff, Blinkerhoft.
Brower, Brouer, Brouwer, Brouyer.
Clasen, Claasen, Claes, Claese, Claesen, Claesse.
Cornelis, Cornelise, Cornelisen, Corneliss, Cornelisse, Cornels.
Cuyper, Cuypers, Kuyper, Kuypers.
De Mare, Damarees, de Mare, De-mare, De Maree, de Maree, De-maree, De Marre, de Marre, Demarre, Marre.
De Mott, de Mot, Demot, De Moth, de Moth, Demoth.
Deryie, der Jee, Deryee.
De Vouw, Devou, Devouw, de vouw, Du vouw, du Vouw.
Diderick, Didericke, Didericks, Didericksе, Diderickx, Didericx, Diderikx, Diderix, Diederick, Diedericks, Diederickx, Diederiks, Diederikx, Diederikz, Diederix, Diedrik, Diedriks, Diedrikx, Diedryck.
Dircks, Diercks, Dierckx, Dirck, Dirckse, Dirckx, Dirkx.
Du Bois, du Bois, Dubois.
Earle, Eerell, Eerle, Eerrel, Eerrell, Erle, Errel.
Edsall, Edsal, Etsel.
Eiddo, Eiddwm, Ido, Idoo, Jddo.
Everts, Eevers, Eeverse, Evers, Everse, Evertsen.
Fielding, Fielden, Fiylden, Tielden.
Franse, Fraensen, Frans, Fransen.
Fredrickse, Fredericksе, Fredericksen, Fredricksen, Fredrickx, Fredrikse, Fredriksen, Fredrikx.
Gerrebrants, Gerbrands, Gerbrans, Gerbranse, Gerbrants, Gerbrantse, Gerbrantsen, Gerbrantz, Gerbrantze, Gerbrentse, Gerrebrands, Gerrebransen, Gerrebrantsen.
Gerretsen, Gerresse, Gerrets, Gerretse, Gerretze, Gerrit, Gerrits, Gerritse, Gerritsen.
Hartmans, Hartmansen, Hertmans.
Helmigs, Heelmigh, Helmens, Helmigh, Helmighse, Helmigsen.
Hendricksen, Hendrick, Hendricks, Hendrickse, Hendrickx, Hendricx, Hendriksen.
Hennion, Hennejon, Henneon, Henneyon.
Hermans, Hermens, Hermense, Hermensen, Hermenz.
Heylhaaken, Heijhaken, Heilhaaken, Heylhaake.
Hoagland, Hoaglant, Hooglant.
Jacobs, Jacobse, Jacobsen, Jacobz.
Jacobusen, Cobase, Kobus.
Jansen, Jan, Jans, Janse.
Joris, Jorise, Jorisen, Jorisz.
Jurrianse, Jureaansen, Juriaansen, Juriaens, Juriaense, Juriaensen, Jurijaense, Jurijaensen, Jurjanje, Jurjanse, Jurreaansen, Jurriansen, Jurrianzen, Jurrijanse, Jurrijansen, Jurriyansen, Jurryyansen.
Klyndinni, Kleydenni, Kleyndini, Kleyndinni, Klyndinney.
Kouwenhoven, Couwenhoof, Kouenove, Kouwenhove, Kouwenove, van Kouwenhoven, van Kouwon-Hove.
Lubberts, Lubbers, Lubberse, Lubbersen, Lubbertse.
Macleen, Macheleyn, Mackeleyn, Mackleyn.
Makdennel, Mekdannel, Mekdannil, Mekdennel, Mekdennil.
Marselus, Marcelisse, Marseelus, Marseeluse, Marselis, Marselisse, Marselissen, Marseluse, Mercelis, Merselis, Merselise, Merselisen, Merselisse, Mersilise.

Marten, Maertens, Martens.
Michielsen, Magielse, Michielse, Migielse.
Niewkerk, Nieukerk, Nieuwkerk, Nieuw kerk, Nieuw-kerk, Niew-kerk, N-Kerk, Nukerck, van Nieukerk, van Nieuw-kerk, van N-Kerk.
Olfers, Olfertse, Olphers.
Oosteroom, oosteroom, Oosterum.
Outwater, Ouwtwaater, Ouytwater.
Pietersen, Pieters, Pieterse.
Pouluse, Paulus, Pouelse, Poulus.
Pryer, Preyer, Preyers, Prier, Pryjer.
Riddenhars, Redde..rs, Reddehars, Reddenhaers, Reddenhars, Reddenhoers.
Roelofs, Roelof, Roelofse, Roelofsen, Roelpfse, Roels.
Sabriske, Sebriske, Sobriska.
Shipper, Sippe, Sipper.
Sickels, Sicgels, Sichels, Sichgels, Sichgelse, Sickel, Sickelsen, Sickkels, Sickles, Sieggels, Siekkels, Siggels, Sikels, Sikkels, Sikkelsen, Zicgelse, Ziggels.
Simmensen, Symmons, Symons.
Sip, Siph, Sippe, Sips, Zip, Ziph.
Smith, de Smidt, Smit, Smits.
Solder, Salders, Solders.
Steegh, Steeghs, Stek.
Streycker, Streyckers, Stryckerz.
Stymets, Steymets, Steynmets, Stynmets.
Thomas, Tamsen, Thomase, Thomasen, Thomasse, Tomansse, Tomas, Tomase, Tomasen, Tomassen.
Tonisen, Tonis, Tonise.
Tysen, Matheus, Matteusse, Mattheeusen, Mattheeussen.
Van Benthuysen, V. Benthuysen, van Benthuyse, van Benthuyze.
Van der Hoef, Oeven van der Hoef, vander Hoef, van der Hoeven, van der Oeven, vander Oeven.
Vanderlinden, van de Linden, vande Linden.
Van Eydestyn, Eydersteyn, Eyderstyn, Eydestyn.
Van Giesen, van Giese, van Giesen.
Van Horn, van Hooren, van Hooreren, van Hoorn, Van Horen, van Horne, van Horren, van Horrn.
Van Vorst, van der Voorst, van de Voorst, van de voorst, vande Voorst, vandevoorst, Van de Vorst, van de Vorst, van Voorst, van voorst, van Vorst.
Van Wagenen, van Wagene, van Wagenen, van Wageneng, van Wagenin, van Wagening, van Wagenyng.
Van Wert, van Waert, van Weert.
Van Winkel, Van Winckel, van Winckel, van Winckelen, van Winkel, van Winkelen, van Winkell.
Verkerk, Verkerck, Verkerke.
Vlierboom, Vliereboom, Vlireboom.
Vreeland, Vreelant, Vreland, Vrelant, Vrelent.
Vreelinghuysen, Vreelinghuyse, Vrelenhuysen, Vrelinghuyse, Vrelmighuysen.
Waldron, Walderon, Waldrum.
Winne, Wennen, Wennem, Winnie, Winning.

Abeel, Davidt, 504
Abrahamse, Cornelis, 28.
Ackerman, Ackermans, Abigail, 438.
Abraham, 276, 581.
Annetje, 102.
Davidt, 276.
Eliesabet, 605.
Hendrick, 913, 942.
Jannetye, 808.
John, 890.
Laurus, Lourus, 102, 161.
Lodewyck, 276.
Palley, 1016.
Sara, Saara, Saertie, Serrey, Zara, 565, 581, 607, 630, 641, 811, 891, 908, 958.
Adolf, Pieter, 654.
Aertse, Aarsen, Hendrickje, 38, 59, 93, 130, 136, 233.
Mattheuz, 609.
Andriesen, Andriesze, Abraham, 462.
Feytje, 244, 268, 300, 370, 399.
Jan, 351.
Lourus, 2.
Merrytje, 521.
Sara, Saartje, 462, 464, 476, 480, 486, 489, 500, 512, 606, 638.

Anton, Antonides, Aldert, 123, 124
Do. Vincentius, 418.
Ariaens, Ariaense, Annetje, 43.
Merreytje, Merritje, 24, 59.
Baelden, Keetye, 898, 975.
Banker, Raagel, 844.
Banta, Arei, 984.
Gerrit, Gerret, 753, 978.
Hendrick, 978.
Hester, 710, 766, 781, 847.
Jannetje, Jannetye, 697, 766.
Margrietje, Grietje, Grietye, 463, 465, 1017.
Marrytie, 776.
Wiert, 868.
Barents, Barentse, Baltus, 129.
Cornelis, 44.
Dierck, 391
Jannetje, 151, 193.
Tys, 45.
Barwey, Catreyna, 248.
Bayard, Baeyert, B., 6, 7, 334.
Merritje, 334.
N., 16.
Been, Heelena, 240.
Beling, Cornelis, 384.
Berberno, Jan, 193.
Berdet, Mary, Polley, Polly, 762, 787, 823.
Samuel, 958.
Bertingh, Jan, 277.
Bertolf, Bartolfs, Elisabet, 875.
Do. Gilam, Gielam, 160, 170, 230, 261, 263, 357.
Hendr., 410.
Joanna, 262.
Zara, 359.
Besset, Bessed, Antye, Nensei, 712, 732, 755, 846, 884.
Leena, 755.
Susanna, 712.
Bevois, Catreyna, 277.
Bisday, Berney, 787, 823.
Boerum, Jannetye, 862.
Bogert, Bongert, Aeltje, Aeltje Toenis, Aeltje Tonissen, 173, 199, 352.
Jan Cornelis, Jan Cornelise, 69, 80, 89, 107.
William, 388.
Boir, Mateys, 248.
Bokee, Bockque, Abraham, 162, 186, 211.
Jannetje, 156, 188.
Bokkenhoove, Annatie, 856.
Bon, Catriena, 604.
Geertruy, Gertruy, 590, 604, 616, 622, 634, 640.
Helena, 634.
Johannis, John, 711, 854.
Bos, Annatje, 679.
Catrientie, 785.
Elizabeth, 692.
Isack, 719.
Jan Pieterse, 193.
Jannetje, Jannetye, 679, 692, 719, 746.
Mateys, 248.
Michiel, 692.
Boskerk, Cornelius, 627.
Braeck, Braack, Claesje, Claesje Dierckx, Claesje Dirckse, 115, 168, 255, 329.
Dirck Claese, Dirck Claesen, 35, 48, 106.
Merritje Diercks, Merritje Dierckx, Merritje Dircks, Merritje Dirckse, Merritje Dirckx, 88, 120, 153, 255, 288, 323.
Metje Derckse, Metje Dierckx, Metje Dirckse, 68, 76, 329 416.
Bras, Braesen, Abraham, 464.
Elysabet, 464.
Geertje, 656.
Brestede, Brestee, Treyntje, 223, 271, 304, 409.
Brinckerhoef, Blinkerhoft, Aagtje, Aacgtje, Aagttje, Aegje, Aegye, 527, 583, 607, 626, 652, 676, 859, 880, 920, 921, 933, 956, 974, 991.
Aaltje, 445.
Claesje, Claasje, Klaase, 508, 515, 535, 593.
Cornelis, Cornelies, 425, 435, 443, 445, 446, 451, 458, 460, 508, 515, 527, 566, 583, 806.
Dirck, Dirk Hendricksen, 435, 468.
Gesie, Geesye, 626, 806.
Hartman, 624, 880.
Hendrick, Hendrik, 626, 806, 880, 921, 933, 962, 1012.
Jacobus, 458, 463.
Jannetye, 927, 956, 985, 1012.
John, 991.
Margrietie, Margrietje, 427, 451, 463, 468, 470, 478.
Martje, 566, 573, 593, 594.
Broeks, Richert, 877.
Sara, 877.
Brower, Brouyer, Abraham, 605.
Hester, 683, 748, 785, 868.
Jacob, Jacop, 517, 522, 548, 577, 578, 633, 683, 713.
Jakobes, Jacop, Kobes, 794, 808, 944.
Jannetye, 821.
Johannis, 713, 727, 729, 748, 754.
Lea, Leeya, 522, 719.
Pekkee, 983.
Ulrick, Uldrik, 346, 357, 373, 404, 577, 578, 605, 618.
Buys, Buis, Ariaen Pieterse, Arien Pieterse, Arien Pietersen, 51, 71, 109, 129, 167, 197, 218.

Catharina, Catrina, 618, 835, 836.
Freyntje Janse, 151.
Hendrickje, 365.
Johannis, John, Jan Cornelise, Jan Cornelisse, 51, 155, 835, 836, 861.
Saara, 874.
Cadmus, Kadmus, Abraham, 656.
Casparis, 1006.
Catharina, Catriena, Catrientie, Catrina, 664, 667. 696, 716, 829.
Dirk, Derck, Derk, 558, 572 584, 591.
Jannetye, Jenneke, Jennetye, 777, 906, 923, 930, 955, 1000.
Joris, Jooris, 647, 659, 662, 667, 681, 696, 698, 704, 707, 739, 777, 800, 826, 895, 906, 950.
Metye, 930.
Neeltie, 800.
Pieter, 869.
Calyer, Kalyer, Annatie, 1003.
Jacobus, James, 685, 745.
Cammegaer, Kammegaar, Rachel, Raechel, Raegel, Raeghel, 670, 725, 740, 747, 752, 768, 805.
Carelse, Carelss, Carel, 20.
Symon, 20.
Caspers, Berber, 54.
Cavelier, Catlyntje, Calyntje, 523, 539.
Johannes, 523, 539.
Cemmel, Christiaen, Cristiaen, 763, 802.
Cerson, Pieter, 81.
Ragel, 67, 81.
Susan, 67.
Cin..., Tanneke, 211.
Clasen, Claesse, Adries, 178, 206, 226.
Andries, 268.
Cornelis, 199, 228, 319, 352.
Elysabet, 228.
Geertje, 352, 387.
Gerbrant, 66, 70, 159, 211, 222, 239, 248, 292.
Hendrick, 387, 414, 437.
Jan, 199, 202, 214, 278, 281, 308, 324, 326.
Merritje, 70, 196, 211, 222, 239, 292.
Pietertje, 202, 214, 319, 341.
Treyntje, 64, 83, 86, 114, 173, 199, 202, 207, 214.
Vroutje, 128, 164, 191.
Coesaerdt, Davidt, 417.
Collard, Callerd, Annatie, Annatye, 946, 953, 980.
Geertruy, 1014.
Jeemes, Jeems, Jemes, Jems, 749, 778, 827, 870, 1014.
Johannis, Johanis, 947, 953, 980, 1014.
Jurrey, 870.
Coetens, see Koerten.
Corle, Adam, 188.
Cornelis, Cornels, Abraham, 144.
Achtje, 390.
Annetje, Aennetje, 11, 22, 39, 55, 86, 119, 191, 281, 319.
Claesje, 65, 89, 253, 302.
Dirckje, 9, 10, 154, 264.
Elysabet, 29.
Feytje, 406.
Gerritje, 30.
Jacob, 41.
Jannetje, 354.
Matheus, 30, 53, 75, 118, 175, 194, 205, 243, 269, 293, 307, 338, 378.
Merritje, 5.
Paulus, 17.
Pieter, 38, 59, 93, 136.
Treyntje, 5.
Weyntje, 107.
Corsen, Cornelus, 800.
Creen, Femmetye, 1015.
Creeven, Thomas, 241.
Crigers, Catreyna, 123, 124.
Cristiaense, Barent, 314.
Cristyn, Jan, 240.
Csi, Marey, 85.
Cubberly, Cubberley, Thomas, Tames, 916, 936.
Cuyper, Kuyper, Catrina, Catryntje, 485, 563, 592.
Eliezabet, 555.
Geertje Klaas, 454.
Hendricus, Hendryck, Hendrik, Klaasen, 454, 555, 563, 735, 797.
Sara, Zara, 563, 592.
Dad, Catlyntie, 1006.
Jeemes, Jeems, Yeems, 934, 945, 997, 1008.
Daniels, Danniels, Aeltje, 42, 61, 91, 108, 111, 133, 165, 174, 195, 201, 242.
Davitse, Jan, 78.
Day, Barnabas, 762.
Willem, William, 221, 280, 320, 342, 361, 381, 387, 404, 413.
De Grauw, de Grau, Abel, 676, 715, 746, 797.
De Groot, de Groot, Aagtje, 620.
Elysabet, 503.
Johannes, 503.
Leeya, 868.
Pieter, 683, 748, 785, 868.
Staets, 54.
De Mare, Damarees, Davit, 67, 77, 81, 85, 359.
Johannes, Jan, 67, 94, 101, 309, 828.

Keetie, Keetye, 873, 907, 931, 957.
Lena, Leena, 796, 801, 828, 915, 963.
Marey, Marrytye, 94, 825.
Nensey, 905.
Raegel, Raagel, Raeghel, Raeghelde, 900, 905, 928, 935, 946.
Samuel, 94.
De Mott, Demoth, Anthony, 427.
Claasie, Klaasje, Klaesye, 580, 632, 648, 744.
Hendrik, 594.
Jacop, 720.
Margrietje, 460.
Matthys, Mateys, 411, 427, 451, 463, 468, 470, 478.
Michiel, Machiel, 673, 998.
Demsei, Antie, 890.
der Pree, Nicola, 101.
Deryie, der Jee, Jannetye, Yannetye, 992, 1002.
Wyntie, 804.
de Schemaker, Kersten, 90.
de Smidt, see Smith, Fransoys, 162.
De Vael, de Vael, Elisabet, 965.
Ned, 988.
De Vouw, du Vouw, Hester, 346, 357, 373, 404.
Nicola, 85, 113.
Susanna, 357.
Dey, John, 1015.
Diderick, Diederikz, Abraham, 590, 604, 616, 622, 634, 640.
Aeltie, Aaltje, Aeltye, 686, 709, 757.
Antie, Antje, Antye, 482, 488, 530, 590, 612, 685, 726, 727, 729, 737, 749, 782, 788, 827, 834, 885, 896, 989.
Cornelis, 547, 595, 686.
Daniel, 764, 780, 820, 902.
Geertruy, Geertye, 685, 745, 749, 778, 827, 870.
Gerret, 585.
Jacob, Jacop, 603, 612, 778, 788, 807, 834, 860.
Jannetye, 784, 902, 1013.
Johannes, Hans, Jan, Johannis, John, 10, 23, 82, 183, 261, 285, 530, 595, 603, 616, 622, 645, 745, 789, 854, 885.
Leeya, 961.
Margrietie, Grietje, Margrietje, Margriety, 509, 525, 538, 542, 562, 564, 574, 640, 978.
Wander, 261, 285, 317, 324, 355, 366, 367, 371, 407, 433,
Dircks, Dirkx, Ariaentje, Adriaentje, 77, 113.
Beelitje, Beeltje, Belitje, 267, 318, 337, 360, 380, 398, 401, 420, 441, 562.
Claesje, 208, 315, 400, 406.
Geertje, 11, 314.
Lucas, 2.
Merritje, 35, 48, 62, 327.
Metje, 48, 106, 168, 270.
Neeltje, Neelt, 268, 347, 351, 362, 388.
Don, Donen, Nensei, 988.
William Androw, 706.
Donkim, Elisabet, 818.
Doremus, Cornelis, 170, 220.
Dortusee, Marya, 188.
Douglas, Doggelis, Elinor, 284, 316.
Leena, 367.
Douwe, Rachel, Raeggel, 970, 1001.
Druwen, Jacomeyn, 101.
Marey, 94.
Du Bois, Dubois, Do., 351, 362, 513, 517.
Dutoiet, Dutout, Abraham, 156, 188.
Duyke, Evert, 434.
Duyts, Lourus, 13.
Earle, Eerrell, Antibby, 897.
Bekye, 833.
Billi, 785.
Corneelus, 818.
Daniel, 811.
Edward, Eduart, Eduwaert, Eduward, Eduwert, 206, 250, 279, 303, 328, 353, 376, 392.
Elysabet, 6, 7.
Hendrick, 965.
Keetye, 843.
Nettennel, 844.
Polley, 844.
Ritsert, 6, 7.
Edsall, Etsel, Annet, 36.
Elisabet, 897.
Janneke, Jenneke, 10, 14, 16, 23, 26, 32.
Rutje, 123, 124.
Samuel, Sam., 6, 7, 16, 32, 34, 123, 124.
Eduwaertse, Hermen, 14.
Egberts, Egbertse, Geertje, 102.
Sander, 251.
Eiddo, Jddo, Saara, Sellei, Selley, Selli, 845, 889, 901, 915, 941, 947.
Eleysbeth, Elizabeth, 235.
Elisen, Tonis, 40.
Ellen, Tammi, 752.
Epkese, Eppekese, Hendrick, 99, 111, 125, 333.
Sibe, Sibi, 82, 99, 111, 131, 150, 201.
Etli, Eth, Benyamen, 983.
Everts, Eeverse, Achtje, Echtje, Barent, 60, 122, 294. 938, 966, 981, 1021.
Catlyntie, Catleyntie, Katleyntie, 878, 940, 954, 979.
Evert, 422.

Jacop, 878, 929, 938, 966, 994.
Johannis, 614, 623, 633, 657, 690, 878, 914, 940, 954, 969, 981, 1010.
Leena, 1010.
Matthys, Mattheys Mattys, 657, 669, 690, 695, 728, 770.
Seydke, 623.
Eysbrants, Emmetje, 241.
Fielding, Fiylden, Aegye, 906, 950.
Debora, 684.
Gorge, 684.
Hendrick, Hendrik, Henry, 660, 684, 702, 726.
Jannetye, 858.
Fish, Daniel, 861.
Franse, Fraensen, Mareytje, Mareya, Marya, Merreytje, Merritje, 90, 121, 144, 169, 182, 198, 236.
Thomas, Tomas, 223, 271, 304, 409.
Fredrickse, Fredericksen, Andries, 389.
Christina, 436, 453.
Dirck, Dirk, 472, 477, 537.
Geertruy, 436, 467, 472, 477, 497, 503.
Jannetje, 472, 477.
Thomas, Tomas, 24, 189, 373, 389, 436.
Freeman, Do. Bernardus, 427.
French, Catherin, 706.
Gardenier, Harmanis, 881.
Gerrebrants, Gerbrans, Catrina, Catrientie, Catrientye, Treyntie, Tryntje, 498, 693, 725, 735, 797.
Claes, Claas, 196, 396, 461.
Cornelis, Corneelus, Cornelius, Cornelus, 466, 474, 475, 484, 497, 499, 504, 532, 572, 665, 691, 699, 705, 735, 742, 753, 790, 899, 972, 1011, 1019.
Elisabet, 838.
Gerbrant, 691.
Harpert, 426, 446.
Jacop, 843.
Jannetye, 972, 990, 1011.
Leena, 895, 909.
Marrytje, Marritye, Martje, 426, 565, 732.
Myndert, Meyndert, 461, 465, 469, 474, 493, 494, 498, 589, 838.
Neeltie, Neeltje, Neeltye, 466, 668, 753, 978.
Theunis, 668.
Gerretsen, Gerresse, Aeltje, Aaltje, 185, 261, 285, 317, 324, 348, 355, 367, 371, 407, 433.
Antje, 549.
Cathareyna, Catreyna, Catryna, 52, 73, 95, 134, 148, 185, 212, 220, 275, 298, 313, 325, 374, 408.
Cornelis, 507, 553, 586.
Dirck, 54.
Elizabeth, Eleysabet, Eliesabet, Elisabeth, Elysabet, 49, 76, 115, 145, 178, 186, 228, 391, 490, 505, 514, 527, 574, 586.
Fytje, Feytje, 176, 234, 258, 286, 287, 290, 312, 331, 348, 364, 366, 383, 385, 405, 412.
Geertruyt, 60.
Geesje, 8, 26, 41, 231.
Gerrit, Gerret, 12, 30, 31, 36, 50, 97, 139, 190, 229, 234, 237, 238, 261, 274, 285, 290, 310, 318, 343, 350, 366, 367, 422, 432.
Gerritje, 40, 243.
Guert, 15, 26.
Hermanus, 212, 312, 385.
Jannetje, 22, 166, 190, 230, 238, 252.
Johannes, Jo., John, 325, 348, 391, 403, 408, 412, 421, 930.
Juriaen, Jureaan, Juriaan, Jurien, Jurjan, Juryan, 492, 501, 509, 525, 538, 542, 554, 562, 564, 574.
Lea, 471, 495, 501, 502, 521.
Gilbert, Loos, 365.
Giljam [Bertolf], Do., 418.
Griffens, Kirffens, Saara, Sellei, Selley, 940, 954, 969, 981, 1010.
Haargjes, Antje, 427.
Hafte, Catlyntje, 582.
Halenbeek, Rebekke, 913, 942.
Hansen, Annetje, 323.
Hester, 131.
Treyntje, 314.
Haring, Maria, 655.
Hartmans, Hertmans, Feytje, Freytje, 35, 106, 458.
Michiel, 502, 505.
Helmigs, Helmens, Catrina, Cataleyntje, Cateleynt, Cateleyntje, Catelyntie, Catelyntje, Catlyntje, 391, 403, 408, 412, 421, 433, 442, 473.
Cornelis, 408.
Gerretje, 441.
Johannes, 473.
Pieter, 382.
Roelof, 384, 390, 406, 420, 421, 428, 467.
Hendricksen, Hendricx, Aeltje, 213, 253, 368, 402.
Annetje, 45.
Barent, 294.
Barentje, 92.
Catreyna, Treyntje, 51, 71, 109, 129, 167, 218, 294.
Claes, 187.

Cornelia, 44, 146. 247, 264, 302, 336, 363, 394.
Dieuwer, 333.
Jacob, 277.
Jan, 526, 528.
Margrietje, Grietje, 289, 291, 309, 330, 333, 349, 395, 411.
Marteyntje, Merteyntje, 160, 230.
Susanna, 146.
Weybrecht, 103.
Willemyntje, 187.
Hennion, Hennejon, Antie, Antje, 632, 655, 668, 694, 722, 754, 810.
Davit, 940, 954, 979.
Fytie, Fytye, 798, 810, 832, 871, 883, 912, 922, 932, 987.
Gerret, 557, 609.
Marytye, 979.
Hermans, Hermensen, ——, 229.
Annetje, Aennetje, An..., 12, 24, 36, 50, 97, 166, 229, 261, 321.
Hermptje, 20, 40.
Jan, 155, 167, 235.
Reyckje, Reychje, Reycke, 49, 101, 133, 155, 227, 254, 267, 293, 378.
Herperingh, Jan, 151.
Herrisnut, Antje, 432.
Benjamin, 432.
Hesselse, Pieter, 40, 49, 76, 115, 145, 178, 186, 228.
Heylhaaken, Heijhaken, Aafje, Aaftje, Aafttje, 584, 600, 615, 670.
Hoagland, Hooglant, Keetye, Knelia, 767, 774, 776, 829, 850, 882, 935.
Homs, Persilla, 389.
Hoppe, Abigail, 424.
Andries, 424, 438.
Catreyna, Catareyna, Catarina, Catryna, 63, 92, 110, 140, 233, 257, 418, 453.
Geertje, 127.
Hendrick, Hendrik, 87, 112, 130, 149, 375, 424.
Hendrikje, 581.
Marrytje, 424.
Matys, Mateys Adolf, 93, 127, 136.
Willem, 59, 130.
Huysman, Sjarel, 77, 113.
Jackson, Jaksen, Anatye, 721.
Patrik, Peterick, Petrik, 672, 741, 759.
Do. Willem, Wilhelmus, William, Wilyem, 672, 693, 721, 722, 741, 759, 769, 795, 816, 852, 893.
Jacobs, Jacobsen, Anna, Annetje, 105, 190, 200, 221, 226, 238, 280, 320, 342, 361, 381, 387, 404, 413.
Bartol, Bertel, 277, 284, 316, 367.
Carel, 415.
Catlyntje, Cateleyntje, 390, 415, 422.
Eytje, 23.
Grietje, 27, 33, 37, 57, 156, 167.
Hillegont, Hellegont, Hilgont, 277, 415, 422.
Jacob, 42, 61, 79, 91, 156, 174, 195, 289, 309, 330, 333, 395.
Merritje, Mettitje, 1, 17, 27, 28, 31, 116, 309.
Simon, Symon, 43, 56, 108, 150, 163.
Styntie, 1.
Tanneke, 186.
Treyntje Hans, 192, 219.
Walingh, 46, 79, 91, 116, 174, 204, 212.
Jacobusen, Cobase, Kobus, Maeyke, 170, 184, 232.
Jansen, Jan, Cathreyna, Catrayna, Catreyna, Treyntje, 25, 181, 193, 197, 322, 339, 356, 358, 372, 375, 405.
Claes, Claesen, 11, 39, 55, 86, 119, 191, 281, 290, 319, 354.
Cornelis, 69, 80.
Doreta, Dorete, 313, 345, 350, 401.
Grietje, 13.
Gysbert, 358.
Hendrickje, 148, 181.
Hester, 358.
Hilletje, Hellitje, Hillitje, 3, 12 34, 90, 100, 161, 234.
Isack, 862.
Jannetje, 2.
Maddeleentje, Maddaleentje, 19, 25, 51, 66, 110, 158.
Marytje, Mareytje, Marya, 87, 112, 130, 149.
Neeltje, 155, 158, 235.
Pieter, 11, 149.
Styntje, Steyntje, 161, 182.
Swaentje, 69, 80.
Tonis, 215.
Willem, 157.
Grietje, 17, 28, 31.
Jaspers, Grietje, 17, 28, 31.
Joris, Jorisen, Hendrick, 65, 89, 213, 253, 302.
Hilgont, 388.
Jannetje, 220.
Jork, see York.
Josephs, Annetje, 249.
Jurrianse, Jurjanje, Aeltje, Aaltje, 398, 501, 697.
Aert, 293.
Cornelis, Cornelius, 597, 611, 628, 638.

Elizabet, Eliezabet, 597, 627, 636.
Gerrit, Gerret, 267, 313, 318, 337, 360, 378, 380, 398, 407, 420, 431, 441, 449, 495, 507, 525, 562, 660.
Geurt, 441.
Hermen, 398.
Johannes, Johannis, 592, 611, 636, 697.
Leya, 628, 643.
Merritje, Martje, 396, 654.
Neeltje, 461.
Thomas, Tomas, 231, 254.
Kabasje, Stoffel, 107.
Kerseboom, Jan Evertse, 17, 28, 31.
Kiersteede, Hans, 18, 123, 124.
Killi, John, 961.
Kip, Blaudina, 869.
Jannetye, 806, 899.
Keetye, 815.
Klopper, Cornel, 3.
Klyndinni, Kleydenni, Antye, Nensi, 976, 993.
Catrientie, Katrienie, Katrientie 886, 904, 926.
Keetye, 959.
Nelley, 904.
Walter, 892, 924, 992.
Koerten, Coetens, Cateleyntje, 162.
Guert, 49, 231, 318.
Kog, Kogh, Geertruy, Geertie, 758, 798, 832, 912, 922, 929.
Kool, Pieter, 822, 851.
Kouwenhoven, Couwenhoof, Aeltje, 6, 7.
Elsje, 516.
Elysabet, Eleysabet, 225, 246, 248.
Sara, Saara, Saartie, Saertie, 703, 756, 794, 841, 894.
Krets, Margarietje, 78.
Kroese, Gerret, 593.
Marrytye, 859.
Kuyper, see Cuyper.
Kuyser, Hendericus, 693.
Lacomba, De Lacombe, Anthoni, 161, 182.
Lattoret, Susanna, 822, 851.
Leroe, Jacob, 103.
Lisier, Nicklaes, 859.
Lisk, Antye, 824.
Loockermans, Merritje, 6, 7.
Loserecht, Jan, 24.
Willem Janse, 45.
Louersen, Louerse, Pieter, 314.
Tomas, 314.
Lubberts, Lubbers, Catarina, 423.
Jan, 19, 66, 110, 112, 148, 197.
Lubbert, 104, 125, 142, 205, 269.
Mareya, 99, 104, 125, 150.
Roelof, 104.
Tys, 25.
Lubi, Anna, 30, 53, 75, 118.
Jacob, 75.
Lucas, Aennetje, 2.
Merritje, 2.
Luperdus, Do., 324.
Macleen, Macheleyn, Sjarel, Charel 105, 239, 240, 262, 296.
Maeds, Gergs, 877.
Maerle, Pieter, 521.
Makdennel, Mekdannil, Jannetye, Jeinie, Yannetye, 938, 966, 981, 1021.
Tammes, 996, 1021.
Makniel, Koobes, 824.
Man, Jan, 430.
Manderviel, Marreytye, 998.
Marse, Josias, 103.
Marselus, Merselisen, Annatie, 861.
Helena, 496.
Hillegont, Hilligont, 414, 420, 426.
Jacop, 952.
Jde, 682.
Jenneke, 528, 711, 724, 736, 765, 792, 809, 840, 892, 924, 992.
Johannis, Jan, John, 653, 867, 888, 918, 952, 1007.
Leena, 835, 836.
Lysbet, 382.
Marselis, Marcelis, Marselisse, Seel, 653, 680, 682, 711, 738, 765, 771, 791, 840, 867, 1002.
Pieter, 13, 29, 60, 97, 100, 480, 496, 524, 528, 541, 556, 564, 992, 1002.
Marten, Maertens, James, 689.
Margrieta, 689.
Treyntje, 14, 68, 192, 269.
Matheus, Mattheeussen, see Tysen.
Matkins, Ann, 877.
Merrit, Willem, 294.
Merry, Willem, 236.
Merse, Pieter, 4.
Mersaro, Misyero, Mary, Pally, 916, 936.
Mesier, Misier, Abraham, 225, 246.
Meyer, Meyers, Dickje, 20.
Elisabet, 839.
John, 839.
Michielsen, Magielse, Ariaentje, 122, 162.
Catryna, Catreyna, 46, 75, 79, 84, 116, 158, 160, 174, 198, 204, 212.
Cornelis, 106.
Elyas, Eleyas, 1, 9, 32, 34, 37, 57, 86, 160.
Hertman, 33, 35, 48, 62, 88, 105, 120, 123, 124, 145, 153, 288.
Jannetje, 32.
Johannes, 76.
Preyntje, 178.
Tades, Tade, 84, 117, 137, 200.

Miller, Ann, 706.
Mutsker, Johannis, 858.
Natanielse, Davidt, 297.
Neefje, Neesje, 642, 654, 674.
Niewkerk, van N-Kerk, Arent, 1010, 1016.
Barent, 772, 871, 879, 987.
Catryntie, 751.
Gerrit, Gerret, 563, 592, 751, 979, 1016.
Hendrick, Hendrik, 813, 919, 927, 948, 955.
Jacop, 798, 810, 832, 871, 883, 912, 922, 932, 987.
Jannetje, Janetye, 585, 695, 813.
Mattheus, Matteewes, Mattewes, Matthewes, Tewes, 695, 714, 751, 758, 775, 793, 798, 799, 813, 832, 912, 919, 922, 929, 969.
Paulus, Poulus, 533, 559, 571, 585, 619, 635, 669.
Olfers, Olphers, Margrietje, 598, 601.
Sjoert, 4.
Oosteroom, Oosterum, Hendrick Janse, 135.
Jan Hendrickse, 135.
Treyntje Hendrickse, 197.
Outwater, Ouwtwaater, Gileam, Gilyaem 866, 920.
Thomas, 596.
Ovenmoef, Eliesabeth, 650.
Parsel, Paersel, ——, 457, 917.
Amela, 917,
Willem, 457.
Pels, Maria, 587.
Pereu, Willem, 282.
Pier, Abraham, 499.
Jacob, 532.
Jannetje, Jannitje, Yannetye, 466, 475, 484, 499, 504, 532, 705, 753.
Selley, 857.
Tomas, 466.
Pietersen, Pieters, ——, 449.
Annetje, 217.
Christiaen, Cristiaen, 5, 6, 7.
Elysabet, 449.
Elsje, 251.
Freyntje, 177.
Hessel, 211, 228, 235.
Jannetje, Joanna, 47, 53, 74, 98, 132, 139, 141, 180, 227, 232, 256, 265, 305, 344.
Johannis, 476, 517.
Merselis, Mersilis, 100, 138, 265, 286, 296, 312, 335, 386, 401, 426.
Neesje, Neisje, Niese, Niesje, Niessi, Nisje, 97, 139, 237, 274, 310, 318, 343, 350, 366.
Paulus, Poulus, 14, 68, 192.
Tenneke, 449.
Treyntje, 144, 152, 215.
Wesselse, 306.
Post, Adriaen, 52, 73, 95, 134, 148, 185, 198, 212, 220, 382, 1005.
Claertje, 382.
Eckbert, Ep, 750, 756, 781, 817, 842, 860, 864, 910, 911, 963, 1005.
Elisabet, 842.
Frans, 232.
Johannis, 743, 750.
Saara, 911.
Santye, 1004.
Pouluse, Pouelse, Annetje, 127.
Catryna, Catarina, Catreyna, 175, 194, 205, 243, 269, 307, 338, 378.
Cristina, 219.
Elisabet, 752.
Hillitje, 104, 142, 205.
Marten, 219, 243.
Mynouw, Minouw, 93, 136.
Pieter, 192, 205, 219.
Pruis, Casper Cornelise, 158.
Pryer, Pryjer, Abraham, 625, 639, 646, 945.
Andries, Anderias, Anderies, Andreas, Andrias, 263, 295, 332, 639, 644, 646, 658, 663, 688, 708, 737.
Annatje, 526, 528.
Arriaentie, 783, 945, 997, 1004, 1020.
Casper, Casparis, Casparus, Casperis, Casperus, Kasparis, Kasparus, 462, 464, 480, 486, 489, 476, 500, 512, 606, 638, 710, 886, 901, 904, 926, 937, 959, 962, 974.
Geertruy, Geertie, 947, 953, 980, 1014.
Hartman, 886, 1004.
Jacop, 845, 889, 901, 915, 941, 947.
Jenneke, Jenneje, 524, 541, 556, 564, 653, 688, 777, 800, 826, 895.
Johannes, Johannis, 630, 641, 663.
Nicklaes, Niclaes, Nicolass, Niklaes, 658, 710, 766, 781, 847.
Pryntje, Printie, Printje, Pryntie, 543, 556, 570, 580, 599, 606, 617, 708.
Sara, Saara, Saertie, 783, 803, 812, 847, 872, 889, 926, 934, 1008.
Selytje, 462, 658.
Tenneke, 480, 496.
Raeft, Leevey, 874.
Ralemont, Jacob, 319, 341.

Rap, Adam, 997, 1004, 1020.
Retan, Abraham, 743.
Catryntie, Catrientye, 743, 750.
Marya, 881.
Sara, 743.
Reycken, Hendrick, 23, 25.
Reyli, Petterick, 965.
Reyniers, Jellitje, Jelitje, 209, 210.
Richard, Samalli, 877.
Riddenhars, Reddenhaers, Abel, 322, 339, 356, 358, 365, 372, 375, 405, 423, 439.
Geertruyt, Geetringt, 245, 272, 311, 340, 365, 375, 393, 450.
Roelofs, Roels, Cornelis, 53, 58, 72, 96, 98, 126, 132, 154, 173, 179, 207.
Helmigh, 47, 74, 98, 141, 180, 203, 217, 227, 232, 256, 265, 305, 344.
Jittje, 4.
Machteltje, 129, 135.
Theunis, Tonis, 64, 83, 114, 154, 173, 199, 202, 214.
Roome, Romme, Geertruy, Geertruyt, 582, 614, 619.
Roos, Antje, 547, 595, 686.
Gerrit, Gerret, 440, 448, 456, 459, 529.
Rutger, Mereytje, 351.
Sabriske, Sobriska, Casparis, 971.
Hendrik, 655.
Joost, 718.
Samuels, Grietje, 15, 291.
Santfort, Frenkye, 779.
Schoonmaker, Martynes, 712.
Seboy, Antje, 434.
Shipper, Sippe, John, 975.
Joris, Jooris, 943, 964, 975, 986, 1018.
Sickels, Ziggels, Aagtje, Aegye, 656, 764, 780, 820, 902.
Abraham, 565, 583, 607, 626, 652, 676, 700, 859, 872, 896, 939, 959, 968, 977, 1007.
Aeltie, 720, 779, 856, 941.
Daniel, 726, 737, 782, 834, 885, 896, 989.
Geertruy, Geertie, 630, 639, 641 644, 646, 658, 663, 688, 708, 737, 768, 780, 843, 853, 876, 886, 901, 925, 967, 986, 989.
Hartman, 688.
Hendrick, Henderick, Hendrik, Hendryck, 467, 472, 475, 477, 497, 503, 565, 581, 607, 630, 641, 796, 801, 814, 830, 856.
Johannes, Johannis, 508, 515, 535, 814.
Leysbet, 282.
Marya, Martje, 311, 625, 639, 646.
Raeggel, 1005.
Robbert, 245, 272, 311, 340, 365, 375, 393, 413, 450, 637, 651, 673, 709, 782, 830.
Sofia, 467.
Willem, 555.
Zacharias, Zagharias, Zagharis, 467, 505, 514, 567, 589, 625, 645, 652, 977, 1003.
Simmensen, Symmons, Catarina, Treyntje, 15, 437.
Pieter, 755.
Sip, Ziph, Adriaantje, 682.
Annatie, Annati, Annatje, Annatye, Antje, Antye, Annetje Ariaens, Annetje Ariaense, Annetje Ariens, 56, 91, 108, 121, 163, 183, 216, 516, 637, 651, 675, 677, 724, 730, 736, 757, 760, 949, 995.
Arien, 412.
Catlyntje, 671.
Cornelis, Corneelus, Cornelius, Cornelus, 723, 730, 731, 760, 792, 809, 846, 925.
Gerrit, Gerret, 724, 736, 765, 792, 809.
Helen, Helena, 602, 617.
Hillegont, 407.
Ide, Jde, Jede, 483, 487, 496, 516, 534, 549, 552, 557, 569, 573, 576, 588, 602, 608.
Jan, Jan Ariaansen, Jan Ariaense, Jan Ariaensen, Jan Ariens, 108, 131, 218, 255, 262, 265, 283, 286, 324, 354, 386, 414, 423, 434.
Jannetye, Jenneke, 717, 995.
Mareytje Ariaense, Mareya Ariaense, Mareyte Ariaense, Marya Ariaens, 82, 111, 131, 150, 201.
Pieter, 995.
Slot, Eva, Evaje, 492, 493, 494, 511, 522, 596, 713.
Jan Pieter, 204.
Lea, Leja, Leya, 517, 548, 577, 578, 633, 683.
Pieter Janse, Pieter Jansen, 1, 27
Sara, 596.
Smee, Hermen, 9.
Smith, Smits, see also de Smidt, Abel, 970, 1001.
Arriaentie, Arriyaentie, 826, 855.
Catrientie, 929, 938, 966, 994.
Jacobus, Jacoobes, 679, 692, 719, 746.
John, 905.
Morgen, 510, 545.
Printje, 432.
Selli, 991.
Solder, Salders, Daniel, 679, 714, 733, 758, 775, 799.

Jakkemeyntie, 1016.
Spier, Spiers, Abraham, 531, 656, 728, 869.
Albertus, Albartus, 613, 620, 635, 642.
Anna, Annatie, Annatje, Annetje, 518, 519, 529, 531, 540, 559, 579, 599, 613, 623, 733, 869.
Barent, 390, 415, 533, 540, 551, 582.
Benjamin, 551, 568.
Catriena, Catelyntje, Catlyntje, Catreyna, Catreyna Hendrickse, 152, 169, 187, 533, 540, 691.
Geesie, Gessie, Gezie, 571, 579, 584.
Helena, Leena, Lena, 506, 533, 559, 571, 585, 619, 635, 657, 669, 690, 695, 728, 770.
Hendrik, Hendryck, 568, 579.
Jannetje, 572.
Johannis, Johannes, Hans, 90, 121, 144, 152, 158, 169, 177, 182, 198, 215, 236, 571, 582, 614 ,619.
Leija, 568.
Maritje, 568.
Sara, Saara, Saera, 876, 887, 964.
Seytje, Zeittje, Zytje, 614, 633, 657, 690.
Tonis Janse, Tonis Jansen, 157, 187, 189.
Willemeyntje Hendrickse, 237.
Steegh, Stek, Jooris, 715.
Margritje, 33.
Tomas, 33.
Steenhalder, Pieter Janse, 19.
Steen-Huys, Engelbert, 36.
Stevens, Stevensen, Albert, 209, 210.
Hendrickje, 209, 210.
Stoothoft, Hendrik, 478
Straetmaker, Straet, Annetje, 297.
Jan, 8, 22, 26, 41, 231, 281.
Jannetje, 231, 254.
Treyntje, 278, 281, 308, 326.
Streycker, Streyckerz, Angenietje, 69, 77, 80, 89, 107.
Jan, 69, 80.
Stuyvesant, Anna, 9.
Casparis, 703, 756, 794, 841, 894.
Catrientie, 864, 911.
Jenneke, 703, 796, 801, 814, 830.
Pieter, Petrus, 543, 556, 570, 580, 599, 606, 617, 703, 708, 796, 801, 828, 915, 963.
Sara, Saara, Saertje, Saertye, 750, 756, 781, 817, 842, 860, 864, 910, 963, 1005.
Stymets, Steynmets, Anna, Annetje, 41, 84, 117, 137, 200, 204.
Ariaentje, 252, 263.
Casper, Casparis, Casparus, Casperus, Kasparis, 8, 12, 22, 252, 263, 489, 844.
Cristoffel, 166, 190, 212, 230, 238, 252, 419.
Gerrit, 128, 164, 191, 200, 252, 275, 298, 313, 325, 374, 408, 433.
Harmanis, 516.
Helena, 489.
Jannetje, Johanna, 3, 263, 295, 332, 373, 413.
Johannes, Johannis, Jo, Jo., Jos., 84, 116, 133, 163, 166, 178, 190, 191, 200, 221, 226, 263, 309.
Ursuleena, 325.
Swaan, Jacob, 404.
Tades, Tadese, Antje, Antye, 510, 715.
Catrina, Catje, 510, 545.
Johannis, 510.
Magiel, 27.
Mayeke, 715, 746.
Tecx, Tecxe, Margrietje, 78.
Tomas, 78.
Terheun, Terhuen, Albert, Albert Albertse, 209, 210, 825.
Annatie, 718.
Elizabeth, Elisabet, Betye, 718, 761, 825, 849, 951, 973, 1009.
Thomas, Tomansse, Arien, 170, 184.
Catreyna, 105, 157, 189, 239, 240, 262, 296.
Cornelis, 92, 452.
Fransyntje, Franseyntje, 143, 171, 172, 184, 189, 203, 266, 301.
Fredrick, Frederick, Fredrik, 63, 92, 140, 184, 233, 257, 418, 453.
Jacob, 524.
Jannetje, 266, 389.
Johannes, Jan, Jo., Johannis, 266, 273, 418, 431, 452.
Juriaen, Jurien, 36, 133, 227, 254, 267, 293, 378.
Marytje, 452, 524.
Thomas, 369.
Tielden, see Fielden.
Tjurckse, Poulus, 127.
Toeder, Polley, 870.
Toers, Tours, Abraham, 779.
Antie, 772, 871, 879, 987.
Arent, 518, 519, 529, 540, 559, 579, 599, 613, 623.
Cateleynt, Catleyntie, Catlyntie, Katlyntie, 714, 728, 751, 775, 793, 799, 813, 919, 969.
Ellener, 977, 1003.
Franseyntje, 266.

Jacomyntje, Jackemeyntie, Jackemyntie, Jackkemeyntie, 448, 714, 733, 758, 775, 799.
Jan Arentse, 171.
Judith, Judik, Judith Arentsen, 440, 448, 456, 459.
Lourus Arentse, Lourus Arentsen, Lowrus Arents, 143, 171, 172, 184, 189, 203, 266, 301.
Nicklaes, Nickklaes, Niklaes, Niklaers, Claes, A., Claes Arents, Claes Arentse, 33, 68, 115, 147, 171, 172, 241, 259, 299, 334, 377, 419, 761, 772, 793, 831, 863, 932, 939, 951, 957, 961.
Tonisen, Tonis, Hendrick, 15, 291.
Merritje, 215.
Tysen, Matheus, Beelitje, 45.
Cornelis, 485.
Gerrit, Garret, Gerret, 20, 40, 102, 485, 506.
Gerritje, 293.
Jannetje, 485, 506.
Poulus, 506, 518.
Willempje, 135.
Valentyn, Tyme Jansen, 357.
Van Benthuysen, van Benthuyze, Pieter, P., 550, 575, 598, 601.
Van Blerkom, van Blerkum, Cataryna, 439.
Elisabet, 837.
Leujkes, 837.
Raegel, Raeggel, 803, 910.
Van Bront, Rut, 819.
Van de Bilt, Jacob Janse, 110.
Jan Aertsen, Jan Aertse, 121, 152.
Van der Hoef, van der Oeven, Gerrit, Gerret, 783, 803, 812, 847, 872, 889, 926, 934, 1008.
Hendrik, 492, 511. 522, 596.
Jakobes, 812.
Johannes, Jan, 313, 345, 350, 401.
Marreytye, Marreyte, 812, 865.
Petrus, Peetrus, Peterus, 783, 803, 837, 910.
Raagel, 837.
Vanderlinden, van de Linden, Jan, 268, 302.
Roelof, 146.
Van der Spiegel, vander Spiegel, Annatie, Anatie, Annatje, Annatye, 672, 741, 759, 769, 795, 852, 893.
Van de Swalme, Constantina, 159.
Van Deusen, van Dueselen, Grietje, 431.
Marytje, Merreytje, 418, 431, 452.
Zaertje, 369.
Van Deventer, Cornelia, 251.
Jan Willemse, 251.
Vandewater, Hendrick, 18.
Van Dien, Gerrit, 233.
Van Elslant, Janetje Joris, 170.
Van Eyderstyn, Eydestyn, Maayke, Maycke, 676, 797.
Styntie, Steyntie, 878, 914.
Van Galen, van Gaalen, Louwrens, Lourus, 359, 379, 410, 425, 446.
Van Gelder, Gerret, 448.
Isack, Isak, 833, 848.
Kobes, Koobes, 833, 891, 908, 958.
Van Giesen, van Giese, Aaltje, 451.
Abraham, 207, 244, 268, 300, 370, 399.
Anna Mary, 224.
Bastiaen, Bastaienen, 132, 213, 253, 368, 402.
Dierckje, 213.
Isaac, Isaack, Isaacq, 247, 264, 302, 336, 363, 394.
Johannes, 44, 268, 302.
Magdalena, Maddaleena, Maddaleentje, Magdaleena, 44, 58, 72, 96, 126, 132, 154, 179, 207.
Marey, 260.
Reynier, R., 9, 10, 44, 253, 264, 311, 365.
Van Horn, van Hooreren, Aagtje, Achtje, Aafje, Effe, 362, 397, 416, 429, 443.
Annatje, Annatie, 648, 665, 699, 744, 773.
Dirk, 471.
Helena, Heeleena, Leena, 534, 819, 952, 972, 1011, 1019.
Jacop, 864, 911.
Jannetje, Jannetye, Jannitje, Jannitye, 537, 558, 572, 591, 665, 691, 699, 705, 735, 742, 790.
Johannis, Jan, John, 362, 385, 386, 534, 536, 552, 602, 617, 742, 773, 786 790, 819, 831, 838, 849, 918, 931, 972, 990, 1011.
Neeltje, 447, 678.
Rutger, Rutgert, Ruth, 347, 351, 362, 388, 417, 429, 447, 500.
Van Houten, van Houte, Catlintje, 560.
Feytye, 720.
Helena, Lena, 488, 549.
Helmig, Helmich, Helmigh, 662, 664, 678, 698, 717, 767, 774.
Jannetje, Jenneke, Janneke Helmigsen, Jenneke Helmegsen, 513, 520, 560, 561, 570, 601, 608, 615, 624, 631, 649.

Johannis, Johanis, Johannes, John, Johannes Helmegsen, Johannes Helmigsen, Johannis Helmegsen, Johannis Helmigsen, 488, 491, 513, 520, 541, 546, 549, 598, 610, 720, 779, 856, 900, 905, 928, 935, 941, 946. 953, 980, 1003.
Klaesje, Klasie, 624, 880.
Van Kleeck, Baltus Barentse, 151, 181, 193, 197.
Van Laer, Abraham, 21.
Aeltje, 276.
Arien, 21.
Van Naamen, Evert, 447.
Wyntje, 447.
Van Neste, Van neste, Jacomyntje, Jacomeyntje, 143, 147, 171, 172, 241, 259, 299, 334, 377, 419.
Merritje, 377.
Saartje, 419.
Van Reenen, van Reene, Gerrit, 60, 122, 249.
Van Reype, van Rype, Aeltie, 740, 784, 786, 805, 853, 867, 888, 918, 949, 952, 1007.
Beelitje, Beeletye, Beelitye, Beletye, Belletye, 702, 742, 773, 786, 790, 819, 831, 838, 849, 918, 931.
Catrientie, Catrientye, 903, 937, 950, 973, 1019.
Corneelus, 1009.
Daniel, 702, 718, 761, 825, 849, 951, 973, 1009.
Gerrit, Gerret, 766, 784, 786, 863, 902, 903, 937, 950, 973, 982, 999, 1013, 1019.
Jannetje, Jannetye, Yannetye, 761, 772, 793, 831, 863, 932, 939, 951, 957, 961.
Johannis, 842.
Marytye, 710.
van Roen, Reynier Josiassen, 159.
Van Saen, van Saan, Jannetye, 794, 808, 944.
Ysack, 808.
Van Schyve, van Scheyve, Annetie, Annatie, 996, 1021.
Marreytye, Marreyti, Marrytye, 934, 945, 997, 1008.
Van Steenwyck, Pieter Cornelise, 233.
Van Tilburg, van Tilburge, Johannes Jansen, Jo. Janse, 224, 260.
Van Tuyl, v. Tuyl, Abraham, 610, 621, 629, 777.
Femmetye, 739.
Van Vechten, Neeltje, Neeltje Dierckx, 302, 417, 429.
Van vogsten, Dirck Janse, 29.
Van Vorst, van der Voorst, Annetje Cornelis, 138, 290.
Cornelis, Cornelius, Cornelus, 138, 176, 185, 234, 258, 286, 287, 290, 312, 331, 348, 352, 364, 366, 383, 385, 405, 412, 439, 442, 479, 580, 632, 648, 665, 699, 744, 773.
Ide, Jde, 3, 5, 10, 234.
Jannetje, Joanna, Johanna, 163, 218, 262, 283, 286, 324, 354, 386, 414, 434.
Maria, Maritje, Marya, 557, 577, 578, 605, 609.
Pietertje, 98, 100, 138, 265, 296, 306, 312, 335, 386.
Sofia, Feytje, 439, 609.
Tenneke, 479.
Van Wagenen, van Wagene, Annatie, Annatje, Antie, Antje, Antye, 483, 487, 534, 557, 558, 569, 573, 576, 588, 591, 600, 602, 608, 631, 644, 650, 659, 666, 677, 789, 815, 854, 885, 937, 962, 974.
Belytje, 627.
Catlyntie, Catleyntie, 789, 854, 863.
Cornelis, Cornelus, 588, 634.
Helmigh, Helmech, Helmeg, Helmigs, 487, 566, 573, 593, 594.
Hessel Pieters, 604.
Jacob, Jacop, Jacob Garretsen, Jacob Gerretsen, Jacob Gerritsen, 471, 490, 495, 501, 502, 521, 539, 553, 608, 624, 628, 640, 643, 649, 666, 701, 734, 770, 855, 880, 920, 921, 933, 956, 974, 991.
Jannetje, 588, 594.
Johannis, Johannes Gerretsen, Johannis Gerresse, Johannis Johannisse, 442, 450, 560, 643, 649, 661, 687, 694, 701, 789, 824, 866.
Leeya, 921, 933, 962, 1012.
Neesje, Neesye, 643, 649, 661, 687, 694, 701, 824.
Van Wert, van Waert, Johannis, 733.
Polley, Palley, Palli, 872, 896, 939, 959, 968, 977, 1007.
Van Winkel, van Winckelen, Aagtje, Aegye, 660, 684, 702, 726.
Aaltje, Altje, 507, 586, 597, 611, 628, 638.
Abraham, 887, 976, 993.
Annatje, 536.
Catryntje, Catrientie, 487, 943, 964, 975, 986, 1018.
Daniel, 444, 455, 469, 544, 567, 697, 740, 784, 805, 853, 943, 949, 982, 1017.
Feytje, 660.
Geertruy, 530.

Hendrick, Hendrik, 465, 493, 494, 544, 575, 587, 821, 857, 876, 887, 964.
Jacob, Jacop, Jacob Jacobse, Jacob Jacobsen, 165, 201, 242, 289, 291, 349, 455, 670, 725, 740, 747, 752, 768, 805, 857.
Jannetje, 544, 603, 612.
Josep, 725, 768, 780, 843, 853, 876, 986.
Jurrie, Jurri, 949, 995.
Margrita, Grietje, Margrietje, Margritie, Mergrietje, 349, 455, 611, 636, 898.
Rachel, 567, 589, 625, 645, 652.
Symon Jacobse, Symon Jacobsen, 183, 201, 216.
Tryntje, Tryntje Jacobsen, Treyntje Jacobsen, 461, 465, 469, 474, 493, 494, 589.
Varlet, N., 3, 9.
Veeder, Veder, Hermanis,Harmanis, Harmanus, Hermanus, 632, 655, 668, 694, 722, 754, 810.
Verkerk, Verkerke, Jannetje, 437, 454, 555.
Roelof, 437.
Vermeule, Vermeulen, Adrian, Adr., 421, 436, 453.
Grietje, 18.
Mareya, 18.
Verplanck, verplanck, Abigel, 21.
Hilgont, 276.
Verveele, Verveel, Daniel, 807.
Dirricke, Dirrickye, 763, 802.
Tietje, Tietye, Titye, 778, 788, 807, 834, 860.
Verwey, Cornelis, 148, 181.
Vlierboom, Vlireboom, Elizabet, Eeliesabet, Eliesabet, Elisabet, 653, 680, 682, 711, 738, 765, 771, 791, 840, 867, 1002.
Vochst, Barent, 243.
Volck, Claes Hendrickse, 237.
Vos, Maria, 618.
Thomas, 618.
Vreeland, Vrelent, ...481.
Aagtje, Aaggie, Aagttje, Aege, Aegye, Achtje, Cornelis, Aagtje Hartmans, Aegtje Hartmans, 384, 421, 428, 435, 445, 446, 458, 460, 515, 566, 583, 647, 662, 664, 666, 678, 698, 701, 717, 734, 767, 770, 774, 855, 948, 999.
Aeltie, Aaltje, Altje, 661, 687, 866.
Abraham, 349, 498.
Annatie, Annatye, Antje, Antye, 542, 546, 704, 707, 716, 734, 866, 909, 920, 971, 985,
Arianntje Hartmansen,Ariaentje Michielse, 208, 505.
Beelitye, Beeletye, Beleetye, Belytje, 671, 723, 730, 731, 760, 792, 809, 846, 925.
Claes, Claas, Klaes, Claas Hartmansen, Claes Hertmanse, Claes Hertmansen, 321, 323, 445, 671, 712, 732, 755, 846, 884.
Cornelis, Cornelus, Cornelis M., Cornelis Machielsen,Cornelis Michielse, 270, 329, 351, 416, 428, 444, 664, 667, 696, 716, 829.
Dirk, Derck, Dirreck, Dirrick, 642, 654, 674, 681, 723, 731, 804, 846.
Elisabet, 967, 1009.
Elsje, Else, 206, 250, 279, 303, 328, 353, 376, 392, 509.
Elyas Magielse, 168, 182.
Enoch, Eenog, Enog., Enoch Machielsen, Enoch Magielse, Enoch Michielse, Enoch Michielsen, 143, 172, 206, 299, 349, 397, 416, 429, 443, 460, 815.
Feytje, Feytje Cornelis, 273, 384, 561.
Gerrit, 671, 906, 923, 930, 955, 1000.
Hartman, Hertman M., Hertman Magielse, Hertman Michgielse, Hertman Michielse, 146, 208, 226, 255, 323, 327, 354, 732.
Helena, Leena, Helena Johannissen, 491, 541, 546, 598, 610, 999.
Helmigh, Helmich, 678, 717.
Hester, 595, 603, 616, 622, 645, 745.
Jacop, Jacob Elyassen, 359, 776, 804, 923.
Jannetje, Jannetye, Jannitje, Jannitye, Jenneke, Jannetje Cornelis, Jannetje Cornelissen, Jannetje Johanissen, 444, 455, 479, 514, 543, 567, 621, 647, 659, 662, 667, 681, 696, 698, 704, 707, 739, 919, 927, 948, 955.
Johannis, Johannes, John, Johannes, Johannessen, Johannes M., Johannes Magielse, Johannes Michielse, Johannis Johanisse, Johannis Johannissen, Jo. M., Jo. Mechgielse, Jo. Michielse, 168, 169, 208, 220, 230, 255, 315, 329, 400, 406, 482, 488, 530, 542, 546, 561, 590, 612, 739, 767, 774, 776, 829, 850, 873, 882, 895, 907, 909, 931, 935, 957, 999.

Joris, Jooris, Joris Enogsen, 536, 558, 569, 576, 591, 600, 631, 644, 650, 659, 666, 677, 815, 927, 956, 985, 1012.
Keetye, 873.
Marreytje, Marretye, Marritie, Marritye, Marr. .ye, Martje, Marretje Harmanssen, 425, 435, 481, 681, 723, 731, 804.
Mettje, 610, 621, 629.
Michiel, Machiel, Maghiel, Machiel Corneluse, Michiel Cor., Michiel Cornelis, Michiel Cornelise, Michiel Cornelisse, Michiel Cornelissen, Michiel Cornellissen, Michiel H., Michiel Hartman, Michiel Hartmans, Michiel Hartmanse, Michiel Hartmansen, Michiel Hartmensen, 490, 509, 513, 514, 520, 527, 543, 554, 560, 561, 570, 574, 586, 597, 601, 615, 621, 627, 631, 636, 647, 704, 707, 716, 721, 734, 909, 925, 967, 971, 985, 989.
Preyntje Michielse, 206, 226.
Rachel, 410.
Tryntje, Treyntje, Tryntje Elyassen, 359, 379, 410, 425, 446.
Vreelinghuysen, Vrelmighuysen, Annatie, Annatje, Annatye, 672, 693, 721, 722, 741, 759, 769, 795, 816, 852, 893.
Waldron, Waldrum, Catrina, Catriena, Catrientie, Catrientye, Catryntje, 544, 575, 587, 713, 727, 729, 748, 754.
Daniel, 587.
Joseph, Josep, 584, 600, 615, 670, 685, 727, 729, 749, 788, 827.
Sara, 814.
Walingh, Annetje, 385.
Wekken, Elisabet, 833, 848.
Wels, Jorg, 865.
Wernaers, Wande, Mayritje, 21.
Margrietje, 183, 285.
Wessels, Grietje, 299.
Hendrickje, 16, 123, 124.
Warnaer, 32.
Westervelt, Johannis, 620.
Leena, 984.
Osseltje, 613, 620, 635, 642.
Roelof, 325.
Susanna, 857, 887.
Wieller, John, 875.
Wiggertse, Hessel, 122.
Willense, Davidt, 377.
Wilyems, Marytye, 811.
Wilson, Gerrit, 960.
Jannetye, 960.
Winne, Wennem, Annetje, Antie, Antje, Antye, 258, 637, 651, 673, 709, 782, 830, 943, 982, 1017.
Clausie, 673.
Jannetye, 982, 1013.
Johannis, 675, 686, 709, 757.
Levynus, Lavynes, Lavynis, Lavynus, Livinas, Livynus, Lyvynus, 637, 651, 675, 677, 724, 730, 736, 757, 760.
Maria, 675.
Marten, Marte, 258, 479, 486, 514, 967, 1013, 1017.
York, Jork, Elisabeth, 674.
John, Jan, 650, 674, 826, 855.

YEAR BOOK

OF

The Holland Society

OF

New York

1914

BERGEN BOOK

2nd Volume

PREPARED BY THE RECORDING SECRETARY

Executive Office
90 WEST STREET
NEW YORK CITY
A

Wm L Brower

PRESIDENT 1913

OF

THE HOLLAND SOCIETY OF NEW YORK

THE FOUNDING OF JERSEY CITY

to and including the

INCORPORATION OF THE VILLAGE OF BERGEN

by

DINGMAN VERSTEEG

SCARCELY anything is known about the history, prior to 1638, of the section whereof Manhattan is the center. Albany is somewhat more fortunate in this respect, the year 1630 opening its unbroken authentic history. In regard to the remainder of New Netherland, the South River (Delaware) and the Fresh River (Connecticut), the early information is even more meager and scattered than about Manhattan and its immediate vicinity. A few fragmentary records, such as about the founding and destruction of the Colony of Swaenendael (Lewes) on the Delaware in 1631, the founding by the Dutch in 1633 and subsequent usurpation by the English of Fort Hope on the Fresh River (Connecticut), and a scanty number of other fragmentary, disconnected, often obscure, but very valuable reports of Dutch activity

activity in the extensive territory once known as New Netherland, contain the sum total of our information about its history prior to 1638.

The chief reason for this scarcity of information lies in the fact that the New Netherland official records before 1638 (excepting a few valuable extracts and excerpts) are missing, while practically all of the West India Company's records in Netherland have disappeared; nor have any of the books and records of the New Netherland Company (founded in or before 1614) been discovered. The proceedings of the States General and other public bodies in Netherland contain very little about New Netherland, chiefly owing to the fact that this Dutch colony was, from the beginning, under private control.

Our chief known sources of information for the period prior to 1638 are contained in the all too meager extracts referred to above, some few letters, occasional reports, remarks or notes by travellers visiting the country, and the very instructive, though often obscure, descriptions of the historians Wassenaer and De Laet.

Nothing really authentic about the territory at present included in Jersey City, Hoboken and Bayonne, prior to 1630, is known to historians and antiquarians, though its close proximity to Manhattan renders it highly probable that adventurous Dutch traders had established themselves there prior to 1614.

Jersey City was founded under Dutch auspices and by the Dutch. Like Greater New York it is an aggregation of distinct and independent settlements, made at different times and under differing impulses, the settlers at the time not even dreaming that their humble beginnings would ever be consolidated and attain to the dignity of powerful, populous cities.

Long before Jersey City was known as such, however, its present territory with many more small settlements, extending from the Kill van Kull to the bounds of Hackensack, had been incorporated, for judicial and civil as well as military purposes, into one government, whose capital was named Bergen, the last but most important of the settlements founded in this section during

during the Dutch rule. Yet it must be kept in mind that with the founding of the Bergen municipality none of the component parts lost any more of their identity than they did when the whole of this territory still resorted under the jurisdiction of the City of New Amsterdam. The chief original settlements Communipaw, Hasimus, Paulus Hook, Pemrepogh, as well as the smaller and more distant ones, retained at least as much of their individuality as before 1661. At the same time, as a consequence of the consolidation and the greater protection promised by it against Indian depredations, their population rapidly increased.

The

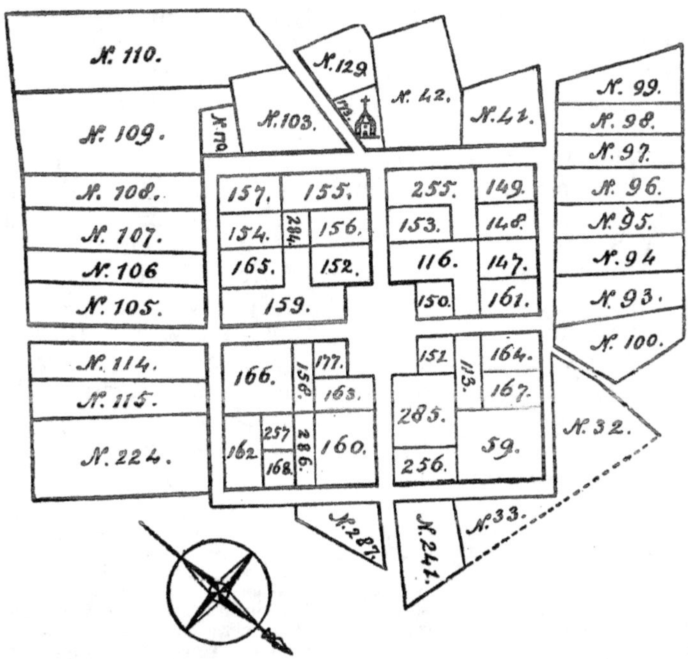

BERGEN AND BUYTEN TUYN, 1660

THE DISTRICT OF PAVONIA

As was stated before the earliest authentic history of Jersey City begins in 1630, when Michael Paauw, Lord of Achttienhoven, caused to be purchased for him from the Indians not only the tract on which Hoboken now stands (July 12) but also Ahasymus (November 22) and the entire territory extending from there to the Kill van Kull. In between these purchases on August 10th of the same year he had acquired Staten Island.

There is, however, no deed in existence showing that he purchased the tract between Hasymus Creek and the Kill van Kull, though there is abundant evidence that he had owned it.[1] The entire tract was named Pavonia, as is evident from many allusions not only in private writings but also in government documents.

It is evident that very early after acquiring his extensive landed estate Pauw set about peopling it in order to comply with the West India Company's conditions.[2] As early as May, 1632,[3] Pauw not only had a permanent officer at Pavonia in the person of Cornelis Van Vorst, who occupied a dwelling there fit to receive and entertain Directors Minuit, Van Twiller and other distinguished guests, but in company with Van Rensselaer—as well as on his own account—Pauw sent out animals and had scoured the country for cattle fit to stock his farms and plantations. And it is to be noted in this connection that Van Vorst was not employed as a farmer or even manager by Pauw but as chief officer (the civil and judicial head of the colony) showing that long before Pavonia was disposed of to the West India Company there was a considerable population residing there.

This

[1]Could it be possible that the Aressik named in Paauw's deed of November 22, 1630, instead of being Paulus Hoock, was in reality the tract between Ahasimus and the Kill Van Kull? It is called Hoeck (corner) in Dutch but it is well known that this word usually designated a pretty large tract of land frequently very much larger than Paulus Hook. There does not appear to be any authority to connect Paulus Hoeck with Aressik. While the deed is translated "the little island Aressick" on page 2, Vol. XIII, "Documents relating to the Colonial History of the State of New York," the translation on page 4 of Winfield's "History of the Land Titles in Hudson County, N. J." reads "the peninsula Aressick." On Oct. 25, 1634, the West India Company reserves to itself........Achassemes, Arasick and Hobokina.

[2]Van Rensselaer Bowier Mss., page 138.

[3]Van Rensselaer Bowier Mss., page 304, question 20.

This is the more probable because Pavonia not only contained very good farming land but also owing to the circumstance that here was the ferry to Fort Amsterdam, "where the Indians are compelled to cross to the Fort with their beavers" according to Captain De Vries,[1] and where Pauw, being a Patroon of New Netherland, was at liberty to erect a trading post and traffic with the natives.[2]

That Pauw, for the purpose of improving his Pavonia holdings, temporarily employed many people under Van Vorst's supervision is evident from a memorandum in the Van Rensselaer Bowier Manuscripts,[3] dated July 20, 1632, reading as follows: "I hear also that Cornelis Van Voorst has laborers whose time is up and that he has engaged new men." From the fact that their "time is up" it may be inferred that Pauw had sent them over at the time that he purchased Hoboken or perhaps even about January 10, 1630, when he first registered with the Chamber of Amsterdam of the West India Company his intended patroonship of the section afterward known as Pavonia.[4]

That Van Voorst was a hospitable entertainer and lover of congenial company is evident from at least two instances, both related by Captain De Vries. During the evening of May 23, 1633, the incoming flood prevented De Vries from reaching his ship, which was waiting for him at Sandy Hook. He consequently directed his men to row him over to Pavonia, there to await the ebb tide. Here they were immediately well received by Van Vorst,[5] who utilized some of the time in writing letters to Holland, which were to be carried over

[1]Narratives of New Netherland, page 210.

[2]Van Rensselaer Bowier Mss., page 145, Art. XV, 2nd clause.

[3]Van Rensselaer Bowier Mss., page 223.

[4]Van Rensselaer Bowier Mss., page 158.

[5]Narratives of New Netherland, page 190. The rendering in English "We were there received by one Michael Poulaz an officer of the company" is absolutely wrong and has given rise to many mistaken statements. The original on page 115 of De Vries' *Korte Historiæ* reads: "Aan Pavonia komende werden wy daer dadelyk wel onthaeld door Michiel Poulusz dienaer." Arriving at Pavonia we were there immediately well received by Michiel Poulusz' [Pauw's] employee." Not a word about the Company. Dienaer in those days meant any employee from a King's minister to a menial servant. It is also correctly translated on page 190 of the Narratives of New Netherland: "We were immediately well entertained by the agent of Michael Poulusz."

over by De Vries. Meanwhile the sailors as well as their captain were most hospitably treated by the host, which resulted in their oversleeping in the morning, so that they would almost have lost the opportunity of profiting much by the ebb, which was to carry them out to the ship, where they arrived about noon.

Hunthum, who had been the West India Company's Director at Fort Orange, appears to have been a troublesome individual. The Indians were exasperated at him, the whites were displeased with him. Some time during 1633 he had occasion to visit Pavonia and there got into difficulties; how or wherefore is not known. Van Vorst as Pavonia's peace officer was drawn into the case, and, as a consequence, swords were used, during which Van Vorst killed Hunthum. Perhaps this is the "killing" (doodslag) referred to by De Vries on page 145 of his "Korte Historiael", describing his entertainment by Van Vorst and the burning down of the latter's house. This killing may have aroused the ire of Director Van Twiller, as indicated by a letter to him dated April 23, 1634, by Kiliaen Van Rensselaer, in which it was stated that Paauw "was also very sorely out of patience with you because of the severe proceedings against Cornelis Van Vorst."

Some three years later, on June 25, 1636, there took place another celebration at Pavonia, which did not terminate as harmlessly as the one mentioned before. De Vries in company with Director Van Twiller and the Reverend Bogardus, together crossed over to Pavonia "where the person in command there for Michiel Pauw was Cornelis Van Vorst."[1] Van Vorst not only had become a farmer and cattle raiser but, like many another enterprising New Netherlander of the period, carried on commercial transactions with the English colonies. He had just returned from New England in a small English bark, loaded with good Bordeaux wine, purchased there by him. It was for the purpose of sampling this wine that De Vries and his distinguished fellow guests crossed over from the fort to Van Vorst's dwelling in Pavonia. The house was enclosed

[1]This must refer to Van Vorst's former station, as Pauw had disposed of his Pavonia holdings prior to Oct. 25, 1634. Van Vorst at the time of this visit was a tenant of the Company.

enclosed by palisades in spots surmounted by "steenstucken" or pedereros. After the guests had taken leave Van Vorst, in honor of Van Twiller, had one of the pedereros discharged. A spark was blown unto the thatched roof, the house caught fire and within half an hour was in ruins. As the whole of Pavonia, with all it contained, had been West India Company's property since the summer of 1634, Van Twiller immediately had a new house built for Van Vorst, while a little earlier he had one erected for Jan Evertsen Bout[1], a former officer of the Company, but who in the beginning of 1634 had entered Pauw's service, and, like Van Vorst, remained at Pavonia after its transfer to the Company, as one of the West India Company's tenants.

The patroonships of New Netherland had become a source of great annoyance to the Company. Its Directors in Netherland desired to eliminate the patroons by buying them out. During the summer session of 1634 some offers were made. Van Rensselaer demanded six thousand pounds Flemish or thirty-six thousand guilders for his colony of Rensselaerswyck, but the sale was not consummated. The partners of Swaenendael (Lewes, Del.) on the South River sold their rights to the Company. Pauw disposed of his colony for the amount of twenty-six thousand guilders, which shows an annual outlay since 1630 of between five thousand and six thousand guilders per annum. And as capital in those days was worth certainly six times as much as at present, Pauw's efforts toward the development of early New Netherland entitle him to greater recognition than he has hitherto received.

It is probable that the news of Pauw's sale of Pavonia to the West India Company reached here about the beginning of September, 1634. Consequently Van Vorst not desiring to quit either New Netherland or his present holding prepared for the life of an independent settler. On September 8th he bought of Mr. Cock[2] a trading sloop on which he paid one-third of the purchase money, giving a note for the remaining two-thirds

[1]Documents relating to the Colonial History of the State of New York, Vol. XIV, page 16; Vol. I, page 432.
[2]Calendar of Dutch Mss., page 8.

thirds. In disposing of Pavonia Pauw had not lost sight of the interests of his former officers. Kiliaen Van Rensselaer in a letter to his Schout Planck, dated May 24, 1635, thus refers to this matter: "The respective patroons of the Colonies of Swanendal and Pavonia have sold and transferred their colonies to the West India Company......Investigate some time what the colony's rights are as the Company having bought the colony of Mr. Pauw *has been obliged to admit and accept the contracts* which Mr. Pauw made with his people concerning the trade in peltries till the expiration and end of their terms."[1] This freedom of trade in the case of Pauw's former officials seemed to have expired before October 21, 1638, when the Fiscal of New Netherland instituted proceedings before the Council against Jan Evertsen Bout, Hendrick Cornelissen Van Vorst and others, "for illicit trading in furs."[2]

It is more than probable that Pauw had stipulated with the West India Company that besides having freedom of trade his former officers also should be permitted to remain on their farms during the time of their contract. This contract, in the case of Jan Evertsen Bout, appears to have terminated on July 20, 1638, when he was secured in the continuous occupancy of the Pavonia farm by a lease executed between himself and Director Kieft. Also in the case of Van Vorst there is no evidence that he ever left his original holding, and he may have been entitled to occupy his farm till the spring of 1639. On March 31st of this year Director Kieft leased "to Vrouwtje Ides, widow of the late Cornelis Van Vorst, the Company's bouwery at Ahasimus for 20 years."[3] On the same date Jan, eldest son of Cornelis Van Vorst, rented a farm on Manhattan, belonging to the Company, while a few days before, on March 12, 1639, Hendrick Cornelissen Van Vorst, another son of the deceased former Schout of Pavonia, rented of Kieft the Company's bouwery at

[1]Van Rensselaer Bowier Mss. page 314.

[2]Calendar of Dutch Mss., page 65.

[3]Calendar of Dutch Mss., page 6.

at Hoboken,[1] which young Van Vorst had occupied before, and which after his death was on February 15, 1640, leased to Aert Teunissen Van Putten.[2]

On May 18, 1639, the West India Company's executive in this country still further favored the widow of Pavonia's former chief officer by providing her with a flock of sheep, which some time previous had arrived from Holland, for distribution among the most responsible and trustworthy of New Netherland farmers.

It would appear that the West India Company kept possession only of the cultivated farms in Pavonia while it made grants of uncultivated lands to prospective settlers or those able and willing to develop the region. Thus on May 1, 1638, Director Kieft granted the whole of Paulus Hook, the eastern extremity of Hasimus, to Abram Isaacksen Verplanck, who on the same date secured a loan from the Director for five hundred and twenty guilders.[3] Verplanck as subsequently shown settled there, at least temporarily, leasing portions of his estate to planters on a small scale. Thus on October 21st of the same year he leased to Gerrit Dircksen and Claes Jansen two acres of land each for tobacco plantations. On May 16th of the following year Verplanck had cleared enough of his Paulus Hook holding to entitle him to receive from the Company two cows on half shares, a practice much followed at the time, and which greatly assisted in increasing New Netherland's herd of domestic animals.

That the West India Company generously supported the independent settlers or free colonists in their struggles to subdue the wilderness is shown by a receipt to Verplanck, the Dutch original of which, with other priceless original Dutch documents, is in the possession of the New York Historical Society, and of which the following is a translation: "Abraham Planck living at Paulus Hoeck has fully satisfied and paid to the Hon. Company all that which he owed to January 1, 1641, according

[1]Hendrick Van Vorst had died without issue, his estate being inherited by his brothers and sisters. This estate must have been considerable as Jacob Stoffelsen, on April 26, 1640, sued the Rev. Bogardus and Jan Damen, administrators, for compensation for feeding fifteen head of cattle, belonging to the estate. Calendar of Dutch Mss. page 71.

[2]Calendar of Dutch Mss. pages, 5 and 12.

[3]Calendar of Dutch Mss. page 2.

according to his account in the free colonists' book, as well for Paulus Hoeck, food, storegoods, as other items in said account. Therefore the present has been delivered to him at his request, this November 25. Executed at Fort Amsterdam, in New Netherland.

By authority of the Hon. Lord Director,
Cornelis Van Tienh: Secretary."

This important document was endorsed: "Receipt of the Company for the payment of Paulus Hoeck."

The fact of Paulus Hoeck being the gateway from the river side to Hasymus, at one time even caused the entire Pavonia district to be comprised under this name. On February 10, 1654, among the twelve New Netherland communities to be taxed for equipping a naval force of forty men for the purpose of suppressing the "robberies by English pirates" Paulus Hoeck was set down for one man. It is evident, however, that Paulus Hoeck was here substituted for the whole of Pavonia, as this Hoeck was one of the least populated sections of the district.

While Hasimus, Communipaw and Paulus Hook were thus being developed by the aid of the West India Company other sections of Pavonia did not lag far behind. Jan De Lacher's Hook, a tongue of land just south of Hasimus or Mill Creek, was occupied by Egbert Woutersen, an early resident there. On June 20, 1640, he received as his share of the general distribution of animals imported by the West India Company, three milch cows and three mares, while his neighbor Jan Evertsen Bout was on the same date provided with an equal number of cows.[1]

Thus affairs prospered at Pavonia. The various settlements slowly increased in population and cultivated area. While neighborly good will and helpful coöperation were the rule among the settlers, sometimes difficulties arose, and once in a while the differences between some of the colonists were rehearsed before the court.

The settlement of Cornelis Van Vorst's estate did not appear to proceed very smoothly and often was a subject for litigation. It would seem that this estate was

[1]Calendar of Dutch Mss. page 13.

was one of the largest private estates in New Netherland at the time, and various complications rendered expert decision necessary. The Council of New Netherland was the natural expert and disinterested arbitrator. In these proceedings, besides the Van Vorst heirs, there figured most of the leading men of New Amsterdam at the time, such as the Reverend Everardus Bogardus, Frederick Lubbertsen, Maryn Adriaensen, Huygh Aertsen Van Rossum, Jan Damen, David Provost, Jacob Stoffelsen, Cornelis Leendertsen, Jan Evertsen Bout, Tymen Jansen, Hendrick Jansen Ostrom and others.

Withal nothing of real magnitude is recorded until the eventful year 1643, when occurrences took place which threatened the colonies in this central portion of New Netherland with total annihilation and for many years to come caused the bitterest antagonism between the people and the government. The regrettable occurrences of this eventful year have been so often rehearsed and so widely commented on by every writer on New Netherland history that it is not necessary to enter into details about them here. The Indians for some years back not only had been very troublesome but had committed several murders on the colonists at Manhattan and neighboring settlements. This even obliged the Council of New Netherland to adopt a resolution[1] on September 12, 1641, "to construct a redoubt on Staten Island for the protection there of the inhabitants" who were daily assaulted and murdered by the Raritans. Far from conducting "themselves like lambs"[2] as stated by Kieft's accusers, the Indians in the neighborhood of Manhattan, even prior to 1643, went often on the warpath against the whites, or at least made many murderous attempts upon the lives of more isolated settlers. The murder of Claes Cornelissen Swits, in 1641, was the immediate cause of this first recorded Indian war. The attack on the Indians by the burghers at Van Curler's bowery on Manhattan, and by the soldiers on the Indians massed at Jan De Lacher's Hook behind Jan Evertsen

[1]Calendar of Dutch Mss. page 77.
[2]Documents relating to the Colonial History of the State of New York Vol. I, page 206, Article 8.

Evertsen Bout's bowery at Pavonia, both on February 24th, 1643, are matters of general knowledge. Nearly all of our information of the deplorable events we get from sources absolutely antagonistic to Director Kieft and the West India Company. Kieft's version, reports, documents and affidavits concerning them were lost with himself in the wreck of the *Princess* on the west coast of England in 1647. The general war with the Indians, following these two attacks, beggared most of the colonists, and rendered it even more dangerous than before to attend to their business in the fields and on the water. Had the war been successful and the Indians rendered harmless without great loss to the settlers Kieft would have been the best loved and most lauded man of the period. He was unsuccessful and his memory has been blackened ever since.

The original board of Twelve Men, convened August 29, 1641, for the purpose of advising the government about the course to be followed in dealing with the Indians, was composed of delegates from Manhattan and surrounding settlements. It contained at least two of Pavonia's early settlers: Gerrit Dircksen Blauw and Abraham Isaacsen Verplanck. Later Jacob Walingsen Van Winkle and Jan Evertsen Bout were added to the Pavonia members. It is probable that Walingsen's property at Pavonia having been destroyed during the war he removed to Rensselaerswyck, where he remained till 1650, when he returned to Pavonia, much to the regret of the authorities of Rensselaer's colony, who made him tempting offers to remain. Among the other Pavonians whose houses or barns were destroyed at the time were Jan Evertsen Bout, Gerrit Dircksen Blauw, whose stepson was killed at the same time, Cornelis Arentsen or Aertsen, the reputed ancestor of Van Schaick and Bryant families, Cornelis Leendertsen, Abraham Planck. Abraham Verplanck's losses were so large that on April 27, 1643, he was obliged to mortgage Paulus Hook to Jan Damen and Cornelis Van Tienhoven as joint securities for a loan which on the same day he had received from the Company to tide him over his difficulties. Three days later he leased Paulus Hook with the house and garden thereto

thereto belonging to Cornelis Arissen or Aertsen, referred to before.[1]

The destruction, by the Indians, of property at Pavonia had been wholesale and extended over the entire region. Aert Teunissen Van Putten of Hoboken who at his farm there, hired from the Company, had "fenced the lands, cleared the fields, erected a suitable brewhouse, brought thither twenty-eight head of large cattle, besides various small stock, swine, goats and sheep, together with many of his own fruit trees," not only lost all his live stock and horses "but the dwelling house, barns and stacks of seed were burnt, the brewhouse alone remaining standing," while he himself "was murdered, with many others who were killed before and after him by the Indians."[2]

Besides a number of plantations four well stocked bouweries at Pavonia were destroyed and worse would have happened but for the fortunate occurrence that "two ships of war and a privateer were here at the time, and saved considerable cattle and grain. Probably it was not possible to prevent the destruction of four bouweries at Pavonia, which were burnt; not by open violence but by stealthily creeping through the bush with fire in hand, and in this way igniting the roofs, which are all either of reed or straw; one, coverėd with plank was preserved at the time." And further "All the Bouweries and plantations at Pavonia with 25 lasts (2000 bushels) of grain and other produce are burnt and the cattle in part destroyed by the Indians."[3]

Among the houses and barns destroyed was the dwelling occupied by Jan Evertsen Bout. Still to him it was not an unmixed evil, for, as if to compensate him for the loss sustained the West India Company "made a free gift to Jan Evertsen, long after the house was burnt, of the land whereon his house stood, and of the bouwery, which produced good wheat."[4] That the soil was very valuable was shown by the fact that after Jan Evertsen removed to Breuckelen, Michel Jansen Vreeland bought the property, not much improved as to

[1]Calendar of Dutch Mss., page 22.

[2]Documents relating to the Colonial History of the State of New York, Voi. I, pages 328, 329.

[3]Documents relating to the Colonial History of the State of New York, Vol. I, pages 185 and 190.

[4]Documents relating to the Colonial History of the State of New York, Vol. I, page 432.

to buildings, for eight thousand guilders, and he made the farm pay not only by the raising of produce but of cattle as well.

Yet notwithstanding the Indian war, which raged more than two years, it would seem that the farmers generally had been able to sow and harvest their crops and attend to their live stock, for on September 30, 1643, when a request had been received from Curaçao for supplies, the Council was able to provide "pork, beef and peas, [they] being plentiful in New Netherland," and it was necessary only "to send to New England for a cargo of dry fish."[1] It was not until August 30, 1645,[2] that a final treaty of peace with all the Indian tribes was concluded, though a partial treaty had been made as early as April 22nd, and celebrated by the firing of the fort's batteries, during which a brass six-pounder burst, badly wounding the right arm of the gunner, Jacob Jacobsen Roy, the future patentee of Constable's Hook.

It is probable that Stoffelsen, Van Vorst's successor at Hasimus, was the only one who had been permitted to remain at Pavonia during the war. The only bouwery not destroyed, probably, was the one occupied by him. Van Vorst, as related previously, not only had taken the precaution of surrounding his buildings with palisades but even had planted batteries of stone cannon or pedereros. This precaution, however, though sufficient against Indian attacks, did not, in 1636, save his house from destruction by fire, owing to the thatched roof. For this reason he had probably induced Van Twiller, at the rebuilding of the house, to cover it with planks. The Van Vorst estate being wealthy, and Stoffelsen himself being a well-paid official of the Company, there were many farm hands employed, able to assist in defending the bouwerie, while Indian fire arrows were powerless to ignite the planked roof. There is no evidence that the Stoffelsen Van Vorst family was driven off, so that there is every reason to believe that this Hasimus farm was the only habitation at Pavonia which escaped unscathed from the

[1]Calendar of Dutch Mss., page 86. | [2]Calendar of Dutch Mss., page 97.

the war of 1643. Nor is there any evidence that the family was forced to leave during the Indian uprising of 1655, so that there is ample ground for the conjecture that the Van Vorst family was the only one uninterruptedly to occupy a Jersey City site from its founding about 1630 to the incorporation of Bergen village in 1661, after which there occurred no more general exodus of the inhabitants either on account of Indian attacks or for other known causes.

That Stoffelsen had not suffered much, if anything, from the Indian attacks is evident from the fact that eight months after the first breaking out of war he was able, on October 8, 1643, to advance, for the use of the privateer *La Garce*, an amount of three hundred and fifty guilders, for which Captain Blauvelt and Anthony Crol gave him a joint note.[1] About a year later Stoffelsen became the custodian of a quantity of valuable plate belonging to Jan Jansen Wanshaer (Wanser, Wanzer) an officer of the *Garce's* crew, while on December 4, 1646, at the reëquipment of the *Garce*, Stoffelsen with eleven others became one of her owners.[2]

For the next three years nothing of any general interest seems to have occurred at Pavonia. But that the Indians had not yet discontinued their occasional attacks on the whites is shown from an occurrence recorded on March 11, 1649, when a resolution was passed by the Council concerning the murder of Simon Walingen, who had only lately arrived from Rensselaerswyck, by Indians at Paulus Hook. This probably was the "mischief" referred to by chief Pennekeck of the "Achter Col" Indians, when at a large conference at Fort Amsterdam on July 19, 1649, he stated that "An Indian of Mechgachkamick had involuntarily or unknowingly lately done mischief at Paulus Hook." He requested forgiveness for the act, which seems to have been granted.[3]

Yet after the restoration of outward peace between the Dutch and the Indians, lands at Pavonia began to be taken up more extensively than ever before. Early in 1646 Jacob Jacobsz Roy, the Constapel (gunner) at Fort

[1]Calendar of Dutch Mss., page 24.
[2]Calendar of Dutch Mss., page 36.
[3]Documents relating to the Colonial History of the State of New York, Vol. XIII, page 25.

Fort Amsterdam, received one of the largest grants yet issued to private individuals, a tract of more than 230 acres on the Kill van Koll, which grant was afterwards known as Constable's (gunner's) Hook. He was soon followed by others and between this date and December 4, 1654, at least sixteen more or less extensive tracts in this neighborhood were granted to Claas Carstens, Egbert Woutersen, Maryn Adriaensen, Dirck Dey,[1] Jacob Walingsen Van Winkle, Michiel Jansen Vreeland, Claes Jansen Backer, Jan Cornelissen Buys (Boys, Boice), Jan Lubbertsen Van Blaricom, Jan Gerritsen Van Immen, Jan Cornelissen, Gerrit Pietersen, Lubbert Gysbertsen, Jan Cornelissen Crynen, Gysbert Lubbertsen, Hendrick Jansen Van Schalckwyck (Ostrom), and probably many others. Some of those receiving grants do not appear to have actually settled thereon; others who had been settled there before were granted extensions of their original holdings, while others soon after moved on their newly acquired property. Crynen soon transferred his grant to Isaack De Forest, who on April 17, 1664, was confirmed in his title by a deed from the Council of New Netherland.

Thus the various settlements comprising the district of Pavonia grew apace and seemed on the highway to uninterrupted prosperity. It even appears from chance reports that conviviality and sociability were occasionally indulged in as at the time of Cornelis Van Vorst. Captain Geurt Tysen, the famous privateer, during one of his occasional stays at New Amsterdam, with some of his officers and a number of other guests, were hospitably entertained by Jacob Stoffelsen, over at Pavonia. After the celebration, at which besides other eatables and drinkables two entire sheep were consumed, Captain Tysen, in recognition of the received generous hospitality, presented Stoffelsen with a negro. Ide Van Vorst, Stoffelsen's stepson, claimed that half of the

[1]Dirck Jansen Siecken Dey, with Claes Carstens, was among the earliest settlers of Greenville, N. J. As shown by an entry in the "Minutes of the Orphanmasters of New Amsterdam," 1655-1663, page 70, he also owned 100 acres of land at Pemmerpoock, before February 19, 1659. Owing to this he or his son Jan Dey, was among the earliest settlers at Bayonne, N. J. Winfield, History of the County of Hudson, page 85 note. N. Y. Genealogical and Biographical Record, Vol. 7, page 57. Winfield calls him Seickan or Sycan, and Sycan's Creek was named for him. Winfield, History of the Land Titles of Hudson County, N. J., page 59.

the sheep belonged to his father's estate, consequently that one-half of the negro belonged to the estate. This Stoffelsen denied and the result was a lawsuit, on September 14, 1654, before the City Court of New Amsterdam.[1] From this chance example we may safely infer that sociability, even at Pavonia at the time, was not a forgotten accomplishment and that Jersey City's pioneers and founders knew how to soften the rigors of their incessant struggles through occasional conviviality.

Just one year after the last related festal occasion, however, another calamity befell the section of which Manhattan was the center, and Pavonia again bore the brunt of the battle. In the latter part of August, 1655, Stuyvesant, with the entire garrison and a considerable force of the militia, had set out to reduce the recently lost South River (Delaware) territory again to the obedience of the Dutch. It is evident that the Indians had only been waiting for some such opportunity. They probably thought that New Amsterdam's entire male population able to bear arms had joined in the South River expedition, and were likely to be either killed or taken prisoner by the foe they had set out to attack. Their runners scoured the woods, calling upon every Indian tribe for scores of miles around to join in a united attack on defenceless New Amsterdam and adjacent settlements. Most of the Indian tribes responded. The most conspicuous exceptions were some of the Long Island tribes. These knew from experience that they had to fear less from the presence of the white man than from the periodical depredations of their own kinsmen of the interior. The whites were their friends and protectors while the distant Indians were always their enemies. Besides, they very well knew that the whites were not defenceless even then, and that the white man's wrath was almost sure to alight on their heads while the more distant tribesmen were safely hidden in their own woods and mountain fastnesses. Consequently whatever they may have done in secret, most of the Long Island tribes remained outwardly

[1]Records of New Amsterdam, Vol. I, page 242.

outwardly neutral in the Indian outbreak of September 15, 1655.

From August, 1645, to September 15, 1655, not less than fourteen whites had been murdered by the Indians around Manhattan.[1]

Early in the morning of September 15, 1655, about a thousand (according to another report, five hundred) Indians, in sixty-four canoes, descended upon New Amsterdam, then and later committing many depredations, which about nine o'clock in the evening resulted in a pitched battle, forcing the savages to retire mostly to Pavonia. Soon from the Manhattan shore they "saw the house at Harboken in flames. This done, whole Pavonia was immediately on fire and everything there is burnt and everybody killed except the family of Michiel Hansen (Michael Jansen Vreeland). On the island [Staten Island] they do nothing but burn and fire. Nine hundred savages are in camp at the end of this island or thereabouts, having joined the others."[2] In nine hours it was said the savages murdered over a hundred people, besides taking many prisoners, seventy-three of whom were still in their hands a month afterward.[3] According to a later report, dated October 31, 1655, "in three days' time about fifty christians were killed and murdered, more than one hundred, mostly women and children, captured, of whom we afterward ransomed 60 to 70 at great expense, the rest being still in their hands; 28 bouweries and some plantations and about twelve to fifteen thousand schepels of grain burned, 500 to 600 head of cattle either killed or taken by the barbarians; have suffered through these barbarous Indians—damage of more than two hundred thousand guilders and more than 200 persons besides those who were killed or are still in captivity, have lost their possessions."[4] Without doubt the largest share of the losses had fallen upon the people of Staten Island and of Pavonia. Their situation

[1]Documents relating to the Colonial History of the State of New York, Vol. XIII, page 56.

[2]Documents relating to the Colonial History of the State of New York, Vol. XII, pages 98, 99.

[3]Documents relating to the Colonial History of the State of New York, Vol. XIII, page 45.

[4]Documents relating to the Colonial History of the State of New York, Vol. XIII, page 50.

situation was most exposed and they were much more scattered than the settlers on Manhattan and Long Island. The settlements on Long Island, also owing to the Indians there remaining neutral, suffered very little as compared with other sections.[1]

From a lawsuit in the New Amsterdam City Court on September 25, 1655, between Lambert Huybertsen Moll (Moal) and Edward Scarborough it appears that the Gemoenepaen (Communipaw) people saved much of their cattle and property by making use of Moll's ample scow, which was put by him at their disposal free of charge "as he was giving it to them through love." The scow had not yet been returned on the day of the suit, and while suing Scarborough for hire of the scow on another occasion, Moll at the same time was anxious to find out who was responsible for the vessel's disappearance.[2]

The earlier statement made in the excitement caused by the tragedy that "everything is burnt and everybody killed except the family of Michiel Hansen" at Pavonia, was somewhat exaggerated. Michael Jansen's property was destroyed either at the time or perhaps a few days later. But it is almost certain that the Company's bouwery at Hasymus then occupied by Stoffelsen and part of the Van Vorst family escaped destruction. But that Stoffelsen must have sustained some losses or perhaps have incurred heavy expenses as a consequence of the Indian attacks is suggested by the fact that he was allowed one year's rent when, on December 21, 1656, the Council renewed his lease for the Company's farm at Hasimus.[3]

After the fray, and when the Indians had apparently disappeared, rescuing and searching parties were sent into the woods to hunt up hidden fugitive whites and stray cattle. How dangerous even this was, is shown by the fate which overtook one of these parties, six strong, who had been surprised and attacked by a force of thirty savages. In the fight four of the whites were wounded and all were taken prisoners. The two unwounded

[1]Documents relating to the Colonial History of the State of New York, Vol. XII, page 99. The letter here referred to is dated 12th September which is evidently a mistake as the attack occurred on the 15th.

[2]Records of New Amsterdam, Vol. I, page 364.

[3]Calendar of Dutch Mss., page 178.

wounded members of the party, Stephen Necker and Cornelis Mourissen, were sent to New Amsterdam to demand a heavy ransom. During the trip through the forest Mourissen was shot in the back by an Indian arrow, the point of which, on his arrival at the Fort, on October 13th, was cut out by the surgeon.[1]

The Indians deputed some of their more prominent prisoners to the Fort, to negotiate about the ransom to be paid. Captain Adriaen Post, the Commander at Staten Island, had been taken prisoner with his wife, five children and some servants. He was one of those dispatched for the said purpose. While he was negotiating about the ransom, some of his Indian captors were to await the result at Paulus Hook. The captain was delayed. Peter Cock, who rowed Captain Post to Paulus Hook, upon his return to the Fort stated "that the savages are not satisfied, that Captain Post had not come over at the fixed time, and that they say, you Dutch people lie so much that you cannot be trusted."[2]

The slow progress of the negotiations as well as the devious ways of the Indians are best illustrated by the following letter, dated October 16, 1655, from Amsterdam in New Netherland: "Captain Post. Whereas the savages often impose on us by displaying the flag, and lure us across the river for trivial matters, which makes our people tired to cross and recross, without getting an answer from them in regard to our prisoners, therefore your Worship or someone else who knows the Indian language must ask the Sachems Pennekeck, Oratany and others, what they really mean and intend, and whether they will return the prisoners or not and when, and that they must not cause any further delay or lie to us."[3] On October 17th following Captain Post was so fortunate as to bring about the release of fourteen prisoners, and the Council were so much pleased with the success of his efforts that he was appointed official negotiator and provided with a leather badge with the initials of the West India Company plainly written on it, as a token to the Indians of his official

[1]Documents relating to the Colonial History of the State of N. Y., Vol. XIII, page 44.

[2]Documents relating to the Colonial History of the State of N. Y., Vol. XIII, pages 45 and 46.

[3]Documents relating to the Colonial History of the State of N. Y. Vol. XIII, page 67.

official status. On October 21st, twenty-eight more prisoners had been returned but many more months elapsed before all the captive whites had been set free.

So dangerous did the situation continue that on March 28, 1656, when Nicholas Verleth had presented a petition to the Council for a convoy of six or eight soldiers to remove the frame of a house at Hoboken, sold by Verleth to Michael Jansen Vreeland for two hundred and thirty guilders, the request had to be refused owing to the danger of Indian opposition which was the more to be feared because "the savages still held in captivity about twenty of our children."[1] This after the Indians had assured Peter Cock on October 13, 1655, that the prisoners were all to be set free in two days.

Even as late as January 22, 1657, the Indian peril had not yet entirely subsided, as is shown by an action in the City Court of New Amsterdam, in which Wolfert Webber endeavored to oblige Claes Pieterszen Cos to employ Webber's son on Manhattan instead of at Pavonia. There, Webber stated, "much danger is to be expected as well by water as from the Indians, of which he has had a sample." Webber continued, "if any misfortune happen to his son, either in passing over, or from the Indians or otherwise, he has done his duty, and shall avenge himself on him,"[2] Kos. Cos or Kos removed to Communipaw where he was one of the wealthiest and most public spirited settlers.

It is evident that the Company, for the purpose of accommodating Indians desiring to cross in order to trade at Manhattan, had erected a rough building or lodge, either at Paulus Hook, Hasimus or Communipaw, as it also had done at the Manhattan side of the North River and at other trading posts. This lodge, called the Company's house at Pavonia, apparently had been destroyed or much damaged during the late Indian uprising. Stuyvesant verbally authorized Stoffelsen to have the lodge rebuilt, and he employed Jan Reidersen for the purpose. When Reidersen sent in his bill for fifty guilders to the Director, the latter had forgotten all

[1]Records of New Amsterdam, Vol. II, page 271.

[2]Records of New Amsterdam, Vol. II, page 363.

all about the matter and refused to pay. Thereupon Reidersen sued Stoffelsen who had set him to work.[1] Stoffelsen was ordered to pay, and he doubtless afterward succeeded in refreshing Stuyvesant's memory regarding the case, and had the amount deducted upon paying his annual rent. If the West India Company's account books had been preserved they doubtless would show this transaction, and very many others, rendering Pavonia's history fuller and much more interesting. Probably the Receiver General Cornelis Van Ruyven, upon his return to Holland after the second English occupation, in November, 1674, carried these books away with him, and they were disposed of with the Company's other records, early in the last century.

As a sample of the buoyancy of the pioneers' disposition the following may serve. Michael Jansen Vreeland apparently had lost everything and been ruined through the Indian uprising of 1655. But he did not lose any time in fruitless wailings. Immediately he set to work, rebuilding his destroyed fortune. After tranquillity had been sufficiently restored, he returned to his deserted Communipaw farm, where he engaged in cattle raising on a large scale. Amsterdam's colony on the South River (Delaware) was in need of cattle, and Director Stuyvesant, at the request of Director Alrichs, during the month of June, 1658, bought of Michael Jansen twenty-seven head of cattle of various descriptions and ages, together costing thirteen hundred and thirty guilders.[2]

A few months prior to this, however, on January 22, 1658, the farmers of Pavonia, Gemoenepa and adjacent settlements, in view of their previously sustained losses, petitioned the government for an exemption from the tenths. On the same day the petition was granted, and the exemption extended for six years under condition that they should form a village for mutual protection and defence.[3] From all appearances Communipaw, as the most centrally located of the settlements, would be the locality fixed upon for such a village, and from all appearances a successful beginning was subsequently

[1]Documents relating to the Colonial History of the State of N. Y., Vol. XII, page 217.

[2]Calendar of Dutch Mss., page 188.

[3]Calendar of Dutch Mss., page 201.

quently made, the settlement even having been surrounded with palisades. As all other seaports, small or large, budding or fully developed, Communipaw soon attracted outsiders, and on September 23, 1658, the Council in the Fort at Manhattan issued an order "to send three Quakers across the river to Gemoenepae, whence they came."[1] However, about three years later a more favorably situated new settlement further inland superseded Communipaw as the capital of the Pavonia district.

It was a common practice with the Indians after the lapse of a number of years subsequent to a sale of land either to have forgotten the sale, or to contend that they had not received the full amount agreed upon, or that they had not granted nearly as much land as was shown by the conveyance. These and similar contentions gave rise to various attacks upon isolated white settlers and were causes of many dangerous outbreaks. The same contention appears to have happened in regard to the Pavonia tract, and may have been the cause of the Raritan and Hackensack Indians joining in the outbreak of 1655. Stuyvesant was ever desirous of placating the Indians and acceding as much as possible to their demands and claims, for the sake of the safety of the colonists. He therefore called together a number of chiefs of the interested Indian tribes, and on January 30, 1658, while securing the title to the whole of Pavonia, as before, obtained a few additional tracts. The price paid was eighty fathoms of seawan, twenty fathoms of cloth, twelve kettles, six guns, two blankets, one double kettle, and one-half barrel of strong beer.[2]

Some years afterward the Indians again were in doubt as to the exact extent of the purchase, which was brought to the attention of the Council of New Netherland in the following manner: "The Councillors, Messrs. Cornelis Steenwyck and Cornelis Van Ruyven have today [March 8, 1674,] heard, by order of the Governor the claims made by some savages that *Sicakus*,

[1]Winfield, History of the County of Hudson, N. J., pages 63-65.
Winfield, History of the Land Titles in Hudson County, N. J., pages 5-7.
Calendar of Dutch Historical Mss., page 190.

[2]Winfield, History of the County of Hudson, N. J., page 63.

Sicakus, a small island lying back of *Bergen*, had not been sold, but only *Espating* and its dependencies and that they were now reproached by the other savages for having sold land, which did not belong to them. The contract of sale was thereupon examined and after hearing further debates, it was found that the said island was included in the sale made in January, 1658, but not in the sale of *Espating*. After Saartie Van Borsim had interpreted and explained the matter to them, they said they had not known it and represent that they were now entitled to have an anker of rum, which the parties in interest agreed to give them to avoid further trouble."[1]

On February 9, 1660, the Council of New Netherland renewed its former orders regarding the abandonment of detached dwellings and farm-houses, and the removal of the occupants into established villages, or the founding of new palisaded villages.[2] Tielman Van Vleck, a prominent Notary Public at New Amsterdam and Pieter Rudolphus, an enterprising merchant of the same place petitioned the Council of New Netherland, on March 1, 1660, "on behalf of several persons, for permission to settle on the maize land behind Gemoenepaen, on the West side of the North River."[3] The petition was refused. On April 12th of the same year the Council renewed its order to "those living scattered throughout the country, to form hamlets and villages." Nothing daunted by the recent refusal, Van Vleck and a number of others on the same date of the renewal of the Council's order, again petitioned "for permission to settle a village and some bouweries on the maizeland behind Gemoenepaen." A second time the petition was refused. Yet it is evident that something in the refusal must have given Van Vleck hopes that even this second refusal was not final. The probability was that the Council, as in other instances, desired to have assurance that enough families would join in the proposed settlement, before being willing to grant the otherwise welcome request. For the same reasons of safety

[1]Documents relating to the Colonial History of the State of N. Y., Vol. XIII, page 479.

[2]Winfield, History of the County of Hudson, N. J., pages 68-69.

[3]Calendar of Dutch Mss., page 208.

safety to the prospective settlers Jacob Walingsen[1] Van Winkle was refused permission to establish a settlement on the Fresh River (Connecticut), even prior to 1635. Had he had followers enough to enable him to gain the consent of the central authorities it would have radically changed the course of the country's history.

ARMORIAL BEARINGS OF THE DESCENDANTS OF JACOB WALINGSEN VAN WINKLE.

THE VILLAGE OF BERGEN

On August 16, 1660, a numerously signed petition was presented and this time the authorities perceived a prospect of a successful beginning. The request was granted under condition that "the village shall be formed and placed on a convenient spot which may be defended with ease, which shall be selected by the Director General and Council or their commissioners."[1] It was further stipulated that those allotted plots in the proposed village "shall be obliged to make a beginning within the time of six weeks after the drawing of lots, and to send hither at least one person able to bear and handle arms, and to keep him there upon a penalty of forfeiting their right, besides a fine of twenty florins in behalf of the village, and to pay besides others his share in all the village taxes, which, during his absence, have been decreed and levied."[1] The settling, after selection of the spot, proceeded satisfactorily. Before the approach of winter, in November, 1660, "the village Berghen in the new maize land" was officially recorded in a survey of land for Douwe Harmansen Taelman (Tallman) though for about a year after its founding it was also frequently referred to as "the new village on the maizeland." This "on" (op) was sufficient indication of its high location.

The probability is that Bergen was founded with the sole or chief object of inducing future settlers to venture further inland, and to make Bergen the center of all communities, within easy reach and easy to defend in case of Indian attack. A refuge in time of need for those who, having taken up their abode further inland, could not in time reach the shelter offered by the palisaded enclosures of Communipaw and Hasimus. The founding of Bergen by offering greater safety would induce the colonists to quit hugging the river bank and to start cultivating the arable lands further in the interior. One of the first requisites in case of an investment by the Indians would be water. The cattle as well as those caring for them would be constantly in danger if obliged to go to the spring, "outside the land gate

[1]Winfield, History of the County of Hudson, N. J., pages 68-69.

gate and fence." Therefore water was to be provided within the enclosure, and on January 28, 1662, Bergen's Magistrates ordered "that a public well be constructed for the public accommodation, on the Square, to water the cattle."

Still it is evident that Bergen was not destined to be the only palisaded stronghold in the region of Pavonia. It was only intended to make it the capital of the district, the seat of government. The Schout was to live at Bergen, the court was to sit at Bergen, the council was to meet at Bergen, the chief officer of the militia was to reside at Bergen. But Communipaw and Hasimus were to retain their individuality as distinct parts of the body politic. The fact of the Company's bouwery being located at Hasimus even rendered it doubtful in the minds of the Bergen magistrates whether or not Hasimus resorted under their court. This doubt they expressed in 1662 in their petition for a minister, as follows: "the petitioners do not know whether the people of Haersimons come under this jurisdiction."[1] This fact of the Company retaining in its own hands at least a large portion of the land at Hasimus, accounts for the granting by the general government, on January 21, 1664, of about ten morgens of woodland, behind the Company's bouwery at Ahasemus to Jacob Stoffelsen's wife, provided it be "not prejudicial to the bouwery;" and on April 5, 1664, to Ide Cornelisz Van Vorst, of "a lot situate at Ahasimus on the Northeast side of Claes Jansen and the Southwest side of the wagonroad."[2] But though the ownership of most of the land at Hasimus was retained by the Company, there is no evidence that its inhabitants were exempt from the jurisdiction of the Bergen Court, or resorted under any other than the Bergen municipality.

That there was not the least intention of deserting Communipaw is shown by the order on September 8, 1660, to Surveyor Cortelyou to survey Gemoenepa and lay it out into village lots.[3] Some of the citizens were backward

[1]Year Book Holland Society of N. Y., 1913, page 13.

[2]Documents relating to the Colo-History of the State of N. Y., Vol. XIII, pages 366-367. Calendar of Dutch Mss., page 258.

[3]Winfield, History of the County of Hudson, N. J., pages 88-89.

backward in their duty toward fortifying Communipaw and on February 10, 1661, in reply to a petition regarding Communipaw the Director General and Council of New Netherland replied: "The persons named in this petition are authorized to promote as well the palisading of the village as that of the land, as they, considering the situation of the place and time, shall deem proper, carefully observing that the palisades which are used are of a due length and thickness, viz: between six and seven feet above the ground, and to communicate this to the inhabitants of the village by affixed billets, commanding them under penalty of two pounds Flanders (12 guilders), to be paid in behalf of the village by anyone, who, at the determined day, shall be found to have neglected the one or the other part of his duty. What regards the waggon road, this may be delayed to a more favorable opportunity."[1]

The impetus given to the development of this section by the founding of Bergen, and the use of Communipaw as the natural shipping point of the district probably soon made the place outgrow its earlier dimensions, so that a considerable number of people were living outside the palisades. This is the more probable because on October 26, 1661, the Director General and Council issued an order to all outlying settlers and especially those of Pemrepogh and Mingackque to remove either to Bergen or to Gemoenepan. This rendered necessary an extension of the original fortifications, and on June 18, 1663, the Director General and Councillor De Sille "listened to the verbal request of Harmen Smeeman, Nicholas Backer and Fytje Harmens, widow of Michiel Jansen (Vreeland), to enclose in consideration of these dangerous times their settlement at Gemoenepa with long palisades for the safety of their houses and barns and that for this purpose one as well as the other should be compelled to contribute pro rata. The Director General and Council praise and approve the request and appoint herewith as commissioners to hasten this necessary work Gerrit Gerritsen, Harmen Smeeman and Dirck Claesen ordering and empowering them, to compel every inhabitant to contribute, as they shall

[1]Winfield, History of the County of Hudson, N. J., pages 88-89.

shall judge it equitable and in proportion to the area and location of the lands and lots."[1] That the putting of Communipaw as well as the other Pavonia settlements in a proper state of defence was no useless proceeding was demonstrated on October 18 of the same year. At about eight o'clock in the evening of that day word was received at the Fort that "two Christians on their way from Bergen to Gamonepa were this day murdered by the Indians." As it was not known what they might or might not do during the night the gunner was forthwith ordered to load two of the loudest voiced pieces of artillery on the walls of the fort with six pounds of gunpowder each, and they immediately were "fired as a warning to the people to be on their guard."[2] While this murder may only have been one of the sporadic, isolated outbreaks of some lawless Indians of the neighborhood, it yet showed that the danger still was imminent, especially since most of the garrison of Fort Amsterdam and a large portion of the male civilians had departed for the Esopus country where the Indians had murdered or captured a large part of the population of Wildwyck (Kingston) and the Niew Dorp (Hurley), entirely destroying the latter and greatly damaging the former settlement.

Yet though the founding of Bergen had been undertaken with the sanction of the supreme authority and for the purpose of creating a distinct civic center, more than a year elapsed before the appointment of municipal and judicial officers (the Court of Schout and Schepens). Consequently lawsuits, as before, had to be decided by the City Court of New Amsterdam, under which Pavonia resorted as long as no distinct court had been erected across the North River. Thus on June 21, 1661, two Bergen residents, Casper Steinmets and Douwe Hermansen, were before the New Amsterdam Court, because Hermansen had stated that Steinmets "has removed the boundary stakes of his land." Hermansen could not substantiate his accusation and he was condemned "to pay to the Poor the sum of twelve Guilders for that he has slandered Caspar Steymits and further in

[1]Documents relating to the Colonial History of the State of N. Y., Vol. XIII, page 252.

[2]Documents relating to the Colonial History of the State of N. Y., Vol. II, page 466.

in the costs and loss of time."[1] This "loss of time" to Pavonia people having law cases to attend to doubtless hastened the establishing of an independent Court across the North River and on September 5, 1661, an ordinance was passed by the Council of New Netherland for the erection of a Court of Justice at Bergen (The Bergen Charter).[2] It was to be a Court of Schout and Schepenen. The Schout was Tielman Van Vleck, the New Amsterdam Notary Public, and the Schepens were Michael Jansen Vreeland, Harman Smeeman and Caspar Steinmets. It is to be noted that Vreeland and Smeeman were Communipaw settlers. The Schout was to be Secretary of the Court and as Court messenger was appointed Jan Tibout who in 1663 was succeeded by Claes Arentse Toers.

In order to increase the dignity of the newly erected municipality the Director General and Council on October 26, 1661, "granted to the inhabitants of the village of Bergen, the lands, with the meadows thereunto annexed, situate on the West Side of the North River in Pavonia, in the same manner as the same was by us underwritten, purchased of the Indians, and as the same was to us delivered, by the said Indians, pursuant to an instrument of sale and delivery thereof, being under the date of the 30th of January A. D. one thousand six hundred and fifty eight."[3] This generosity immediately provided the newly founded Municipality with a source of revenue as the authorities were privileged to charge for the grants of the ownerless tracts in the region it had acquired.

Down to this time there had been no regularly established or officially regulated communication between Manhattan and Pavonia, every person desiring to cross to either side of the river making use of whatever means of transfer proved most convenient. The actual and prospective influx of new settlers, however, rendered necessary and promised to make paying the establishing of more regular means of communication, and before the winter of 1661, Willem Jansen was appointed ferrymaster

[1]Records of New Amsterdam, Vol. III, page 324.

[2]Winfield, History of the County of Hudson, N. J., pages 74-80.

[3]Winfield, History of Land Titles in Hudson Co., N. J., pages 7-8.

ferrymaster between Manhattan and Communipaw.[1] Legal rates of ferriage were established by the central authorities in the fort, but those living near the river bank and possessing boats were not disposed to forego their occasional chance of adding a few stivers to their regular earnings, or employing the official ferryman when they themselves or their friends or servants had occasion to cross over to Manhattan and back. Jansen applied to the Bergen authorities,[2] but they upheld the claims of the boat owners. The ferryman thereupon appealed to the Council of New Netherland. On December 28, 1662, the case was argued before the supreme authority, and on January 4, 1663, a decision was handed down which practically proclaimed a victory for Jansen. It is recorded as follows: "Pursuant to the order of the 28th Decbr. Willem Jansen ferryman at Bergen, appeared on one side and the Schout Van Vleeck and Engelbert Steenhuysen on the other; the said ferryman stating in his complaint, that the Schout Van Vleeck and Engelbert Steenhuysen had given permission to all and everyone of the inhabitants there to carry over goods for others, etc.

"Whereupon the said Schout and his companion answered that they had not done it without reason, as the ferryman had refused to carry over.

"The ferryman says that he left nobody behind except those who would not pay him, etc.

"After hearing the parties, the Schout was directed to assist the ferryman, that he may obtain the ferriage earned by him and if he should forget himself and act unbecomingly, to report it to the Director-General and Council, who will then issue such orders as occasion may require."[2] Jansen remained in charge of the ferry for nearly eight years and on June 25, 1669, was succeeded by Pieter Hetfelsen.

Differences of a more serious nature, however, had been developing in regard to land matters, and at about the same date of the ferryman's complaint another was sent in to the Council, containing not less than twenty-one signatures. This complaint was as follows: "Show with

[1]Documents relating to the Colonial History of the State of N. Y., Vol. XIII, page 214.

[2]Documents relating to the Colonial History of the State of N. Y. Vol. XIII, pages 234-5.

with due reverence the inhabitants of the villages of Bergen and Gemoenepa that they, the petitioners have seen, that the Schout Van Vleeck, Caspar Steinmets and Harman Smeeman have fenced in a parcel of highland situate at the South end of the village enclosure, in the best part of the pasture, which they appropriate to themselves; it is also said that Mr. Nicholas Varleth desires a piece of highland, situate at the north of the aforesaid village back of Hoboocken, which, if it is done, would tend to the ruin and destruction of this village, because they would be entirely deprived of an outlet for their cattle and nothing but a marshy underwood would remain to them, where already three or four animals have been smothered. Hence there would hardly be any pasture left for the draught beasts, for the Mincqkaghoue people are also fencing in their land, so that this village will be enclosed in a fence all round. They therefore respectfully request, that Your Honors will please to make some provision and guard the common interests of the aforesaid village and of Gemoenepa." The following reply was given: "The petitioners or a committee of them shall appear with Tielman Van Vleeck, Casper Steinmets and Harmen Smeeman, mentioned in the foregoing petition, personally before the Director General and Council." On January 4, 1663, Michiel Jansen Vreeland, Captain Adriaen Post and Jan Scholten appeared before the Council with their opponents, and it was found that the main cause for contention was the interpretation of a grant to Van Vleck and others dated December 22, 1661. Therefore: "After hearing the parties, it was ordered that the piece of land in dispute, granted to the said Van Vleck upon his petition, by the order of the 22d December, 1661, should be surveyed and that the surveyor shall make a report of its situation and area to their Honors, the Director General and Council. After that directions will be given upon the petition."[1]

Yet in the heat of all their local differences the Bergen authorities did not forget the dangers by which they were surrounded. The recent happenings in the Esopus

[1]Documents relating to the Colonial History of the State of N. Y. Vol. XIII, pages 234-5.

Esopus and elsewhere served as object lessons to them. Consequently a committee was appointed consisting of Arent Lourens, Jacob Luby, Harmen Edwards, Laurens Andriessen Van Boskerck (Van Buskirk), Poulus Pietersen, Jan Swaen (Swann) and Jan Lubbertsen Van Blaricum, who, on February 21, 1664, sent the following petition to the Council of New Netherland: "The Community of the village of Bergen have unanimously decided, to erect for the maintenance and necessary protection of this village a blockhouse at each gate and in order to have it undertaken and promoted with diligence the Hon. Court here has directed and authorized us, the undersigned, to promote each in his quarter the work as much as possible and to take good care of it. For the better prosecution of this much needed improvement we have ordered that the men, who absent themselves, shall pay part of the expenses, and besides a fine of six guilders for each day on which they are absent." And further: "The tenants are opposed to pay their share of the expense of the new work, though willing to assist in maintaining it, unless it is especially expressed and stipulated in their contracts." On this the following decision was taken, dated February 21, 1664: "The Director General and Council of New Netherland approve, praise and consent to the enclosed resolution and order; they therefore command all, whom it may concern, to govern themselves accordingly under the penalty fixed by it. As to the exception taken by the tenants, it is conceived, that the same are bound to assist in making the fortifications in question; but if they believe to have any action in law against their landlords in this regard (which for the present is not quite evident to the Director General and Council) they may institute legal proceedings before the proper tribunal."[1]

Still it would appear that those farmers employing enough hands, or having a numerous enough family to assist in defence against Indian attacks, had been permitted to remain on their farms, without being obliged to remove into fortified towns. On the same February

[1]Documents relating to the Colonial History of the State of N. Y., Vol. XIII, pages 360-1.

ary 21, 1664, there appealed to the Council "the wife of Samuel Edsal, producing an order from the Schout of the village of Bergen, by which she was directed to send another man there.

"It was ordered as follows:

"Our above friend appeared before our secretary and declared, she had there four men able to work on her lands, namely the farmer and his servant and two soldiers on furlough. If it is so, the Director General and Council consent that during her husband's absence she may go on with them, without being troubled about sending any more men until her husband's return."

Some months prior to this time, however, the males of the two most populous communities of Pavonia, on June 21, 1663, had been formed into military companies. Bergen being the capital and having the larger population was to be the residence of the commanding officer. Caspar Steinmets (Stymus) upon the request of the Bergen Magistrates was appointed captain, while on June 30, following, the inferior officers were designated. Adriaen Post, living at Bergen, was appointed ensign with Jan Swaen as sergeant. At Communipaw only two sergeants were appointed in the persons of Harmen Smeeman and Gerrit Gerritsen Van Wageningen. This arrangement in case of need would put the entire Pavonia militia under command of Captain Steinmets. Ensign Post was probably not the former commander at Staten Island but his son Adriaen. It is to be noted that the nomination for their office had been presented to the Council by the magistrates of Bergen. With the Council's appointment was sent a request for assistance of men in the expedition against the Esopus Indians. In answer to this request, Tielman Van Vleeck, as Secretary for the Council of War of Bergen, on July 4th wrote back that instead of being able to assist in the expedition, Bergen "too requires assistance, considering the dangerous location." Still the drum had been beaten and as a result six volunteers from Bergen and two from Communipaw had offered their services but under express condition "that the volunteers are not to go any farther, than the neighbor-

ing

ing villages, if they are in need and attacked and expressly excluding the Esopus."[1] Thus, even if the Pavonia volunteers themselves did want to serve near their own homes only, it set free eight other men from the Fort Amsterdam garrison. Nor was their precaution superfluous. Many rumors and open threats by Indians to residents both of New Amsterdam and Communipaw in the course of the summer foreshadowed a general Indian attack. On August 30, 1663, Sara Kierstede was informed by a savage that not less than eight Indian tribes had united to destroy all the white settlements along the North River, while the widow of Michael Jansen Vreeland had been warned by another savage that several Indian tribes had joined forces for the purpose of securing more Dutch prisoners. Fortunately the war remained confined to Esopus, but none at the time could foresee how soon and how far it would spread.

As Pavonia was near enough to New Amsterdam for the people occasionally to go to church there or for the ministers to cross over to Pavonia during the week days the petition in the latter part of 1662 for a pastor[2] had to be ignored by the central authorities, especially since the subscription list amounted to only four hundred and seventeen guilders, about one-third of the usual salary, and the general government would either be responsible for or be required to supply the balance, which was a pretty hard problem owing to the generally low state of the country's finances. Therefore Bergen, and the entire Pavonia district, would have to be provisionally satisfied with a *Voorleser* and schoolmaster who could read sermons in church. Whenever there was an opportunity the preachers from Manhattan or Long Island administered to the spiritual needs of the Bergen congregation such as the sacraments of baptism and the Lord's supper, as well as conducting services in commemoration of special events.

Engelbert Steenhuysen was a well-to-do and respected burgher of Bergen. Probably more for the sake of the additional distinction and gratitude of his

fellow-citizens

[1] Documents relating to the Colonial history of the State of N. Y., Vol. XIII, pages 268, 271.

[2] Year Book Holland Society of N. Y. 1913, pages 13-15.

fellow-citizens than for the money there was in it, Steenhuysen agreed to accept the office of Voorleser and schoolmaster. But if he should consent to fill the office he also wanted to enjoy the privileges he thought went with it. This brought him in conflict with the village authorities as is shown by the following petition, dated December 17, 1663, to the Council of New Netherland: "Show humbly the Schout and Commissaries of Bergen, that, as Your Honors undoubtedly know, before the going out of office and the election of new Commissaries, Michael Jansen, deceased, had been before Your Honors and requested that we might have a precentor who could also keep school for the instruction and education of our young children, and that Your Honors proposing one Engelbert Steenhuysen as a suitable person the Schout and Commissaries repeated this proposition more than a year ago to the community, which resolved to employ him not only as precentor, but also, this was expressly stipulated, to keep school. The said Steenhuysen accepted this and has now served for more than fifteen months for which he was allowed a salary of 250 Guilders in seawan annually and some other emoluments, besides the school fees, considered proper and fair. Now being the owner of a house and lot and of a double bouwery in the jurisdiction of the village of Bergen, the said Engelbert Steenhuysen has upon the complaint of the majority of the community been directed to maintain a soldier like the other inhabitants; this has aggrieved the said Engelbert Steenhuysen so much, that he has resigned his office, asserting that a schoolmaster should be exempt from all village taxes and burdens, as it is customary, he says, everywhere in Christendom. The Schout and Commissaries interpret this to be the case, when a precentor has only the school lot, but not when a schoolmaster owns a lot and a double bouwery; the community is also opposed to his being exempted for his lot and lands, for he receives a salary as precentor and is bound not only to serve as a precentor, but also to select himself and provide a fit and convenient place to keep school in, which he has failed to do until this day, pretending the community must designate and provide

provide such a place fit for a schoolhouse. The petitioners are of opinion that Engelbert Steenhuysen cannot resign his office without giving a notice of six months of his intention to do so and therefore the petitioners address themselves to Your Honors with the humble request, to direct said Engelbert Steenhuysen that he must continue to serve during the second year now commenced, and to decide whether he is not bound to maintain on behalf of his lot and land a soldier like the other inhabitants." The Council took speedy action in the matter as is shown by the following extract: "The Schout, Commissaries and Engelbert Steenhuysen, mentioned in the foregoing petition, having been summoned before the Council and heard, the parties were made to agree after divers debates and it was arranged that Engelbert Steenhuysen should duly serve the rest of his term according to contract as mentioned above."[1] Steenhuysen probably served till January 1, 1666, when he was succeeded by Bastiaen Van Giesen, who on February 8, 1708, was succeeded by Adriaen Vermeule. P. Van Benthuysen, on April 3, 1736, succeeded Mr. Vermeule and on April 3, 1761, Abraham Sickels succeeded Mr. Van Benthuysen. Mr. Sickels was Bergen's last Voorleser and in 1789 his successor, John Collard, received the title of "clerk" with only the duties usually expressed by this title.[2]

In the absence of a regular pastor Bergen continued to be considered as a kind of out-station of New Amsterdam and its pastors frequently supplied the spiritual needs of Pavonia's population. They either were paid a regular salary or, what is more probable, had their expenses paid for every time they officiated at Bergen. The two Megapolensis, father and son, statedly used to cross over from Manhattan and from the following entries in the Council Minutes it is evident that the Bergen church treasury was not always in a condition to discharge its debts to them when due:

"Whereas it has been represented to us that the Widow of deceased Dom^e^ Megapolensis, and Dom^e^ Samuel Megapolensis, late Ministers in this city, have still

[1]Documents relating to the Colonial History of the State of N. Y., Vol. XIII, pages 318 and 319.

[2]Versteeg, Sketch of Early Bergen, page 25.

still due to each of them for earned salary from the town of Bergen the sum of 100 guilders, Seawan value, requesting that the same may be paid her, the rather as said widow is on the eve of going to Patria; therefore the Magistrates of the said Town are, on her presented petition, recommended to use all possible means that said arrears may be forthwith paid and discharged." Still, Bergen was not the only delinquent, the New Orange congregation owing considerably more.

Less than two weeks later, on June 27, 1674, "On petition presented by Mr. Cornelis Van Ruyven, on behalf of the widow of dec[d] Dom[e] Johannis Megapolensis and of Dom[e] Samuel Megapolensis, requesting that what still is due them for earned salary both from the West India Company from this City, and the Town of Bergen, may be ordered to be handed and paid him, etc.; Ordered by the Governor General of New Netherland; As regards the claim against the estate of the West India Company the petitioner is referred to the Commissioners appointed on the 21st instant for the settlement of its books and payment of its debts; regarding the debt of the city, and of the Town of Bergen, it is already recommended to the respective Courts, in order that some means may be found, if possible to pay the same."

Like the town records of many other early New Netherland settlements, those of Bergen have disappeared. That they were kept is quite evident from the following entry in the Council Minutes, dated May 29, 1664: "The petition of Arent Lawrensen residing at Bergen, was taken up and read, who requests, that a piece of low land, close to his plantation, may be given and granted to him; he exhibits besides an extract from the minutes of the village of Bergen, whereby it appears that the Court there has promised it to him subject to approval.

"It was decided

"The petitioner may have the said piece of low land surveyed by the surveyor, and after that a patent shall be granted him."[1] How important these lost minutes would

[1]Documents relating to the Colonial History of the State of N. Y., Vol. XIII, page 383.

would have been for a more intimate knowledge of Bergen's early history is further demonstrated in relation to Bergen's first sawmill. Bartel Lott and Egbert Sandersen on October 20, 1661, had been referred to Bergen's Schepens in connection with their petition for permission to erect a sawmill in Bergen. What decision the Schepens took on this petition the minutes would show. From the fact that Bartel Lott on March 20, 1663, and on November 22, 1665, was living at Bergen it would appear that the Schepens' decision had been favorable. Again on January 17, 1662, when Paulus Pietersen sued Joost Vander Linde in the New Amsterdam Court, reference was made to a "condemnation by the Schepens of the village of Bergen."[1] On December 19, 1662, when Schout Tonneman was suing Pietersen before the New Amsterdam Court it was stated that "the weather does not permit the defendant, who resides in the village of Bergen, to cross over." The following case, also recorded in the Amsterdam Court Minutes, under date of March 20, 1663, contains additional evidence of the existence at the time of Bergen records "Bartelott (Bartel Lott) entering, requests that his canoe attached by Jan Rutgersen may be released from attachment, as the case in question is pending before the Court of the Town of Bergen and says he cannot be sued at two different places. Burgomaster Olof Stevensen Van Cortlant exhibits a letter from Secretary Van Vleeck and in addition an extract from the Minutes of the Court of the Town of Bergen, whereby it appears that the cause is litigated there."[2] About six weeks later, on May 8, 1663, another Bergen case came up before the New Amsterdam Court and was disposed of in the same manner. The plaintiff in the case was Jan Rutgersen, the defendant no less a person than Bergen's Schout Van Vleck. The defendant wrote "that the case is entered before the Court of the Town of Bergen and must be there disposed of." The New Amsterdam magistrates thought the same, discharging "the defendant from arrest as the case is prosecuted before the Bench of the Town of Bergen."

Another

[1]Records of New Amsterdam, Vol. IV, page 15.

[2]Records of New Amsterdam, Vol. IV, page 217.

Another case, upon which the Bergen Court records probably would throw much light, was the suit by Reynier Vander Coele against Balthasar De Hart, on March 10, 1668, in which it was decided "that the two mares of this Plt: at Bergen in New Garsie shal be Sold towards the Paiment of the debt wch this Plt: is indebted to the deft."[1]

The various communities comprising the municipality of Bergen increased in wealth and population, and the people were beginning to congratulate each other upon the bright prospect before them under the continuance of the beneficent rule of the much reviled Dutch West India Company, when suddenly the intrusion upon New Netherland by an alien usurper altered not only their political allegiance but also put a stop to whatever assistance their government had been rendering them, and would have continued to render them, until they were strong enough to stand by themselves. On September 9, 1664, the English took possession of the Fort and the City of Amsterdam on the Island of Manhattan. The surrounding territory went with it. A few weeks later Fort Orange, Schenectady, Wildwyck, the City of Amsterdam's colonies on the South River (Delaware) were included in the surrender. New Netherland had been wiped off the map. The Duke of York, in 1666, took possession of all of the West India Company's corporate property in this country, including the Company's farm at Hasimus.

On October 17, 1664, Bergen's magistrates received the following English order: "You are hereby required to receive into your town Corporal Powell with the soldiers under his command and them to accommodate with lodging, not above two of them to bed in any one house and further you are required to joyne six of the inhabitants with three of the soldiers to be upon constant guard, to secure the peace of the said town until further order, whereof you are not to faill. Given under my hand at Fort James."[2] Even after the distribution of the English soldiery among the various more distant

[1]Records of New Amsterdam, Vol. VI, page 120.

[2]Documents relating to the Colonial History of the State of N. Y., Vol. XIII, page 395.

distant sections of New Netherland, and the quartering of large bodies of them upon New Amsterdam's reluctant inhabitants, there remained too many soldiers in ancient Fort Amsterdam and Nicolls thought it most expedient to inflict them on the surrounding villages.

New Netherland was divided up into two parts, New York and New Jersey. Philip Carteret was appointed Governor of New Jersey. Shortly after his arrival here, on August 30, 1665, he appointed Captain Nicholas Verlett president of the Bergen Court, which was composed of the settlements of Bergen, Gemoenepaen, Ahasymus and Hooboocken.[1] With him as associate magistrates had been appointed Herman Smeeman, Caspar Steinmets, Elias Michielsen Vreeland, Ide Cornelissen Van Vorst, with Hans Diedricks as constable.

On November 22, 1665, thirty-three of Bergen's most representative men took the oath of allegiance to the English.[2] Many more appear to have been unavoidably absent. Outward conditions under English rule did not greatly change, though increase of population was temporarily checked. Nothing remarkable or noteworthy happened to Pavonia's inhabitants for the next few years to come. The district had been settled, the population slowly increased; the Indian peril, after 1655, fortunately was steadily growing less. The only really sore point with the people was the obnoxious display of the alien flag and thc giving of commands in a foreign tongue. But this could not be helped and with true Dutch philosophy the New Netherlanders submitted to a state of things they could not then change. Quarrels and dissensions between the English authorities were frequent and the following order by Governor Carteret to the Bergen authorities was one of the consequences. The order is here reproduced in modern orthography: "These are in his Majesty's name to will and require you that in case any writt or writts should be set up or otherwise published within the Town and Corporation of Bergen by or under any other authority than myself as your Governor that neither

[1]Winfield, History of the County of Hudson, N. J., pages 94-96.

[2]New Jersey Archives, 1st series, Vol. I, page 49.

neither you nor any other person within your jurisdiction yield any obedience thereunto. But that you forthwith pull down all or any such writt or writts or other writings so published and cause the same forthwith to be conveyed unto me, as you will answer the contempt of this my special warrant. Given under my hand and seal the day and year above written"[1] (June 17, 1672.) Still a return to the old allegiance—if only temporary—was close at hand.

On August 10, 1673, admirals Cornelis Everts of Zeeland and Jacob Benckes of Holland again reduced the colony to its former allegiance, which "at once startled and overjoyed the Dutch" settlements of New Netherland. In the words of Secretary Van der Vin of New Haerlem "This day, 10th August, 1673, new style, have the Holland and Zeeland fleets captured the fort at N. York, in the name of their High Mightinesses the Lords States General of the United Netherlands and his Highness the Lord Prince of Orange; and the Fort is renamed Willem Hendrick, and the City obtained the name New Orange."[2] He expressed himself very soberly for it was not known when the enemy might return. And he was right, as was shown in the case of Schout Pieter Alrichs of the South River (Delaware) a couple years later, who was disciplined by the English for having extended too hearty a welcome to the forces of the Dutch liberators.

Immediately Bergen looms up somewhat larger than during English times. The second act of the first session of the Council of War at New Orange, on August 12, 1673, consisted of the following missive "To the inhabitants of the village of Bergen, and the Hamlets and Bouweries thereon depending:

"You are hereby ordered and instructed to dispatch delegates from your village here to us, to treat with us on next Tuesday, respecting the surrender of your town to the obedience of their High Mightinesses, the Lords States General of the United Netherlands, his serene Highness the Prince of Orange, or on refusal so to do, we shall be obliged to constrain you thereunto by force of arms."

In

[1]New Jersey Archives, 1st series, Vol. I, page 93.

[2]James Riker, Harlem its Origin and Early Annals, page 336.

In reply, among other things, Bergen's inhabitants sent to the Council a double nomination for magistrates and from among them, on August 18, 1673, the central authorities appointed as magistrates: Schout and Secretary Claes Arentse Toers and as schepens Gerrit Gerrits Van Wageningen, Thomas Fredericks, Elias Michielsen Vreeland and Peter Marcelissen. Three days later the newly appointed magistrates repaired to New Orange to take the oath, and at the same time were "told that the commanders shall visit their town on Sunday after the sermon in order to administer the oath of allegiance to all their people." Schout Toers after the same ceremonies petitioned the war Council to grant him the office of auctioneer and this favor was immediately conferred upon him.

On August 25, 1673, the Council met again and delegates from several neighboring towns appear to have been present, besides those of the original Dutch settlements. As these settlements were deemed to be more deeply interested than the English towns in a successful defence in case of attack, it was thought that they ought to assist in furnishing the means, and Secretary Bayard thus records the decision of the Council as well as the answer to it: "The Delegates from Midwout, Amesfort, Breukelen, Utreght, Boswyck, Bergen and Staten Island are notified of the necessity of fortifying the city and of each contributing to said necessary work according to its means, which they undertake and promise; whereupon they are referred to the Burgomasters and Schepens of this city to confer with them thereupon." Besides assisting in the fortifying of New Orange, the people of the surrounding towns also sent squads to strengthen the city's garrison, and besides maintained daily and nightly patrols along their shores, as shown by this missive: "Whereas, I remark that the good people of the Towns of Amesfoort, Midwout, Breuckelen, Utrecht and Bushwick on Long Island [and Bergen] do, according to the permission granted by the Magistrates and officers, daily betake themselves hither; which zeal of theirs in the discharge of their sworn oath and bounden duty for the public good is most pleasing to me. I have therefore thought it necessary

necessary on the proposals submitted to me on the part of some inhabitants of sundry of the said towns, that at first some men shall remain in each of the aforesaid towns, to prevent further damage until additional news be received of the enemy's approach or designs; and in order that such be executed for the greatest security of the public and in good order, the respective Captains, Lieutenants and Ensigns of the said towns are hereby ordered to appear with their companies fully armed next Friday being the 29th inst. in the forenoon, in the city of New Orange, in front of Fort Willem Hendrick, leaving six men in each town, which being done, one-third of each company shall be furloughed for the present and at liberty to return to their respective towns, to remain there until relieved by another Corporal's guard, which shall until further order be on the third day; and the officers and magistrates are hereby authorized to give such orders respecting threshing and the foddering of cattle as each in his district shall consider best, above all taking good care that proper guard be kept, and patrolled both day and night, so that they may not be surprised by the enemy or cut off from us." This letter which was dated December 26, 1673, was sent to the five Dutch Towns on Long Island, and the village of Bergen. Meantime the Commanders of the fleet as well as the members of the Council of War on August 27th had gone in a body to Bergen. As befitted so solemn an occasion and so august a body they were accompanied by a sufficient escort and Bergen never in its history had beheld so splendid an array of brilliant uniforms. Upon arriving in Bergen Square the drum was beat, sixty-nine out of Bergen's seventy-eight Burghers responded to the roll call and took the required oath of allegiance. The magistrates promised to forward the oaths of the nine absentees to the Council at New Orange. It is quite probable that during their visit the Bergen militia had been drawn up as a kind of guard of honor to the distinguished visitors and their escort. Captain Colve, who was a pretty good judge of military points, doubtless had noted the merits of the various probable candidates for offices in the Bergen militia forces and at a subsequent meeting of the

the Council of War it was not a hard task to select the men who were deemed most fit to fill the positions. Casper Stymets again was appointed captain with Hans Diedricks as lieutenant and Adriaen Post as ensign. It would appear that the appointment of the petty officers had been left to Captain Stynmets and his officers. On the same date of Captain Steynmets' appointment a petition was received from Ide Van Vorst and Claes Jans "requesting substantially that Casper Steynmets may not be allowed any more privileges than were granted him under Mr. Stuyvesant's government." The reply of the Council was: "Caspar Steynmets of whom the petitioner complains, shall not be allowed any more privileges than have been granted him by Mr. Stuyvesant's government."

Captain Colve, in view of the early departure of the Admirals had, on August 12, 1673, been appointed Governor General of New Netherland, though his commission was not published until September 19, following. At a meeting of his Council, on October 23rd, next, the first business to be disposed of was recorded as follows by Secretary Bayard: "The Schout and Schepens of the Town of Bergen exhibiting to the Council some ordinances drawn up by them for the observance of the Sabbath, respecting fences, etc., requesting thereupon the approval of the governor and Council; which being read and examined, the same is approved; with the reserve that works of charity and necessity on the Sabbath, with the knowledge of the officer, shall be tolerated." The next act of Bergen's magistrates and the decision of the Council in regard to it, serves as an additional illustration of the less magnanimous spirit of the times, in regard to religious matters. It was dated December 24, 1673, and reads as follows: "The Schout and Magistrates of the Town of Bergen requesting that the inhabitants of all the settlements dependent on them, of what religious persuasion soever they may be, shall be bound to pay their share towards the support of the Precentor and Schoolmaster, etc., which being taken into consideration by the Governor and Council.

"It is ordered:

"That

"That all the said inhabitants, without any exception, shall pursuant to the resolution of the Magistrate of the Town of Bergen, dated 18th X^{ber}, 1672, and subsequent confirmation, pay their share for the support of said Precentor and Schoolmaster." This order, like similar orders in previous times, was either absolutely or partially disobeyed and on May 24, 1674, there was a complaint about it for action by the Council. The minutes concerning the case read as follows: "The Schout and Magistrates of the town of Bergen complain by petition that some of the inhabitants of their dependent hamlets, in disparagement of the previous order of the Governor General and Council dated the 24th X^{ber} last obstinately refuse to pay their quota to the support of the Precentor and Schoolmaster." The Council ordered: "The Governor General and Council persist in their previous mandate of the 24th X^{ber} last and order the Schout to proceed to immediate execution against all unwilling debtors." Still even after this peremptory command the opposition did not give in, as can be seen from an order, dated June 15, 1674: "On petition of Lourens Andries, and Joost Vander Linde, agents for the inhabitants of Mingagque and Pemrepogh, requesting to be excused from contributing to the support of the Schoolmaster at Bergen, etc., ordered: Copy hereof to be furnished the Magistrates of the town of Bergen to answer the same."

The return of the English or the invasion by the French was continually feared, and as the entire country, owing to the Anglo-French-Dutch war, was under martial law, the following proclamation was sent by Governor Colve to the magistrates of Midwout, Amesfordt, Breuckelen, Utrecht, Boswyck, Haerlem, Fordham and Bergen: "Whereas the fortifications of the City of New Orange are, by the good zeal and industry of its burghers, so far completed as to be now on the eve of perfection when this city will be in such a state of defence that it will be capable (under God) of resisting all attacks of any enemies which might be expected to come hither; nevertheless, considering that in such case it would not be possible to defend all the surrounding villages and out places of this Province, but that their

their safety must depend alone on the preservation of said city as previous experience has clearly made manifest; therefore I have deemed it necessary hereby strictly to order and to command all out-people of the Dutch nation, dwelling in the respective circumjacent towns, and on the Flat land that they repair to the aforesaid city of New Orange without any delay, provided with proper hand and side arms, on the first notice they shall receive of the enemy's approach, or even of the coming of more than one ship at the same time, whether it be with the Prince's flag or otherwise on penalty that all who will be found negligent therein, shall be declared traitors and perjurers, and consequently be proceeded against as enemies, or be punished with death and confiscation of all their goods, as an example to others; and all Schouts, Magistrates and Militia officers of the respective towns to whom these shall be transmitted, are ordered and commanded to make known this our order without any delay, in their respective towns and the dependencies thereof, by publishing and posting the same, to the end that no man plead ignorance in the premises, and furthermore take care that this our order be duly observed and executed according to the precise tenor thereof. Done Fort Willem Hendrick, this 13th March, 1674." About one month prior to this proclamation peace had been reëstablished between the Dutch and the English though they could not yet know about it here. However, the French did not conclude peace with the Dutch until 1678, four years later.

On March 22, 1674, the following notice was sent to the Schouts of Bergen, the Dutch towns on Long Island, and Haerlem: "You are hereby required and ordered to notify the Dutch Towns situated in your district, to commission each of them a Militia officer and Magistrate from their respective towns, with whom you will repair, on Monday next at ten o'clock in the forenoon, to the City Hall of this City, when I intend to have some conference with you on the present state of the country." The town of Bergen sent Schout Claes Arentse Toers and Captain Caspar Steynmits. The Dutch inhabitants of the English villages on Long Island were represented

represented by their own Dutch Schout Frans Bloodgood. In regard to the proclamation of March 13, the various deputies stated: "that they were altogether resolved to obey it, and to observe their honor and oath, requesting only that notice be sent them in time, and some sloops and boats dispatched to the following towns to convey the people hither, viz.: to Bergen some boats, to Utrecht and Gowanis, two sloops; to Bushwick, one sloop or boat."

Immediately after the breaking up of the meeting Governor Colve issued the following commission: "Whereas it is necessary that good care be taken that the neighboring Out-people be provided, on the arrival of any enemies, with proper boats to convey themselves and families hither; therefore have I thought proper thereunto to commission and empower Messrs. Cornelis Steenwyck and Cornelis Van Ruyven, who are hereby required to take care that in such case the neighboring towns, or those of them that have applied, may be provided and accommodated with suitable vessels; and the skippers and boatmen of this city are ordered and commanded promptly to obey whatever orders they may receive from those gentlemen in the premises. Done Fort Willem Hendrick, this 26th March, 1674."

That population had been growing slowly is shown by the following extract from the minutes dated May 24, 1674, where it is apparent that the settlers at what were afterward called Bayonne and Greenville had become numerous enough to be reckoned with: "The Schout, Magistrates and Commonalty of the Town of Bergen, complaining, by petition, that over two years ago a question arose between the petitioners and their dependent hamlets of Gemoenepa, Mingaghque and Pemrepogh respecting the making and maintaining of a certain common fence to separate the heifers and steers from the milch cows and draft oxen; which question was referred, by the late government, to four arbitrators chosen by both sides, who decided on the 10th of April, 1672, according to the certificate produced in Court, which decision petitioners allege their constant willingness to obey, but it was at once rejected

jected by their opponents; therefore, request that they may be ordered to comply with said arbitration, or show cause for their refusal." The Council of New Netherland, in reply, issued the following order: "The inhabitants of the hamlets Gemoenepa, Pemrepogh and Mingaghque are hereby ordered and commanded promptly to regulate themselves according to the decision of the arbitrators dated the 10th April, 1672, or deliver in to the Court of the Governor-General and Council within the space of 14 days from the date thereof, any objection they will be able to produce against that decision."

This fact of the growth of the borough of Minckaque and Pemerpoch is rendered still more obvious from the fact that on August 15th following the people of these two hamlets, for the first time in the town's history, had two candidates in the field for schepen, viz., Jan Dircksen Siecken Dey and Hessel Weigertsen. The candidates for Bergen were: Adriaen Post, Waling Jacobse Van Winkle, Engelbert Steenhuys and Douwe Hartmans; those for Gemoenepa, Enoch Michielse Vreeland and Hartman Michielse Vreeland. That Ahasymus was considered a borough of Bergen is shown from the fact that Ide Cornelissen Van Vorst and Claes Jansen were candidates for that place. The central government appointed as magistrates: Waling Van Winkle and Engelbert Steenhuys for Bergen, Enoch Vreeland for Gemoenepa, Claes Jansen for Ahasymus and Jan Dey for Michkaque and Pemrepock.[1]

After the re-conquest of New Netherland the Company's former bouwery at Hasymus had been taken from the Duke of York, and, temporarily at least, annexed for the benefit of the government of New Netherland. After Stoffelsen's death[2] Captain Stymets had

[1]Winfield, History of the County of Hudson, N. J., page 85.

[2]Jacob Stoffelsen, of Zierikzee, in the Province of Zeeland, where he was born in 1601, was one of New Netherland's most remarkable pioneers. He is first mentioned in 1633 when he was appointed Commissary of Stores and Overseer of the Company's laborers. Though chief among Kieft's opponents he was, in 1645, temporarily a member of the Council of New Netherland, owing to his familiarity with Indian affairs. But even before this distinction he had been a member of the Board of Twelve and of Eight Men. Though he owned land in Breuckelen on Long Island, his marriage to the widow of Cornelis Van Vorst was the means of per-

had leased the bouwery from the Duke of York's representative, and he continued to occupy it after the Dutch re-conquest. Differences arose between him and other Hasymus residents, and under date of May 26, 1674, had been submitted for decision by the Council, as follows: "The Governor-General and Council of New Netherland having heard the dispute between Casper Steynmits, lessee of the public Bouwery, situate at Ahasymus, on the one part, and Claes Jansen and Yde Van Vorst, residing at Ahasymus aforesaid on the other, in regard to their valley and pasture lands; It is by the Governor-General and Council decreed and ordered that Casper Steymits, the lessee, shall be allowed provisionally and until the Governor-General and Council, either by themselves or their deputies shall have occasion to investigate the circumstances there, to fence in all the ungranted valley appertaining to Ahasymus, or so much thereof as he shall have need to use; also Claes Jansen and Yde Cornelissen are at liberty to fence in for their particular use all the arable and valley lands there belonging to them in lawful ownership; in regard to the pasture and woodland of Ahasymus, they remain as heretofore for common pasturage of the cattle of said parties, and in fencing off the valleys, all persons are most expressly forbid to set up any fence (on the pasture and woodland)."

Fences in other parts of Bergen also continued as from the beginning to stir up bad blood between the various inhabitants, and on June 15th another case was before the Council, reading thus: "On petition of Lourens Andriese (Van Boskerck), Samuel Edsal and Dirck Claesen, agents of some hamlets dependent on the town of Bergen, requesting that the Schout and Schepens of said town be ordered to leave the petitioners undisturbed, respecting a certain fence in dispute

manently identifying himself with Ahasymus. After the death of his first wife, he married, on August 16, 1657, Tryntje Jacobs, the widow of Jacob Walingsen Van Winkel. With her Stoffelsen had at least two sons: Stoffel baptized December 29, 1660, and Jacobus baptized January 28, 1665. Jacob Stoffelsen had died before June 17, 1668, when his widow married Michiel Tadens. Upon her marriage to Stoffelsen in 1657 their former neighbor at Communipaw, Michiel Jansen Vreeland, and Burgomaster Van der Grift of New Amsterdam had been appointed guardians of the six children she had with Jacob Walingsen Van Winkel.

pute between them, or to cause the petitioners to be summoned, and to institute their action in this case before the Governor, etc.: Petitioners are again ordered pursuant to the previous instruction, to deliver into Court within 14 days their objections in writing to the award given by the arbitrators, on pain of discontinuance without being heard any more in the premises." On the same date a petition was read "of Joost Van der Linde, Hendrick Jansen Spier, Hendrick De Backer and Harmen Edewartse requesting that each of them may be given and granted a piece of ground on Staten Island at the mouth of the Kill van Koll." Like other settlers from other sections these four Bergen petitioners were provisionally refused in the following manner: "Petitioners are deferred in the matter of their request, to the time of the disposal of lands."

On the same day, July 7, 1674, that the Council was called upon to decide an appeal by Captain John Berry against W. Sandfort and Schout Claes Arentsen Toers, two of the Bergen men named above "Joost Van der Linde and Hendrick Spiers each allowed a piece of land for a bouwerie, each piece 25 morgens, beginning opposite Schutter's Island, and further westerly along the Kill van Koll."

The objections of some of the boroughs, composing the Bergen municipality, against being obliged to contribute toward the salary of the schoolmaster and Voorleser again resulted in open rebellion, and one of the last recorded acts of the retiring Dutch authorities, prior to the reëntrance of the English was concerned with this troublesome question. That the central government was decided, once for all, to stamp out the opposition is evident from the following minute of the Council: "The Governor and Council of New Netherland, having seen the complaint of the town of Bergen against the inhabitants of the villages of Pemrepogh and Mangagquy, etc., and the answer given by them, in regard to what the inhabitants of Pemrepogh and Mingagquy aforesaid, owe for the support of the Schoolmaster and Precentor of the town of Bergen, it is after due inquiry resolved and ordered, that the inhabitants of Pemrepogh and Mingagquy shall promptly pay their share

share for the support aforesaid, on pain of proceeding against them with immediate execution."[1]

With the ushering in of the new English government, on November 10, 1674, when the province of New Netherland was "surrendered by Governor Colve to Governor Major Edmund Andros in behalf of his Majesty of Great Britain," Bergen entered upon the fourth stage of its career. The various boroughs in the course of events, continued to develop, until the municipalities of Jersey City, Hoboken and Bayonne were evolved from the original pioneer settlements. When, in the fulness of time, the whole of this extensive district should again be welded into one civic community Pauw's faith in its future will have been triumphantly vindicated. Could not then something be done to honor and perpetuate the name of the original founder? This would be only doing justice to the memory of the man who had the courage and foresight to begin reclaiming this marshy wilderness for the benefit of yet unborn generations. What does it matter that he did not himself settle here? His invested capital furnished the motive power, and the pioneers he engaged were the first known permanent settlers of the influential state of New Jersey.

ARMORIAL BEARINGS OF THE DESCENDANTS OF MICHAEL JANSEN AND SOFIA HARTMAN-VREELAND.

[1]The quotations and statements referring to the period between August 12, 1673, and July 7, 1674, are based on "Documents relating to the Colonial History of the State of N. Y." Vol. II, Pages 570-730.

THE FIRST STONE CHURCH AT BERGEN

DIRECTOR GENERAL

OF

NIEUW NETHERLAND

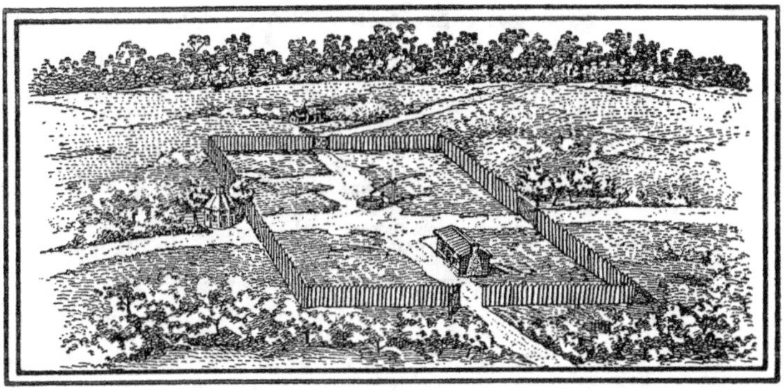

The

PETER STUYVESANT STATUE

at

BERGEN

IN the autumn of 1910 the Two Hundred and Fiftieth Anniversary of the founding of the village of Bergen, New Jersey, was observed with great enthusiasm. It was the recognition of the beginning of civilization in what is now the state of New Jersey.

As a fitting climax to the celebration, it was determined to erect a permanent monument to perpetuate the establishment of the first church, the first school and the first permanent municipal organization in the northern part of the state. A Committee was appointed and a design submitted by J. Massey Rhind was accepted. (See page 54.) It represents Peter Stuyvesant, Director-General of New Netherland, which included the states now known as New York, New Jersey, Delaware and Pennsylvania, in the act of delivering a charter to the representatives of the Burghers of "Old Bergen." The statue is of bronze, eight feet in height, standing on a base, twelve feet in length and eight feet high, bearing the following inscriptions:

In

In the year of our Lord 1660,
by permission of
PETRUS STUYVESANT, Director-General,
and the Council of New Netherland,
around this Square, was founded and built
the Village of BERGEN,
the first permanent settlement in
NEW JERSEY.

On January the Thirtieth, 1658,
the Peninsula between
the Hudson and Hackensack Rivers,
south from Weehawken,
was finally
purchased from the Indians,
and granted
to the inhabitants of BERGEN
in the year 1661.

On September the Fifth, 1661,
the first civic government
in the colony was here established.
Schout Tielman Van Vleck
Schepens { Michel Jansen (Vreeland), Harmanus Smeeman, Caspar Stynmets }
Here also were located
the first organized church
and the first school in New Jersey.

The unveiling of the monument took place Saturday, October 18, 1913, in the presence of a large and patriotic gathering. Reverend Dr. Cornelius Brett, Pastor of the old Bergen Reformed Church making the presentation to the city, on behalf of the Monument Committee.

MARRIAGES IN THE VILLAGE OF BERGEN IN NEW JERSEY BEGINNING 1665

NO. The bans of the following persons have been published for three Sundays, and as no objections have been raised, they have been married on the date and in the years, as follows: 1665

1 December 3. Laurens Duyts and Grietje Jans. On the date as in margin their bans were proclaimed for the first time. As no objections have been raised, after three proclamations, their marriage has been concluded on January 1, 1666, by the minister or preacher.

1666

2 January 14. Jan Dirckse Straetmaker, Y. M., and Geesje Gerritse, Y. D.

3 May 9. Hendrick Janse Oosteroom (widower) and Geesje Jacobs (widow). Married May 23, 1666, at Bergen.

1667

4 May 8. Juriaen Tomassen, Y. M., and Reyckje Hermen, Y. D. Married May 25, 1667.

1668

5 February 25. Andries Claesen, Y. M., and Preyntje Machielse, Y. D. Married March 25, 1668.

All the above couples were married by the minister at Bergen.

6 May 17. Machiel Tades (widower) and Treyntje Jacobs (widow). Married June 8, 1668.

1668 NO.

7 November 25. Hermen Smeeman (widower) and Annetje Dame (widow). Received, Dec. 9, 1668, certificate to New York.

1669

8 June 9. Hendrick Cornelisse, Y. M., and Neeltje Cornelis, Y. D. Married June 9, 1669. Came here with certificate and were married by the court.

1670

9 June 5. Enoch Machielse Vreeland, Y. M., and Dirckje Meyers, Y. D. Received, June 20, certificate to New York.

10 June 19. Johannes Magielse, Y. M., and Neeltje Hermens, Y. D. Received, July 23, 1670, certificate to ——?

11 July 10. Piet Cornelisse Van Steenwyk, Y. M., and Hendrickje Arentse, Y. D. Married July 31, before court at Bergen.

12 November 27. Matheus Cornelisse Van Nukerck, Y. M., and Anna Lubi, Y. D. Married December 14, 1670, by court at Bergen.

1671

13 February 26. Casper Steynmets (widower) and Treyntje Jacobs (widow). Married March 15, before court at Bergen.

14 February 26. Walingh Jacobse Van Winckel, Y. M., and Catharyna Machielse, Y. D. Married March 15, by court at Bergen.

15 November 5. Andries Meyer, Y. M., and Vroutje Vande Voorst, Y. D. Were married upon certificate at New York.

1672

16 January 14. Dirck Janse Van Oogsten, Y. M., and Elisabeth Cornelis, Y. D. Were married upon certificate at New York.

17 July 28. Lourus Arense Toers, Y. M., from Amsterdam, Holland, and Francyntje Tomas, Y. D., from New York. Married at New York Aug. 15, 1672.

18 August 18. Jacob Lubi (widower of Geertruyt Leons?) and Gerritje Cornelis (widow of Roelof Corneliss). Married by the minister at New York, September 4, 1672.

19 September 15. Arien Pieterse Buys, Y. M., from Tiel, and Treyntje Hendrickx Oosteroom, Y. D., from New Jersey. Married September 30, 1672, by the minister, at Bergen.

NO. 1672

20 September 22. Fredrick Thomasse, Y. M., and Catharyna Hoppe, Y. D. Married October 23, by minister at New York.

21 Dircks Braack, Y. D. (rest illegible).

22 November 10. Jan Roelofse Eltingh, Y. M., and Jacomyntje Slech (widow of Gerrit Fooken) both living at Esopus. Received certificate to be married at Esopus, November 24, 1672.

1674

23 August 11.—New Style. Gerbrant Claese, Y. M., from Amersfoort on Long Island, and Merritje Claes, Y. D., from Gemenepa. Received certificate August 25, to Amersfoort, L. I.

1675

24 November 14[1]—Old Style. Jacob Jacobse Van Winckel, Y. M., from New Albany, and Aaltje Daniels, Y. D., from New York. Have been married December 15, by the "Voorlezer" R. Van Giesen, in presence of the court.

25 November 14. Symon Jacobse Van Winckel, Y. M., from New Jersey, and Annetie Ariaense Sips, Y. D., from New York. Have been married December 15, by R. Van Giesen, "Voorlezer" in presence of court.

1676

26 September 3. Helmigh Roelofs, Y. M., from Bergen, and Jannetje Pieters, Y. D., from Gelderland. Married Oct. 2 by preacher at Bergen.

27 October 29. Johannes Steynmets, Y. M., from Manhatans, and Annetje Jacobse Van Winkel, Y. D., from New York. Received, November 30, certificate to New York.

28 December 17. Albert Zaberoski, Y. M., from Enghstburgh, and Machtelt Vander Linden, Y. D., from New York. Received certificate January 8, 1677.

1677

29 March 18. Adriaan Post, Y. M., from the Hague in Holland, and Catryna Gerrits, Y. D., from Wageninge in Gelderland. Married April 17, 1677, at Bergen by the minister.

[1] Ed. Note:—September, 1752: The (3rd) day of September then became the (14th)—and in 1675 they were ten days behind the right time according to the "New Style," therefore the above date is properly November 24, 1675..

1677 NO.

30 May 27. Johannes Meyer, Y. M., from New York, and Annetje Vande Voorst, Y. D., from Hasymus. Received certificate June 12 to New York.

31 December 23. Teunis Roelofse, Y. M., from Amersfoort on Long Island, and Tryntje Claes, Y. D., from Manatans Isl[d]. Received certificate January 8, 1678, to New York.

32 October 14. Cornelis Roelofs, Y. M., from Amersfoort on Long Island, and Maddaleena Van Giesen, Y. D., from New York. Received certificate November 13, 1677, to New York.

1678

33 March 11. Charles Macheleen, Y. M., from Scotland, and Catryna Thomas, Y. D., from Barbadoes. Received certificate March 26, 1678.

34 May 26. Joseph Arsele, Y. M., from London, O. England, and Elisabeth Walinghs, Y. D., from Wickham in O. England.

35 August 11. Hermen Eduwaerts, Y. M., from East Friesland, and Jannetje Hendrickx Oosteroom, Y. D., from Amersfoort; certificate on August 25.

36 October 13. Sibe Epkese, Y. M., from Esterbirum in W. Friesland, and Marytje Ariaense Sips, Y. D., from New York. Married Nov. 6, by Voorlezer R. Van Giesen, in presence of court.

37 October. 27. Hendrick Epkese, Y. M., from Minnersche in W. Friesland, and Mareytje Lubberts, Y. D., from Meppel in Drenthe. Married November 17 by the Voorlezer R. Van Giesen in presence of the court of Bergen.

1679

38 July 5. Lourus Ackerman, Y. M., from Geffen, in the Meiery of 's Hertogenbosch, and Geertje Egbers, Y. D., from N. Albany. Married August 3, by Voorlezer R. Van Giesen in presence of court.

39 July 27. Johannis Spier, Y. M., and Marya Franse, Y. D., from Beest in Gelderland. Received certificate to N. Y., Aug. 12, 1679.

40 September 21. Tades Magiels, Y. M., from New York, and Anna Steynmets, Y. D., from New York. Married by the preacher at Bergen.

NO. 1680

41 March 14. Lubbert Lubberts, Jr., Y. M., from Stapperhut[1], in Overysel, and Hilletje Poulusse, Y. D., from Bergen. Married by the preacher at Bergen.

42 March 14. Hendrick Hoppe, Y. M., from New York, and Maria Jans, Y. D., from Bergen. Married by the preacher at Bergen.

1681

43 January 2. Jacob Lerou, Y. M., from Mannheim in the Palz and Wybrecht Hendricks, Y. D., from Bergen. Received certificate January 25, 1681, to New York.

44 April 17. Cornelis Machiels Vreeland, Y. M., from New York, and Metje Dircks Braeck, Y. D., from New York. Received certificate to New York, May 11.

45 April 24. Marcelis Pieters, Y. M., from Beest in Gelderland, and Pietertje Vande Voorst, Y. D., from New York. Received certificate to New York, May 11th.

46 April 24. Gerrit Gerrits, Jr., Y. M., from Wageninge in Gelderland, and Niesje Pieters, Y. D., from Beest in Gelderland. Received certificate to New York, May 11.

47 September 18. Dirck Epkese, Y. M., from Minnertsche in West Friesland, and Hester Hanse, Y. D., from Bergen in N. Jersey. (See note below *Wiert* Epkese.)[2]

48 September 25. Wiert Epkese, Y. M., from Minnertsche in West Friesland, and Geertje Jelise (Van Mandeviel), Y. D.[2]

49 November 13. Jan Aertsen Vande Bilt (widower) and Maddeleentje Hanse (widow). Received certificate to Breuckelen on Dec. 10.

50 November 20. Cornelis Claesz, Y. M., from New York, and Aeltje Teunise, Y. D., from Breuckelen. Received certificate to Breuckelen on December 10. Married December 11.

1682

51 April 30. Johannes Machielse Vreeland, Y. M., from New York, and Claesje Dirckse Braeck, Y. D., from Manhattan Island. Married May 14, by the preacher from Esopus at Bergen.

---

[1] Present name Staphorst.

[2] Ed. Note:—These two couples were married on October 3, by the preacher at Bergen; the first in the church.

1682 NO.

52 September 10. Roelof Vanderlinde, Y. M., from Wageningen in Gelderland and Susanna Hendricks Bronckhorst [Brinkerhoff], Y. D., from Midwout on Long Island. Married at Bergen by preacher October 2.

1683

53 April 15. Mathys Adolphus Hoppe, Y. M., from New York, and Anna Poulusse, Y. D., from N. Albany. Married at N. Y., May 2, by preacher.

54 May 13. Abraham Ackerman, Y. M., from Berlicum in the Meiery of Bois le duc, and Aaltje Van Laer, Y. D., from New York. Received certificate May 27, to Breuckelen; married May 28.

55 May 20. Thonis Hendricks, Y. M., from New York, and Susanna Lerou, Y. D., from Mannheim in the Palz. Received certificate June 11.

56 July 8. Hans Hendricks, Y. M., from N. Jersey and Tryntje Pieters, Y. D., from Long Island. Received certificate on July 31, and were married at New York by the preacher, August 1.

57 July 22. Jan Hendrickse Van Oosteroom, Y. M., from New York, and Mechteltje Roelofse, Y. D., from Breuckelen on Long Island. Received certificate to Midwout on August 18, and married August 19.

58 October 21. Hans Alberts, Y. M., from Bronswyck, and Annetje Gysbertse, Y. D., from Bergen in New Jersey. Received certificate November 12.

59 November 4. Pieter Pieterse Haeswout, Y. M., from Dyckhuysen in Overysel, and Dirckje Egberts, Y. D., from Midwout on Long Island. Received certificate to Staten Island, November 18.

1684

60 February 24. Gerrit Steynmets, Y. M., from New York, and Vrouwtje Claes, Y. D., from Bergen Jurisdiction. Received certificate to New York, March 11, and were married March 12 at New York.

61 April 6. Jan Ariaens Sips, Y. M., from Bergen in New Jersey, and Johanna Vande Voorst, Y. D., from Ahasymus. Recd. certif. to N. Y. on April 22.

62 April 25. Eduard Harrel, Y. M., from Laster-Charre[?] in Old England, and Elisabeth Marschal, both living at Captain Berry's plantation in Bergen Co., N. J. Received certificate May 11.

NO. 1684

63 June 1. Jan Hermens, Y. M., from Gerder in Gelderland, and Neeltje Janse Buys from Midwout, L. Island. Married June 23, in presence of court and congregation of Bergen by R. Van Giesen.

64 June 22. Claes Arentse Toers, Y. M., from Amsterdam, Holland, and Jacomyntje Van Neste, Y. D., from New York. Received certificate to Breuckelen July 8, and were married there July 13.

65 September 14. Teunis Jansen Spier, Y. M., from New York, and Catharyna Thomasse, Y. D., from Bergen, N. J. Married October 6 by the minister at Bergen.

66 September 21. Christoffel Steynmets, Y. M., from New York, and Jannetje Gerrits, Y. D., from Gemonepa. Married October 6, by minister at Bergen.

67 November 2. Isaac Billau, Y. M., born at sea, and Ida Sueberingh, Y. D., from Midwout, L. I. Received certificate to Staten Is. Nov. 25.

1685

68 March 8. Cornelis Van Voorst, Y. M., from Hasymus, and Feytje Gerrits, Y. D., from Gemonepa. Married Apr. 6 by minister at Bergen.

69 May 24. Pieter Jansz, Y. M., from Bergen, and Elisabeth Symons from Uythuyse[1]. Married June 22 at Bergen by the minister.

70 August 2. Tammes Larens, Y. M., from Southole, L. I., and Francyntje Berreys (wid. of Michiel Smit).

71 September 27. Hendrick Jansz van den Bos, Y. M., from New York, and Maria Booaas, Y. D., from Leiden, Holland. Received certificate to Staten Island on October 17.

1686

72 March 7. Johannes Jansz, Y. M., from N. Utrecht on L. I., and Anna Mary Van Giesen, Y. D., from Midwout on L. I. Married upon certificate at New York on March 24.

73 Pieter Josi, Y. M., and Cornelia Damen, Y. D. Married by the minister here upon certificate April 6, 1868, from Breuckelen and S. I.

74 April 11. Jochem Anthony Robbert, Y. M., from New York, and Mary Jeems (wid. of Jaems Bensen). Married April 28 by R. v. Giesen in the school, in presence of the court.

[1] Ed. Note:—Present name Uithuizen in the province of Groningen.

NO.

1686 75 May 30. Arien Thomasen, Y. M., from New York, and Maaike Cobussen, Y. D., from Albany, both living at Bergen. Married June 21, by the minister at Bergen.

76 June 21. Hermen Douwese, Y. M., and Gerritje Minnes (?), Y. D. Married June 21 by the minister at Bergen.

77 July 5. Matheus Cornelisse Van Nieuwkerk (widower of Anna Lubi) born at Slechtenhorst in Gelderland, and Catryna Poulus, Y. D., from Bergen, N. J., both living at Bergen. Married August 15 at Bergen by the Voorlezer R. Van Giesen, in presence of the court at Bergen in the church.

1687

78 February 13. Jan Criscel and Nicolis Ager. Were married at Bergen by Justice Claes Arentse Toers.

79 June 26. Johannis Van Giesen, Y. M., from Utrecht (Netherland), and Aeltje Schepmoes (wid. of Jan Evertse Keteltas). Received certificate to New York July 11, 1687.

80 September 18. Pieter Poulussen, Y. M., from New York, and Tryntje Hans Jacobse, Y. D., from Stuyvesants Bowery, both living here. Were married October 3, at Bergen.

81 September 20. Pieter Pierra, Y. M., from Sedan, France, living at Hackensack, and Weyntje Cornelis (widow of Poulis Jansen) living at Bergen, had certificate, that they had been registered by the French preacher at New York, to have their first bans published on September 25. After the publication of bans on three Sundays and without objections having been raised they were married October 19, by R. Van Giesen in presence of the Bergen court.

1688

82 January 8. Mathys Gerritse, Y. M., from Bergen, and Catryna Eduwaert, Y. D., from Boston in New England, both living in Bergen. Were married February 5 by R. Van Giesen, in presence of court.

83 January 29. Edward Earle, Y. M., from Maryland, living on Sicakis Island, and Elsje Vreeland, Y. D., from Gemonepa, living at Minkachquee. Were married Feb. 13 by Rev. Selyns of New York.

84 March 11. Roelof Lubbertse Westervelt, Y. M., from Meppel, living at Hackensack, and Urselena Stynmets, Y. D., from Bergen, living at Hasymus. Were married April 11, by Rev. Selyns at New York.

NO. 1688

85 May 13. Andries Preyer, Y. M., from Crevelt in County Meurs, and Johanna Steynmetz, Y. D., from Bergen, both living at Ahasymus. Were married after three proclamations of bans.

86 June 10. Pieter Gerritse, Y. M., and Constantia Vander Swalme (widow of Reynier Josiasse Van Roen), both living here. Were married by D° Tessemaker June 25 at Bergen.

87 June 10. Bastiaen Van Giesen, Y. M., living at Achquechnonk, and Aeltje Hendrickx, Y. D., living at Hackensack; both from Midwout. Were married June 25, at Bergen by D° Tessemaker.

1689

88 March 30. Wouter Willemsz, Y. M., from New York, living at Hoboken, and Dieuwer Joons, Y. D., from Bergen, living there. Were married at Bergen April 22.

1690

89 April 6. Lucas Suberingh, Y. M., from Midwout, L. I., living at Minkachquee, and Merritje Dorlant, Y. D., from Breuckelen, living at St. I. Received certificate April 30, 1690.

90 Frans Post and Maeyke Cobus with certificate from Achqueck-nonk. Were married April 22, 1690.

91 Juriaen Van Westervelt and Geeske Bongert, with certificate from Hackensack. Were married April 22, 1690.

92 June 8. Hessel Pieterse, Y. M., from Bergen, and Lysbeth Claes, Y. D., from Hasymus. Received certificate June 24, 1690, to New York.

93 July 27. Isaack Van Giesen, Y. M., from Bergen, and Cornelia Hendrickx, Y. D., from Midwout, L. I., living at Hackensack. Were married August 10, 1690, at Bergen.

94 August 24. Jan Borton, Y. M., from London, O. England, and Hillegont Jacobs, Y. D., from Midwout, both living at Pem-merepoch. Received certificate September 8, 1690.

95 September 21. Hermanus Gerrits, Y. M., from Bergen, and Anna Walinghs, Y. D., living at Achquechnonk, both from Bergen. Were married October 6 at Bergen.

1691

96 April 5. Willem Day, Y. M., born on Barbadus Island, living near Hackensack, and Annatje Jacobs, Y. D., born near Davids plantation in Bergen County, living at Hasymus. Were married April 14, at Bergen by D° Selyns.

1691 NO.

97 May 3. Johannis Edsal, Y. M., living at Major Davids plantation, and Charity Smit, Y. D., living on Cap. Berry's plantation, both from New York.

98 May 17. Thomas Juriaense, Y. M., living at Bergen, and Jannetje Straetmakers, Y. D., living at Hoboken, both from Bergen. Were married June 2 by D° Selyns at Bergen.

99 May 31. Jan Nickelis, Y. M., born on Barbadus, and Barbara Hartoch (wid. of Jan Ensels) both living on Cap. J. Berry's plantation.

100 July 12. Gerrit Steynmets (widower of Vrouwtje Claes) living at Hasymus, and Catryna Gerrits (widow of Adriaan Post) living at Achquechnonk. Received certificate July 31, 1691.

101 August 23. Enoch Michiels Vreeland (wid. of Dierckie Myers) living at Minkachqwee, and Grietje Wessels (wid. of Jan Janse Langedyk) living at New York.

102 October 4. Abraham Van Giesen, Y. M., from Bergen, and Fytje Andriesse, Y. D., from Gemonepa. Were married October 25, 1691, at Bergen by Voorlezer R. Van Giesen, before the congregation, in the presence of the court.

103 October 11. Michiel Vreelant, Y. M., and Marya Joris, Y. D. Received certificate November 27.

104 November 22. Roelof Swartwout (wid. of Eva Albers) and Francyntje Andries (wid. of Ab. Lubbers), with certificate from D° Selyns. Were married by R. Van Giesen.

105 December 20. Nicasius Kip, Y. M., and Annetje Bryant, Y. D., with certificate from Hackinsack. Were married by R. Van Giesen.

1692

106 March 13. David Nataniels, Y. M., from New York, living at Gemoenepa, and Annetje Straetmaecker, Y. D., from Bergen, living at Hoboken. Were married March 29, 1692, by D° Selyns at Bergen.

107 May 29. Aart Albertse, Y. M., from New York, and Catharina Vreeland, Y. D., from Gemonepa. Were married June 26, by R. Van Giesen.

108 November 6. Mathys Cornelisse, Y. M., from New Harlem, living at Hackensack, and Tryntje Hendricks, born and living at Bergen. Were married Nov. 13, 1692, by R. Van Giesen, Voorlezer, in presence of the court at Bergen.

NO. 1693

109 Daniel De Voor (widower) and Engeltje Cornelis, with letters from the French Church at Kinkachgemeck, Bergen County. Were married by R. Van Giesen, Voorlezer.

110 Jan Webbe (?), Y. M., and Annetje Cornelis (widow) with letters from the French Church at Kinkachgemeck in Bergen County, N. J. Were married by R. Van Giesen in presence of court.

111 April 30. Anthony Swertwout, Y. M., from Kingstown, Esopus, and Jannetje Cobus, Y. D., from N. Albany, both living at Bergen. Received certificate to Esopus, May 8, 1693.

112 May 7. Jacob Van Giesen, Y. M., from Bergen and living there, and Rusje Pluvier, Y. D., from New York and living there. Were married upon certificate at New York June 1.

113 May 14. Gerrit Juriaens, Y. M., from Bergen, and Beelitje Dirckx Van Oogsten, Y. D., from Hoboken, both living at Bergen. Were married June 6, in the church at Bergen by D° Selyns.

114 June 11. Johannes Jansz Van Blarcom, Y. M., from Bergen, and Metje Jans, Y. D. First proclamation at Midwout, L. I., by D° Varick; June 18, first proclamation at Bergen. Married July 16 by R. Van Giesen, Bergen.

115 November 5. Wander Diedrickx, Y. M., and Aaltje Gerrits, Y. D., both from Bergen. Were married November 27 by R. Van Giesen, in presence of court.

1694

116 March 25. Maerten Poulussen, Y. M., from Bergen, living there, and Margrietje Westervelt, Y. D., from Betvoort, L. I., living at Hackensack. Received certificate April 8, to Hackensack and were married there at same date.

117 September 23. Jan Claessen, Y. M., from Hesymus, living there, and Tryntje Straetmaker, Y. D., from Hoboken, living there. Were married Oct. 1 by Rev. Selyns, at Bergen.

1695

118 March 10. Jacob Jacobsen Van Winkel (wid. of Aaltje Daniels) and Grietje Hendrickx Hellingh, Y. D., both living at Bergen. Were married March 26.

119 March 31. Bartel Jacobs, Y. M., from Midwout, L. I., and Ellinor Douglas (wid. of Jan De Lenni), both living at Pemmerepoch. Received certificate April 14, 1695.

1695 NO.

120 June 16. Aalt Juriaensen, Y. M., and Gerritje Matheuse, Y. D., both from Bergen and living there. Received certificate to, and were married at New York, July 7, by D° Selyns.

1696

121 July 12. Abel Reddenhars, Y. M., from Hackemack, Virg., and Catrina Jans from Bergen, both living at Bergen. Were married July 26 at Bergen.

122 November 22. Jacobus Jansen Ralemon, Y. M., from N. Albany, and Pietertje Claes, Y. D., from Ahasymus. Received certificate to Hackensack December 12, 1696.

1697

123 March 7. Wilhem Hermensen Van Borckeloo, Y. M., from N. Utrecht, living at Constapels Hoeck, and Maria Cordeljou, Y. D., from N. Utrecht, living there. Received certificate April 1, and were married April 5 at Amersfoort.

124 April 25. Claes Hertmanse Vreeland, Y. M., from Gemonepa, and Annetje Hansen, Y. D., from N. Utrecht, L. I. Received certificate May 24, and were married May 25 at Gemonepa by D° Bertholf.

125 April 25. Rutger Van Hooren, Y. M., from New York, living at Hackinsack, and Neeltje Dirckx (wid. of Jan Vanderlinden), living at Gemonepa. Received certificate June 28.

126 June 27. Johannes Jansen Bandt, Y. M., and Willemijntje Philips, Y. D., both from New York, had three proclamations and no objections.

127 August 15. James Simse, Y. M., born at Gravesend, living at Bergen, and Martha Janse Daamen (wid. of Jan Remse) living at Midwout, L. I. Received certificate September 10, 1697.

1698

128 June 26. Pieter Gerbrants, Y. M., from Gemonepa, and Christyntje Juriaense, Y. D., from Bergen. Received certificate Aug. 7 to Hackensack.

129 July 31. Barend Hendrickse Spier, Y. M., and Kathalyntje Hendrickx, Y. D., both living at Pemmerpoch. Received certificate August 26, to Achquegnonck.

130 November 6. Dirck Straetmaker, Y. M., and Tryntje Buys, Y. D. Received certificate Nov. 24 to be married Nov. 27.

NO. 1699

131 Christoffel Steynmets (widower of Jannitje Gerrits) and Sara Van Neste, Y. D.

132 April 12. Rutger Jansen, Y. M., from New York, living at Nassau Island, Queens Co., and Annetje Gerrits, Y. D., from Pemmerepoch. Received certificate April 10 (?) 1699.

133 July 30. Dirck Poulussen, Y. M., born at Bergen, living there, and Fytje Hertmans Vreelant, Y. D., from Gemonepa, living there. Received certificate August 19, to Hackensack.

134 August 6. Claes Hertmans (wid. of Annetje Hermans) and Elsje Pieters, Y. D. Received certificate August 19, to Hackensack.

135 October 1. Reynier Van Giesen (wid. of Dirckje Cornelis Van Groenlinde) and Hendrickje Janse Buys (wid. of Cornelis Verwey). Groom "Voorlezer" at Bergen; were married October 17 on the "Polvly" by D° Bertholf.

136 October 8. Abraham Vreelant, Y. M., and Margrietje Jacobs Van Winkel, Y. D. Received certificate October 28, 1699, to Hackensack.

1700

137 March 10. Jan Slot, Y. M., from Bergen and J—— Andriesse, Y. D., from New York; both living at Bergen. Were married April 2, 1700, at Bergen by D° Du Bois.

138 June 16. Hendrick Teunissen Hellingh (wid. of Grietje Sammels) and Styntje Jans (wid. of Pieter Pera); groom living at Bergen, and bride at Hackensack.

The above couple were first registered by D° Bertholf at Hackensack, who gave them a certificate for Bergen; then they went to Bergen where their bans were published; and received, June 30, certificate from Bergen to Hackensack to be married there.

1701

139 March 16. Hendrick Gerritsen, Y. M., and Margrieta Straetmaker, Y. D., both living at Bergen. Were married April 3, by D° Dubois.

140 March 30. Adriaen Post, Y. M., and Elisabeth Mersilis, Y. D. Were married April 21, 1701, by D° Dubois.

141 April 6. Roelof Helmighsz, Y. M., and Achtje Cornelis Vreelant, Y. D. Were married April 21, 1701, by D° Dubois.

1701 NO.

142 April 7. Jacob Symonsen Van Winkel, Y. M., and Jacomyntje Matheus, Y. D. Received certificate to Achquecknonck April 20.

143 August 17. Thomas Thomasen, Y. M., from Bergen, and Sara Van Dueselen, Y. D., from Albany. Received certificate September 17 to Achquechnonck.

1702

144 March 22. Jan Juriaensen, Y. M., from Bergen and living there, and Neeltje Gerbrants, Y. D., from Gemonepa and living there. Were married April 7, by D° Du Bois.

145 April 12. Poulus Douwesen (widower of Aeltje Jacobs) and Zeytje Hendrickse (widow of Hendrick Van Reynne). Received certificate to New York May 3.

146 October 18. Dirck Hertmanse Vreelant, Y. M., born at Gemonepa, and Margrieta Dircks Banta, Y. D., born at Hackensack. Were married December 2, after receiving certificate November 21 to Hackensack.

1703

147 March 7. Jacob Jacobsen, Jr., Van Winkel, Y. M., and Eegje Poulus, Y. D., both born at Bergen and living at Achquecknonck. Received certificate March 26 and were married at Achquecknonck April 11.

148 March 21. Pieter Helmighs, Y. M., and Claertje Post, Y. D., both from Bergen. Were married at Bergen, April 8, by Rev. Vreedeman from Schoonechte.

149 October 17. Johannes Gerritsen, Y. M., and Cathalyntje Helmighs, Y. D., both from Bergen. Were married November 4, by D° Dubois.

1704

150 March 5. Claes Gerbrants, Y. M., from Gamonepa, and Merritje Juriaens, Y. D., from Bergen. Were married April 11, at Bergen by D° Dubois.

151 March 19. Andries Fredricksen, Y. M., from Bergen, and Priscilla Homs, Y. D., from Manhattan Island. Were married April 11 at Bergen by D° Dubois.

152 March 19. Dirck Barentsen, Y. M., from Pemmerepoch, and Elisabeth Gerrits, Y. D., from Bergen. Were married April 11 at Bergen by D° Dubois.

NO. 1704

153 December 10. Gerrit Post, Y. M., and Lea Straet, Y. D. Received certificate December 25 and were married December 27 at New York.

1705

154 January 13. Enoch M. Vreeland (widower of Grietje Wessels) and Achtje Van Hooren, Y. D., both living at Minhachquee in Bergen Co. Were married at New York by D° Dubois.

155 April 15. Mathys De Mot, Y. M., born at Kingstown, living at Bergen, and Margrita Blinckerhof, Y. D., living at Hackensack. Were married May 6, at Hackensack.

156 December 9. Johannes Tomasse, Y. M., born and living at Bergen, and Marytje Van Deusen (wid. of Tymen Van Valensyn) living in Newark, Essex County. Received certificate December 24, 1705, and were married January 1, 1706, at Achquechnonck.

1706

157 May 12. Gysbert Jansen Van Blerekom, Y. M., and Magdalena Lakomba, Y. D., both living at Bergen. Were married June 16, at Bergen by R. Van Giesen, in presence of the court.

158 September 15. Tomas Fransen Outwater (widower of Tryntje Breestede) and Metje Pieters, Y. D. Groom living at Monachie; bride living at Bergen. Were married September 29, 1706, at Achquechnonk.

1707

159 January 12. Jan Straetmaker (widower of Geesje Van Steenwyck) and Neeltje Buys (widow of Jacob Vygoor). Received certificate January 27, and were married by D° Bertholf.

160 January 19. [Hendrick Claasz Cuyper], Y. M., from Ahasymus, and Jannetje Verkerck, Y. D., from Midwout. Received certificate February 2, 1707, and were married by D° Freeman at Midwout.

161 April 27. Jacob Mattheeus, Y. M., from Bergen, and Sara Cornelis, Y. D., from N. Haerlem. Received certificate to Hackensack, May 15.

162 April 27. Daniel Van Winkel, Y. M., from Bergen, and Rachel Straetmaeckers, Y. D., from Hoboken. Received certificate to New York May 15.

1707 NO.

163 May 4. Herpert Gerbrants, Y. M., from Gemoenepaen, and Hillegont Marcelis, Y. D., from Bergen. Received certificate May 29 to New York.

164 May 11. Evert Evertse Van Beukelaer and Hillegond Jacobs. Received certificate June 7th, to be married June 8th by Justice Enoch Mighielse.

165 August 27. Lourens Barents from Vlissingen, Zeeland (widower of Isabella Govera? Zee [or Sea] man) and Hester Van Blercom, Y. D., from Bergen. Received certificate September 8th to New York.

166 September 7. Dirck Phillipse Conyn, Y. M., from Albany, and living at Bergen, and Rachel Andriesse, Y. D., from New York. Received certificate October 21st to New York.

1708

167 May 1. Pieter Van Hoorn (widower of Tryntje Van Dyck) born at Pemmebogh and Elisabeth Gabriels born at N. Albany. Were married May 9, 1708, in presence of Justice Helmig Roelofsen, by Adrian Vermeule.

168 May 1. Cornelis Hendricksen Blinkerhoff, Y. M., born at Witmond, Kings Co., and Aagje Hartmans Vreeland, Y. D., born at Gemoenepan. Were married May 24, 1708, in presence of Justice Enoch Vreeland, by Adrian Vermeule.

169 June 13. Adriaan Vermeule, born at Vlissingen, Zeeland (widower of Dina Swarts), and Christina Fredericks, Y. D., born at Bergen. Were married July 1, 1708, by D° Guilliaem Bertholf of Hackensack.

170 September 26. Isaack Van Giesen (widower of Cornelia Hendriks Blinkerhoff), and Hillegont Klaasen Kampen [?], Y. D., born at Hasemes.

1709

171 May 14. Herman Juriaensen, Y. M., and Marrytie Fredericks, Y. D., both born and living at Bergen. Were married June 20th by D° Dubois.

172 August 14. Daniel Van Winkel (widower of Rachel Straetmaacker) and Jannetje Cornelis Vreelant, Y. D., both born under Bergen. Were married at New York, by G. Dubois, September 3rd.

173 September 18. Lourens Van Boskerk, Y. M., born at Hackensack, and Fytje Cornelissen Vreelant, Y. D., born at Gemoenepan, both living at Pemmerpoch.

NO. 1710

174 May 27. Simon Jacobsen Van Winkel, Y. M., born at Bergen, and Jannetje Aljee (widow of Steven Albertse) born at Hackensack.

175 August 12. Cornelis Cornelisse Doremus, Y. M., born at Middelburg, Zeeland, and living at Achquechnonck, and Rachel Pietersen, Y. D., born and living at Bergen.

176 September 23. Johannis Neefjes, Y. M., born and living at Staten Island, and Antje Gerritsen Van Wageningen, Y. D., born and living at Pemmerpog. Were married October 9, 1710, by D° Dubois.

177 September 30. Johannis Walings Van Winckel, Y. M., and Hillegond Sippe, Y. D. Groom from Achquechnonck and living there. Bride from Bergen and living there.

178 November 17. Pieter Post, Y. M., from Akkwegnonk and living at Ahasemus, and Catharina Beekman (widow) living near N. Y.

1711

179 March 24. Cornelis Helmigsen, Y. M., from Bergen, and Aegtie Johannissen Vreeland, Y. D., born at (?).

180 Thomas Fredriksen (?), Y. M., born at Bergen, and Marytje Hartmansen Vreeland, Y. D., born and living at Gemoenepan.

181 Ary Sip, Y. M., and Gerretje Helmigsen, Y. D., both born and living at Bergen.

182 September 9. Dirck Helmigse Van Houte, Y. M., born and living at Bergen, and Metje Gerrebrantse, Y. D., born and living at Gemoenepan.

183 December 15. Roelof Helmigsen Van Houten (widower of Eegje Corn. Vreeland) and Feytje Sikkels, born at N. Albany and living at Bergen.

1712

184 February 23. Barent Barentsen Van Hoorn, Y. M., born at Pemmerpog, and Jenneken Pieters, Y. D., born and living at Bergen. These persons were married by Adrian Vermeule, in presence of Justice I. Sip.

1714

185 March 13. Casparus Preyer, Y. M., born at Pemmerpoch and living at Ahasemus, and Sara Andriessen (widow of H. Braes?).

1715 NO.

186 March 25. Ary Van Wouglim (?), Y. M., born on Staten Island, and Seleytje Preyer, Y. D., born at Bergen and living at Ahasemus.

187 May 7. Meyndert Gerrebrant, Y. M., born and living at Gemoenepan, and Tryntje Jacobsen Van Winkel, Y. D., born and living at Bergen.

188 October 30, 1713 (sic). Gerrit Harmanse Van Wageningen, Y. M., born and living at Achquechnonk, and Antje Sip, born and living at Bergen.

189 Johannis Post, Y. M., and Elisabeth Helm: Van Houte, Y. D., born and living at Bergen.

190 March 27, 1714 (sic). Barend Bruyn, Y. M., and Antje Borten, Y. D., both born and living at Pemmerpoch.

1719

191 May 2. Jacob Gerritsen Van Wageningen, Y. M., born and living at Pemmerpog, and Lea Gerrits, Y. D., born and living at Bergen.

192 May 4. Michiel Hartmansen Vreeland, Y. M., born and living at Gemoenepan, and Elisabeth Gerrits, Y. D., born and living at Bergen.

193 May 30. Johannis Helmigsen Van Houten, Y. M., born and living at Bergen, and Helena Johannissen Vreeland, Y. D., born and living at Gemoenepa.

194 November 7. Zacharias Sickels, Y. M., born and living at Bergen, and Ariaantje Hartmanse Vreeland, Y. D., born and living at Gemoenepa.

1720

195 Eduard Jefferys, Y. M., born in O. England, and Mary Tamsen (widow of Joseph Tamsen) both living at Sikaakes.

1723

196 May 11. Elias Johannissen Vreeland, Y. M., born at Gemoenepan, and Marytje Van Hoorn, Y. D., born at Pemmerpog and both living at Gemoenepan.

197 May 11. Hendrik Vander Hoeven, Y. M., and Eva Jacobussen Slot, Y. D., born at Hackensack and living at Bergen.

NO. 1725

198 May 23. Ide Sip (widower of Ariaantje Cornelissen Cadmus) and Antje Van Wageningen, Y. D., both born and living at Bergen.

199 October 22. Andries Frederiksen Cadmus (widower of Priscilla Hooms) born and living at Bergen, and Geertje Claassen Kuyper, Y. D., born and living at Ahasymus.

1726

200 May. Hendrik Van Winkel, Y. M., born at Bergen, and Catryntje Waldron, Y. D., born at New York; both living at Bergen.

201 May 2, 1724. (sic) Johannes Didericks, Y. M., born and living at Bergen, and Geertruy Van Winkel, Y. D., born and living at Achqueknonk.

1726

202 Johannis Johannissen Vreeland, Y. M., born and living at Gemonepan, and Antje Didericks, Y. D., born and living at Bergen.

203 [?] Isaac Hennion, Y. M., born at Hackensack, and Helena Stynmets, Y. D., born and living at Ahasemes.

204 [?] Banns. Gerrit Hennion, Y. M., born at Akkingsak and living at Ahasemus, and Marrytje Van Vorst, Y. D., born and living at Ahasemus.

205 [?] Cornelis Van Vorst, Y. M., born and living at Ahasemis, and Claasje De Moth, Y. D., born and living at Bergen.

1727

206 August 5. Casparus Stymets, Y. M., born and living at Ahasymis, and Marytje Hendricksen, Y. D., born at Port Royal and living at Bergen.

1728

207 June 29. Cornelis Gerritsen, Y. M., and Aaltje Van Winkel, Y. D., both born and living at Bergen.

208 June 18. Paulus Van Nieuwkerke, Y. M., born and living at Bergen, and Helena Spiers [?], Y. D., born and living at Pemmerpog.

1730 NO.

209 March 18. Pieter Makale [?] (widower of Antje Vyle) born on Staten Island, and Maria Andriese [?], Y. D., born at Frankfort, Germany, both living at Pemmerpog.

210 March 28. Jacob Brouwer, Y. M., born at Bergen, and Lea Slot, Y. D., born at Ackinsack, both living at Bergen.

211 July 19. Arent Toers, Y. M., born and living at Bergen, and Annatje Spier, Y. D., born and living at Pemmerpog.

212 September 5. Gerrit Mattheussen Van Nieuwkerk, Y. M., born and living at Bergen, and Catryntje Kuypers, Y. D., born and living at Ahasemus.

1732

213 August 10. Willem Zikkels, Y. M., born and living at Bergen, and Elisabeth Kuyper, Y. D., born and living at Ahasymus.

1733

214 April 21. Gerrit Dideriks, Y. M., and Jannitje Van Nieuwkerk, Y. D., both born and living at Bergen.

215 October 27. Petrus Stuyvesand, Y. M., born at New York, and Pryntje Preyer, Y. D., born and living at Bergen.

1735

216 June 7. Cornelis Diedrikx, Y. M., and Antje Roos, Y. D., both born and living at Bergen.

217 September 26. Helmigh Van Wagenen, Y. M., from Bergen, and Martje Brinkerhof, Y. D., born at Gemoenepan.

1737

218 April 17. Reynier Van Giesen, Y. M., born at 2nd River, living at Totua, and Catryntje Marselis, Y. D., born at and living at Bergen.

1738

219 April 22. Johannis Vander Hoef, Y. M., born at Hackensack, and Maria Eertsie, Y. D., born at Kinderhoek.

220 May 5. Hendrik Coejeman, Y. M., born at 2nd River, and Martje Gerbrantse, Y. D., born and living at Gemoenepa.

221 October 8. Uldrik Brouwer, Y. M., born and living at Bergen, and Marya Vander Vorst, Y. D., born at New York, living at Bergen.

1738

NO.

222 November 26. Jacob Diedriks, Y. M., from Bergen, and Jannetje Van Winkel, Y. D., born at Bergen, living at Pemmerpog.

223 December 8. Abraham Van Tuyl, Y. M., from Staten Island, and Metje Vreeland, Y. D., born at Stony Point.

1739

224 April 1. Abraham Sikels, Y. M., born and living at Bergen, and Agie Blinckerhof, Y. D., born and living at Gemoenepan.

225 April 14. Johannes Diedriks (widower), born and living at Bergen, and Hester Vreeland, Y. D., born and living at Wesel.

226 April 29. Johannis Spier, Y. M., and Geertruy Roome (widow of Hendrik Meyer).

227 September 24. Robert Ido, Y. M., born at Westchester, and Annetje Roome, Y. D., born at N. York.

228 November 20. Hartman Vrelant, Y. M., and Martje Gerbrants, Y. D., both born at Gemoenepan.

1740

229 October 30. Hendrik Demoth, Y. M., and Jannetje Van Wagenen, Y. D., both born and living at Bergen.

230 December 2. Johannes Juryansen, Y. M., and Sara Cuyper,. Y. D., were married. She was born at Ahasymus.

231 September 5 [?]. Johannes Jurriansen (widower) and Margrietje Van Winkel, Y. D., both from Bergen.

1742

232 October 17. Cornelis Van Wagenen, Y. M., and Catrina Seggels, Y. D., both born and living at Bergen.

233 October 17. Jacob Van Wagenen, Y. M., and Jannetje Van Houten, Y. D., both born and living at Bergen.

1744

234 June 5. Albertus Spier, Y. M., born and living at Pemmerpog, and Orseltje Westervelt, Y. D., born and living at Hackensack.

235 August 20. Johannis Evers, Y. M., and Seytje Spier, Y. D.

236 October 20. Hartman Blinckerhoff, Y. M., and Claasie Van Houten, Y. D.

1745 NO.

237 June 14. Johannis Pryer, Y. M., and Geertruyt Siggelse, Y. D.

1746

238 March 22. Gerrit Van Wagenen, Y. M., and Margrietje Van Winkel, Y. D.

239 December 18. Abraham Pryer, Y. M., and Martje Sickels, Y. D. Were married in presence of Justices Michiel Vreeland and Pieter Marselis.

1747

240 October 11. Jacob Demoth, Y. M., and Feytje Van Houten, Y. D., both from Bergen.

1748

241 October 17. Johannis Van Wagenen, Y. M., and Aaltje Vreeland, Y. D.

1749

242 October 8. Livynus Winne, Y. M., and Annatje Zip, Y. D.

243 October 8. Robbert Sikkels, Y. M., and Antje Winne, Y. D.

244 October 8. Andries Preyer, Y. M., and Geertruy Sickels, Y. D.

1750

245 November 8. Johannis Van Wagenen, Y. M., and Neesje Van Wagenen, Y. D.

1754

246 April 11. Ide Marcelisse, Y. M., and Ariaantje Siph, Y. D., both born and living at Bergen.

1757

247 November 13. Klaas Vreland, Y. M., born at Gemoenepan, and Cattintje Ziph, Y. D., born at Bergen, were married December 1st by D° Jackson.

248 December 3. Joseph Waldron, Y. M., born at Rey, living at Pemmerpoch, and Antje Diedericks, Y. D., born and living at Bergen.

NO. 1758

249 December 10. Johannis Winne, Y. M., and Aaltje Diedericks, Y. D., both born at Bergen.

1765

250 November 9. Egbert Post, Y. M., born at Ackquegnk, living at Gemoenepa, and Saertje Stuyvesant, Y. D., born and living at Bergen. Were married November 30th by D W. Jackson.

1766

251 May 11. Nicklaas Toers, Y. M., and Jannetje Van Reype, Y. D., both born and living at Bergen. Were married May 31st by D° W. Jackson.

252 August 3. Machiel van Tuil, Y. M., and Saertie Hoeper, Y. D., both born on Staten Island and living at Pemmeropog. Were married August 24th by D° W. Jackson.

1767

253 February 1. Hendrick Sikkels, Y. M., and Jenneke Stuyvesant, Y. D., both born and living at Bergen. Were married February 21st by D° W. Jackson.

254 June 20. John Lisk, Y. M., born on Staten Island and living at Bergen point, and Catrientje Huysman, Y. D., born and living on Staten Island.

255 May 15. Jacobus Meckniel, Y. M., born at Raritan, and Antie Lisk, Y. D., born on Staten Island, both living at Bergen. Were married by D° Jackson.

1768

256 December 17. Johannis Diderix, Y. M., and Antie Van Wagenen, Y. D., both born and living at Bergen. Were married by D° Jackson.

1769

257 Jacob Nieuwkerk, Y. M., born at Bergen, and Feytje Hennyon, Y. D., born at Hoboken, both living at Bergen. Were married February 13th by D° W. Jackson.

1771

258 Thomas Jacobusse, Y. M., born at Pompton, living at Newtown, and Saertie Toers, Y. D., born at Nuwork, living at Barbadoes. Were married January 13th by D° W. Jackson.

1778 NO.

259 Johannis Vreeland, Y. M., born at Pemmerepog, and Helena Gerbrantse, Y. D., born at Gemoenepa. Were married June 21st by D° W. Jackson.

1779

260 Gerrit Van Reype (widower) and Catrientie Van Reype, Y. D., both born and living at Bergen. Were married May 2nd by D° Gerrit Leydekker, New York.

261 Hendrick Blinkerhoff, Y. M., and Lea Van Wagenen, Y. D. Were married June 19th by D° Gerrit Leydekker.

1781

262 Machiel Vreeland, Y. M., and Geertie Sickels, Y. D. Were married September 16th by D° Willem Jackson.

1782

263 Kobus Ackerman, Y. M., and Betje Belser, Y. D. Were married November 27th by D° Wm. Jackson.

264 Johannis Callerd, Y. M., and Gertie Pryer, Y. D. Were married December 19th by D° Wm. Jackson.

265 Johannes Van Houte, Y. M., and Annatie Callerd, Y. D. Were married December 19th by D° Wm. Jackson.

266 Johannis Everse (widower) and Sally Griffens (widow). Were married by D° Wm. Jackson, December 21st.

267 David Hennion, Y. M., and Cathalyntie Everse, Y. D. Were married by D° Wm. Jackson, December 21st.

1783

268 Abraham Woed, Y. M., and Rutie Kleyndini, Y. D. Were married October 12th by D° Wm. Jackson.

1785

269 Gerrit Van Reype, Y. M., and Jannetje Winne, Y. D. Were married November 19th by D° Wm. Jackson.

270 Adam Rap, Y. M., and Arriaentje Pryer, Y. D. Were married by D° Wm. Jackson, November 19th.

1788

271 Cornelis Vreelant, Y. M., and Jenneke Sip, Y. D. Were married by D° W. Jackson, October 5th.

INDEX OF THE MARRIAGE REGISTER

of the

REFORMED PROTESTANT DUTCH CHURCH OF BERGEN

Prepared and Arranged by

DINGMAN VERSTEEG

Ackerman, Abraham, 54.
Kobus, 263.
Lourus, 38.
Ager, Nicolis, 78.
Albertse, Albers, Alberts, Aart, 107.
Eva, 104.
Hans, 58.
Steven, 174.
Aljee, Jannetje, 174.
Andries, Andriesse, Andriese, Andriessen, Francyntje, 104.
Fytje, 102.
J. 137.
Maria, 209.
Rachel, 166.
Sara, 185.
Arentse, Hendrickje, 11.
Arsele, Joseph, 34.
Bandt, Johannes Jansen, 126.
Banta, Margrieta Dircks, 146.
Barentsen, Barents, Dirck, 152.
Lourens, 165.
Beekman, Catharina, 178.
Belser, Betje, 263.
Bensen, Jaems, 74.
Berry, Berreys, Captain, Cap. 62, 97.
Francyntje, 70.
J. 99.
Bertholf, D°, Guilliaem, 124, 135, 138, 159, 169.
Billau, Isaac, 67.
Bongert, Geeske, 91.
Booaas, Maria, 71.
Borten, Borton, Antje, 190.
Jan, 94.
Braeck, Braack, Claesje Dirckse, 51.
Dircks, 21.
Metje Dircks, 44.
Braes, H., 185.
Breestede, Tryntje, 158.
Brinkerhof, Blinckerhof, Blinkerhoff, Agie, 224.
Cornelia Hendricks, 170.
Cornelis Hendricksen, 168.
Hartman, 236.
Hendrick, 261.
Margrita, 155.
Martje, 217.
Bronckhorst [Brinkerhoff], Susanna Hendricks, 52.
Brouwer, Jacob, 210.
Uldrik, 221.
Bruyn, Barend, 190.
Bryant, Annetje, 105.
Buys, Arien Pieterse, 19.
Hendrickje Janse, 135.
Neeltje, 63, 159.
Tryntje, 130.
Cadmus, Andries Fredericksen, 199.
Ariaantje Cornelissen, 198.
Callerd, Annatie, 265.
Johannis, 264.
Claesen, Claezs, Claese, Claessen, Claes, Andries, 5.
Cornelis, 50.
Gerbrant, 23.
Jan, 117.
Lysbeth, 92.
Merritje, 23.
Pietertje, 122.
Tryntje, 31.
Vrouwtje, 60, 100.
Cobus, Cobussen, Jannetje, 111.
Maaike, Maeyke, 75, 90.
Coejeman, Hendrick, 220.
Conyn, Dirck Phillipse, 166.
Cordeljou, Maria, 123.
Cornelis, Cornelisse, Corneliss, Annetje, 110.
Elisabeth, 16.
Engeltje, 109.
Gerritje, 18.
Hendrick, 8.
Mathys, 108.
Neeltje, 8.
Roelof, 18.
Sara, 161.
Weyntje, 81.
Criscel, Jan, 78.
Cuyper, Kuypers, Kuyper, Catryntje, 212.
Elisabet, 213.
Geertje Claassen, 199.
Hendrick Claaz, 160.
Sara, 230.

Dame, Damen, Daamen, Annetje, 7.
Cornelia, 73.
Martha Janse, 127.
Daniels, Aaltje, 24, 118.
Davids, 96.
Major, 97.
Day, Willem, 96.
De Lenni, Jan, 119.
De Moth, De Mot, Claasje, 205.
Hendrik, 229.
Jacob, 240.
Mathys, 155.
De Voor, Daniel, 109.
Diedericks, Didericks, Diedrikx, Dideriks, Diedriks, Diderix, Diedrickx, Aaltje, 249.
Antje, 202, 248.
Cornelis, 216.
Gerrit, 214.
Jacob, 222.
Johannes, Johannis, 201, 225, 256.
Wander, 115.
Dirckx, Neeltje, 125.
Doremus, Cornelis Cornelisse, 175.
Dorlant, Merritje, 89.
Douglas, Ellinor, 119.
Douwese, Douwesen, Hermen, 76.
Poulus, 145.
Du Bois, Dubois, D°, D°. G., 137, 139, 140, 141, 144, 149, 150, 151, 152, 154, 171, 172, 176.
Duyts, Lourens, 1.
Earle, Edward, 83.
Edsal, Johannis, 97.
Eduwaert, Eduwaerts, Catryna, 82.
Hermen, 35.
Eertsie, Maria, 219.
Egberts, Egbers, Dirckje, 59.
Geertje, 38.
Eltingh, Jan Roelofse, 22.
Ensels, Jan, 99.
Epkese, Dirck, 47.
Hendrick, 37.
Sibe, 36.
Wiert, 48.
Everse, Evers, Cathalyntie, 267.
Johannis, 235, 266.
Fooken, Gerrit, 22.
Franse, Marya, 39.
Fredricksen, Fredericks, Fredriksen, Andries, 151.
Christina, 169.
Marrytie, 171.
Thomas, 180.
Freeman [see Vreedeman], D°., 160.
Gabriels, Elisabeth, 167.
Gerbrantse, Gerbrants, Gerrebrantse, Gerrebrant, Claes, 150.
Helena, 259.
Herpert, 163.
Martje, 220, 228.
Metje, 182.
Meyndert, 187.
Neeltje, 144.
Pieter, 128.
Gerrits, Gerritsen, Gerritse, Aaltje, 115.
Annetje, 132.
Catryna, 29, 100.
Cornelis, 207.
Elisabeth, 152, 192.
Feytje, 68.
Geesje, 2.
Gerrit, 46.
Hendrick, 139.
Hermanus, 95.
Jannetje, Jannitje, 66, 131.
Johannes, 149.
Lea, 191.
Mathys, 82.
Pieter, 86.
Griffens, Sally, 266.
Gysbertse, Annetje, 58.
Haeswout, Pieter Pieterse, 59.
Hansen, Hanse, Annetje, 124.
Hester, 47.
Maddeleentje, 49.
Harrel, Eduard, 62.
Hartoch, Barbara, 99.
Hellingh, Grietje Hendrickx, 118.
Hendrick Teunissen, 138.
Helmighs, Helmigsen, Helmighsz, Cathalyntje, 149.
Cornelis, 179.
Gerretje, 181.
Pieter, 148.
Roelof, 141.
Hendrickx, Hendricks, Hendricksen, Hendrickse, Aeltje, 87.
Cornelia, 93.
Hans, 56.
Kathalyntje, 129.
Marytje, 206.
Thonis, 55.
Tryntje, 108.
Wybrecht, 43.
Zeytje, 145.
Hennion, Hennyon, David, 267.
Feytje, 257.
Gerrit, 204.
Isaac, 203.
Hermans, Hertmans, Hermens, Hermen, Annetje, 134.
Claes, 134.
Jan, 63.
Neeltje, 10.
Reyckje, 4.
Hoeper, Saertie, 252.
Homs, Hooms, Priscilla, 151, 199.
Hoppe, Catharyna, 20.
Hendrick, 42.
Mathys Adolphus, 53.
Huysman, Catrientje, 254.
Ido, Robert, 227.
Jackson, D°., D°. W., D°. Willem, 247, 250, 251, 252, 253, 255,

256, 257, 258, 259, 262, 263, 264, 265, 266, 267, 268, 269, 270, 271.
Jacobs, Jacobse, Aeltje, 145.
Annatje, 96.
Bartel, 119.
Geesje, 3.
Hillegont, Hillegond, 94, 164.
Treyntje, Tryntje, 6, 13, 80.
Jacobusse, Thomas, 258.
Jans, Jansz, Jansen, Catrina, 121.
Grietje, 1.
Johannes, 72.
Maria, 42.
Metje, 114.
Pieter, 69.
Poulis, 81.
Rutger, 132.
Styntje, 138.
Jeems, Mary, 74.
Jefferys, Eduard, 195.
Jelise, Geertje, 48.
Joons, Dieuwer, 88.
Joris, Marya, 103.
Josi, Pieter, 73.
Juriaensen, Juriaense, Juriaens, Juryansen, Jurriansen, Aalt, 120.
Christyntje, 128.
Gerrit, 113.
Herman, 171.
Jan, 144.
Johannes, 230, 231.
Merritje, 150.
Thomas, 98.
Kampen, Hillegont Klaasen, 170.
Keteltas, Jan Evertse, 79.
Kip, Nicasius, 105.
Kleyndini, Rutie, 268.
Lakomba, Magdalena, 157.
Langedyk, Jan Janse, 101.
Larens, Tammes, 70.
Leons, Geertruyt, 18.
Lerou, Jacob, 43.
Susanna, 55.
Leydekker, Gerrit, 260, 261.
Lisk, Antie, 255.
John, 254.
Lubbers, Lubberts, Ab., 104.
Lubbert, 41.
Mareytje, 37.
Lubi, Anna, 12, 77.
Jacob, 18.
Macheleen, Charles, 33.
Machielse, Mighielse, Magielse, Magiels, Catharyna, 14.
Enoch, 164.
Johannes, 10.
Preyntje, 5.
Tades, 40.
Makale, Pieter, 209.
Marschal, Elisabeth, 62.
Marselis, Mersilis, Marcelis, Marcelisse, Catryntje, 218.
Elisabeth, 140.
Hillegont, 163.
Ide, 246.
Pieter, 239.
Matheuse, Mattheeus, Matheus, Gerritje, 120.
Jacob, 161.
Jacomyntje, 142.
Meckniel, Jacobus, 255.
Meyer, Meyers, Andries, 15.
Dirckje, Dierckje, 9, 101.
Hendrik, 226.
Johannes, 30.
Minnes, Gerritje, 76.
Nataniels, David, 106.
Neefjes, Johannis, 176.
Nickelis, Jan, 99.
Oosteroom, Van Oosteroom, Hendrick Janse, 3.
Jan Hendrickse, 57.
Jannetje Hendrickx, 35.
Treyntje Hendrickx, 19.
Outwater, Tomas Fransen, 158.
Philips, Willemyntje, 126.
Pierra, Pera, Pieter, 81, 138.
Pieters, Pieterse, Pietersen, Elsje, 134.
Hessel, 92.
Jannetje, 26.
Jenneken, 184.
Marcelis, 45.
Metje, 158.
Niesje, 46.
Rachel, 175.
Tryntje, 56.
Pluvier, Rusje, 112.
Post, Adriaan, Adriaen, 29, 100, 140.
Claertje, 148.
Egbert, 250.
Frans, 90.
Gerrit, 153.
Johannis, 189.
Pieter, 178.
Poulusse, Poulussen, Poulus, Anna, 53.
Catryna, 77.
Dirck, 133.
Eegje, 147.
Hilletje, 41.
Maerten, 116.
Pieter, 80.
Pryer, Preyer, Abraham, 239.
Andries, 85, 244.
Arriaentje, 270.
Casparus, 185.
Gertie, 264.
Johannis, 237.
Pryntje, 215.
Seleytje, 186.
Ralemon, Jacobus Jansen, 122.
Rap, Adam, 270.
Reddenhars, Abel, 121.
Remse, Jan, 127.

Robbert, Jochem Anthony, 74.
Roelofs, Roelofsen, Roelofse, Cornelis, 32.
Helmigh, Helmig, 26, 167.
Mechteltje, 57.
Teunis, 31.
Roome, Annetje, 227.
Geertruy, 226.
Roos, Antje, 216.
Sammels, Grietje, 138.
Schepmoes, Aeltje, 79.
Selyns, Rev., D°., 83, 84, 96, 98, 104, 106, 113, 117, 120.
Sickels, Sikels, Seggels, Sikkels, Siggelse, Zikkels, Abraham, 224.
Catrina, 232.
Feytje, 183.
Geertie, 262.
Geertruyt, Geertruy, 237, 244.
Hendrick, 253.
Martje, 239.
Robbert, 243.
Willem, 213.
Zacharias, 194.
Simse, James, 127.
Sips, Sip, Zip, Siph, Ziph, Sippe, Annetie, Antje, Annatje, 25, 188, 242.
Ariaantje, 246.
Ary, 181.
Cattintje, 247.
Hillegond, 177.
I., 184.
Ide, 198.
Jan Ariaens, 61.
Jenneke, 271.
Marytje Ariaense, 36.
Slech, Jacomyntje, 22.
Slot, Eva Jacobussen, 197.
Jan, 137.
Lea, 210.
Smeeman, Hermen, 7.
Smit, Charity, 97.
Michiel, 70.
Spier, Spiers, Albertus, 234.
Annatje, 211.
Barend Hendrickse, 129.
Helena, 208.
Johannis, 39, 226.
Seytje, 235.
Teunis Jansen, 65.
Steynmets, Stymets, Stynmets, Steynmetz, Anna, 40.
Casper, Casparus, 13, 206.
Christoffel, 66, 131.
Gerrit, 60, 100.
Helena, 203.
Johanna, 85.
Johannes, 27.
Urselena, 84.
Straet, Lea, 153.
Straetmaecker, Straetmaker, Straetmaacker, Straetmaeckers, Annetje, 106.
Dirck, 130.
Jan, 2, 159.
Jannetje, 98.
Margrieta, 139.
Rachel, 162, 172.
Tryntje, 117.
Stuyvesant, Stuyvesand, Jenneke, 253.
Petrus, 215.
Saertje, 250.
Sueberingh, Suberingh, Ida, 67.
Lucas, 89.
Swarts, Dina, 169.
Swartwout, Swertwout, Anthony, 111.
Roelof, 104.
Symons, Elisabeth, 69.
Tades, Machiel, 6.
Tamsen, Joseph, 195.
Mary, 195.
Tessemaker, D°., 86, 87.
Teunise, Aeltje, 50.
Thomasen, Thomasse, Thomas, Tomas, Tomasse, Tomassen, Arien, 75.
Catryna, Catharyna, 33, 65.
Francyntje, 17.
Fredrick, 20.
Johannes, 156.
Juriaen, 4.
Thomas, 143.
Toers, Arent, 211.
Claes, Nicklaas, 64, 78, 251.
Lourus Arense, 17.
Saertie, 258.
Van Beukelaer, Evert Evertse, 164.
Van Blarcom, Van Blerekom, Van Blercom, Gysbert Jansen, 157.
Hester, 165.
Johannes Jansz, 114.
Van Borckeloo, Wilhem Hermensen, 123.
Van Boskerk, Lourens, 173.
Van de Bilt, Jan Aertsen, 49.
Van den Bos, Hendrick Jansz, 71.
Van der Hoeven, Van der Hoef, Hendrik, 197.
Johannis, 219.
Vanderlinden, Van der Linden, Van der Linde, Jan, 125.
Machtelt, 28.
Roelof, 52.
Van der Swalme, Constantia, 86.
Van Deusen, Van Dueselen, Marytje, 156.
Sara, 143.
Van Dyck, Tryntje, 167.
Van Giesen, Abraham, 102.
Anna Mary, 72.
Bastiaen, 87.
Isaack, 93, 170.
Jacob, 112.
Johannis, 79.

Maddaleena, 32.
R., 24, 25, 36, 37, 38, 63, 74, 77, 81, 82, 102, 104, 105, 108, 109, 110, 114, 115, 157.
Reynier, 135, 218.
Van Groenlinde, Dirckje Cornelis, 135.
Van Hooren, Van Hoorn, Achtje, 154.
Barent Barentsen, 184.
Marytje, 196.
Pieter, 167.
Rutger, 125.
Van Houten, Van Houte, Claasie, 236.
Dirck Helmigse, 182.
Elisabeth Helm, 189.
Feytje, 240.
Jannetje, 233.
Johannes, Johannis, 193, 265.
Roelof Helmigsen, 183.
Van Laer, Aaltje, 54.
Van Mandeviel, Geertje Jelise, 48.
Van Neste, Jacomyntje, 64.
Sara, 131.
Van Nieuwkerk, Nieuwkerk, Van Nukerck, Van Nieuwkerke, Gerrit Mattheussen, 212.
Jacob, 257.
Jannitje, 214.
Matheus Cornelisse, 12, 77.
Paulus, 208.
Van Oogsten, Beelitje Dirckx, 113.
Dirck Janse, 16.
Van Reynne, Hendrick, 145.
Van Reype, Catrientie, 260.
Gerrit, 260, 269.
Jannetje, 251.
Van Roen, Reynier Josiasse, 86.
Van Steenwyck, Van Steenwyk, Geesje, 159.
Piet Cornelisse, 11.
Van Tuyl, Van Tuil, Abraham, 223.
Machiel, 252.
Van Valensyn, Tymen, 156.
Van Voorst, Van Vorst, Van de Voorst, Van der Vorst, Annetje, 30.
Cornelis, 68, 205.
Johanna, 61.
Marrytje, Marya, 204, 221.
Pietertje, 45.
Vroutje, 15.
Van Wageningen, Van Wagenen, Antje, Antie, 176, 198, 256.
Cornelis, 232.
Gerrit, 188, 238.
Helmigh, 217.
Jacob, 191, 233.
Jannetje, 229.
Johannis, 241, 245.
Lea, 261.
Neesje, 245.
Van Winkel, Van Winckel, Aaltje, 207.
Annetje Jacobse, 27.
Daniel, 162, 172.
Geertruy, 201.
Hendrik, 200.
Jacob, 24, 118, 142, 147.
Jannetje, 222.
Johannis Walings, 177.
Margrietje, 136, 231, 238.
Symon, Simon, 25, 174.
Tryntje Jacobsen, 187.
Walingh Jacobse, 14.
Van Wouglim, Ary, 186.
Varick, D°., 114.
Verkerck, Jannetje, 160.
Vermeule, Adriaan, Adrian, 167, 168, 169, 184.
Verwey, Cornelis, 135.
Vreedeman [see Freeman], Rev., 148.
Vreeland, Vreelant, Aagje, Achtje, Aegtie, Eegje, 141, 168, 179, 183.
Aaltje, 241.
Abraham, 136.
Ariaantje Hartmanse, 194.
Catharina, 107.
Claes, Klaas, 124, 247.
Cornelis, 44, 271.
Dirck Hertmanse, 146.
Elias Johannissen, 196.
Elsje, 83.
Enoch, 9, 101, 154, 168.
Fytje, 133, 173.
Hartman, 228.
Helena Johannissen, 193.
Hester, 225.
Jannetje Cornelis, 172.
Johannis, 51, 202, 259.
Marytje Hartmansen, 180.
Metje, 223.
Michiel, Machiel, 103, 192, 239, 262.
Vygoor, Jacob, 159.
Vyle, Antje, 209.
Waldron, Catryntje, 200.
Joseph, 248.
Walinghs, Anna, 95.
Elisabeth, 34.
Webbe, Jan, 110.
Wessels, Grietje, 101, 154.
Westervelt, Van Westervelt, Juriaen, 91.
Margrietje, 116.
Orseltje, 234.
Roelof Lubbertse, 84.
Willemsz, Wouter, 88.
Winne, Antje, 243.
Jannetje, 269.
Johannis, 249.
Livynus, 242.
Woed, Abraham, 268.
Zaberoski, Albert, 28.
Zeeman, Isabella Govera, 165.

John Grier Hibben

PRESIDENT

OF

NASSAU HALL

PRINCETON UNIVERSITY

YEAR BOOK

OF

The Holland Society

OF

New York

1915

BERGEN BOOK

3rd Volume

PREPARED BY THE RECORDING SECRETARY

Executive Office
90 West Street
NEW YORK CITY
A

PRESIDENT 1914

OF

THE HOLLAND SOCIETY OF NEW YORK

THE FIRST SETTLERS OF BERGEN

by

NICHOLAS GARRETSON VREELAND

WHILE Gemonepan (Communipaw), the "Village on the Shore," was settled as early as 1630, the formally recognized Village of Bergen was not so known until 1660. Both of these, with other settlements, were officially incorporated as the Village of Bergen. What might be called the Village of Communipaw was, in reality, a row of houses[1] facing New York Bay from Mill Creek southerly, later outlined by the present Phillips Street, with scattered houses between the shore and the hill to the westward.

Jan Evertson Bout was the first known settler in this section, who in 1634 came there as an official of Michael Pauw, the Patroon. Six years later, Egbert Wouterson came into possession of "Jan de Lacher's Hook," later known as Mill Creek Point, the ancestral home of the Van Horne family. Jacob Walling Van Winkle was a settler as early as 1641 but removed to Rensselaerswyck, returning nine years later. Bout sold in 1646 a portion of his farm to Michael Jansen, the common ancestor of the Vreeland family, and moved to Breuckelen.

In

[1] See heading cut.

In 1655, the Indians drove out all of the Communipaw people, killing or capturing nearly every white person. A few families escaped by boat to New Amsterdam, among them that of Michael Jansen, who lived for three years on the corner of what is now William and Stone Streets, and returned to Communipaw in 1658, where he lived until the year of his death in 1663.

Constable Hook, named for Constable (gunner) Jacob Jacobsen Roy, was first occupied for residence in 1646.

To Greenville came Dirck Jansen Dey, Claes Carstens and others prior to 1659. Other names are mentioned as among the early owners of land in this section, but many of these never settled upon the land, being possibly only speculators.

Early in 1660 petitions were sent to the Governor and Council of New Netherland, for permission to settle upon the lands on the "Berg" (Hill) back of Communipaw, but Governor Stuyvesant was so fearful of the safety of the people, owing to the numerous Indian invasions, that he refused to give the permission desired. Later in the year, Michael Jansen, as representative of the district on the west side of the river in the council of "Nine Men," made such strong representations to him, that he gave permission to form a settlement, provided it was protected by a strong palisadoed fence built around it. This was done, and the tract inside the fence was divided into thirty-two plots[1] facing the six roads which are now known as Bergen Avenue, Academy Street, Tuers Avenue, Newkirk Street, Vroom Street, and Van Reypen Street. This map was made by Jacques Cortelyou, the surveyor of New Amsterdam; but though the most diligent search has been prosecuted, no trace of it has been found, nor has there been discovered any list of the names of the original patentees. In accordance with Dutch custom, a church and school were established and service was conducted by volunteers until 1663, when a petition to the Council of New Netherland[2] was signed by the

[1] See map in HOLLAND SOCIETY YEAR BOOK 1914, page 3.

[2] See pages 13–19 of HOLLAND SOCIETY YEAR BOOK 1913.

the Magistrates of Bergen, asking that a clergyman be formally assigned, and annexing as evidence of the good faith of the petitioners a subscription list of four hundred and seventeen guilders, in seawan, as a nucleus for the support of the proposed institution. The names of the subscribers give us our earliest clue to the names of the more prominent earliest settlers of Bergen, which title then officially covered not only the settlement inside the palisades but also the districts of Communipaw, Greenville, and Bergen Point; actually all of the present Hudson County reaching from Kill van Kull on the south to the Bergen woods on the north, with the exception of the people of Harsimus and Paulus Hook, who, by reason of propinquity, worshipped in New Amsterdam. This conclusion is more readily assured because none of the names of the settlers of these last named sections appeared on the petition. We think that we may safely deduce, therefore, that the names appearing on this list[1] covered a great proportion of the First Settlers of Bergen, especially as we later trace up the future history of each one and his connection with the future ruling families.

Taking them up in the order written, we find at the top Tielman Van Vleck, Michael Jansen, Harman Smeeman and Caspar Steynmets. These were the Magistrates of Bergen and were given the preference, which was emphasized by their becoming the largest contributors.

TRANSPOSITION OF FAMILY NAMES

At the time of the settlement of New Netherland, surnames were comparatively unknown; many of the family names now in use were not known in the old country as such; out of our list only the names Post, Van Vleck and Steynmets existed as recognized family names, the others being used for a generation only, to be replaced optionally by the father's name, his occupation, or the name of the old home town. The sons took for their last names the names of their fathers, with the syllable "sen" (son) annexed. Thus, Michael Jansen,

[1] See complete list on pages 14 and 15 of HOLLAND SOCIETY YEAR BOOK 1913.

Jansen, son of Jan or John; Gerrit Gerritsen, son of Gerrit; and so on. Sometimes the occupation of the father was continued in his son's name, thus: Jan Bleecker; John the Bleacher, and again the home town was often tacked on to the surname.

In the Vreeland family is found first Michael Jansen, son of Jan or John van Vreeland; then Michael Jansen van Schrabbekerke, the last being the familiar name of the church home town in Zeeland with which he was connected. Upon landing here, he first went to Rensselaerswyck, opposite Albany, and settled on the "Hooge Berg" (High Hill) farm; when he left there to come to New Jersey he was put down as Michael Jansen van der Burgh. Being a plain Dutchman, however, he dropped all the extra titles and stuck to the plain Jansen all the rest of his life. His children were all Michelsons, and it was not until the third generation in this country that the real and original family name was used by all of the Vreelands.

While the choice of family patronymics varied, a method prevailed in the choice of the first name of the children. The first son was almost always named for his paternal grandfather, the second after his maternal grandfather, and after these the uncles were honored. The girl's maternal grandmother was first honored, then the paternal grandmother and so on. This makes it comparatively easy for the genealogist to locate family lines. Certain names were maintained through many generations, such as Adrian, among the Posts; Garret among the Garretsons or Van Wagenens—primarily the same family; Michael among the descendants of the original Michael Jansen Vreeland; Walling in the Van Winkle family; Henry among the Brinkerhoffs, and so on. In one family we find Elias Adrian and Adrian Elias alternating with each succeeding generation for a hundred years and more. Sometimes one can tell by the middle name pretty near who the father was. Thus, John Jacobs was son of Jacob, and so forth. Adrian has been perpetuated in the Adriance family; Reyer in the Ryerson; Pieter in the Petersons; The Dutch Jurriaen, taken for a corruption of of Yurrie, by easy gradations became Yerry, Jerry and Jeremiah or in other instances Uriah; Yerry's son would be called Yearance, and here we have another family name. Anderson, as a family name, sounds Scotch, but the original Andersons were sons of Andries Claussen who married Michael Jansen's daughter Pryntje (Penelope). Johnson is often thought to be of English stock, but Rut Jansen, who settled in Somerset County, is generally credited with being the head of the line. A man named De Gray prided himself on being a Frenchman but his grandfather was De Grauw, which is surely Dutch; Longfield, another English name, was originally Langeveldt.

DUTCH REVERENCE

As one writer has stated, "The Jersey Dutch were a God-fearing people, constant in their church going. These men and women had the strongest kind of faith in the doctrines of their church. Their piety was exemplified in their wills."

Here is one of Nicholas Vreeland, filed in 1757:

> "I, Nicholas Vreeland, being in health of body and a perfect mind and memory blessed of God, therefore, and calling to mind the mortality of my body, and knowing it is appointed for all men to die, do make and ordain this my last will and testament:
> First: I recommend my immortal spirit in the hands of my great Creator, trusting in the merits of the blessed Saviour for pardon and remission of my sins, and a happy admission to the regions of bliss and immortality."

Their simple faith was also often inscribed upon their tombstones:

> "When overwhelmed with grief,
> My heart within me dies;
> Helpless and far from all on earth,
> To Heaven I lift my eyes."

RACE

RACE SUICIDE

Symon Jacobs Van Winkle dying in 1732, left twelve children, and one of these had twenty, of which thirteen survived their father. A story is told of how he started to carve their initials on the front door posts, and running short of space used the stone doorstep to complete his list. There must have been necessitated a roll call at bed time: Abraham, Johannes, Simeon, Jacob, Antje, Feytje, Saertje, Tryntje, Rachel, Jannetje, Lena, Margrietje, Gertje and half a dozen others whose early demise prevented a record of their names.

Michael Jansen had six sons and two daughters. The Vreeland Book records the birth of sixty-three grandchildren among the sons, and it is fair to assume that the two daughters did their share, which would indicate that not less than seventy-five grandchildren perpetuated the memory of the founder of the Vreeland family in this country.

Of the twenty-seven subscribers to the church establishment added to the nine others who were evidently too modest to state an exact sum they would contribute, less than a score seem to have been eligible to the list of "First Settlers" or heads of families, and of these I have been enabled to acquire information of eleven distinct families among the original subscribers and to these I have added four who were equally prominent and eminent in the good work of building up the country later on. In preparing the brief family histories the assistance of representative descendants now living was invoked for details and data. The families whose brief records are given were represented on the petition by: [1]Tielman Van Vleck, Michael Jansen (Vreeland), Caspar Steynmets, Van Winkle, Tallman, Gerrit Gerritsen (Van Wagenen), Paulus Pietersen (Newkirk), Adrian Post, Lourens Andries (Van Buskirk), Jan Cornelius (Van Horn), Claes Arentsen (Sip).

Those

[1] The original list appears on page 19, and a translation on page 14 of the 1913 YEAR BOOK OF THE HOLLAND SOCIETY.

Those whose stories are also related, who came upon the scenes, at subsequent dates, were: Garabrant, Van Reypen, Winner, Brinkerhoff. This by no means ends the list of the settlers, but time forbids us going deeper into the story at this period.

VAN VLECK

Tielman Van Vleck was a descendant of a noble family whose estate, called "Vlieck," was located near the city of Maastricht in the Province of Limburg.

The Tielman Van Vleck of Bergen fame, according to court records of the city of Amsterdam, dated February 23, 1635, is described as being twenty-one years old, and the only child of Tielman Van Vleck and Maria Moors. He married Magdelena Herlin of Bremen, in the church of St. Augustine. Eight children blessed their union. On June 3, 1656, he was enrolled as a shopkeeper of Bremen. The date of his arrival in this country is not obtainable, but it is supposed that he came over on the ship *De Vergulde Bever* (*The Gilded Beaver*), which sailed from Amsterdam May 15, 1658, and arrived at New Amsterdam in July. On July 29, he was licensed as a Notary of New Netherland. On December 16, 1658, he purchased from Mighiel Paulissen, the ancestor of the Vandervoort family, a house and lot on the north side of the Hooge (High) Street, later Stone Street, near what is now Hanover Square. Two petitions drawn up by him and headed by his name were presented to Governor Stuyvesant in 1660, for the establishment of the Village of Bergen but were denied because of the fear of Indian attacks. The third paper, drawn up by Van Vleck and urged in person by Michael Jansen Vreeland, the New Jersey representative in the Council, was agreed to upon promise of having the village surrounded by a strong palisade. Van Vleck was named as the first "Schout," or President, of the court of Bergen. On May 25, 1668, Van Vleck appeared before the Magistrates of the Village of Bergen and declared that he had deeded to Ide Cornelissen, a resident of Harsimus, a parcel of land

land lying between those of Hendrick Jansen van Ostrum and Adrian van Laer. Governor Philip Carteret in 1670 gave him a deed to a plot of upland and meadow between Jan Lubbertsen, Frederick Phillips, Harman Edwards and Thomas Fredericks, facing on the "Common," the present Van Vorst Square. This would locate Van Vleck as a resident of Paulus Hook.

VREELAND

Michael Jansen Vreeland, the common ancestor of the Vreeland family, came from Holland on the ship *Het Wapen van Norwegen* (*Arms of Norway*) in 1638. He owned a farm or polder in South Beveland, one of the islands of the Province of Zeeland, but his church home was in the village of 'sHeer Abtskerke, three miles from his farm, the common name of the village being Schrabbekerke. From here he went to Bergen-op-Zoom, in Brabant, and took boat to Amsterdam, from whence he sailed in May, 1638, and arrived in New Amsterdam on August 4. Arrangements had previously been made with Patroon Killian van Rensselaer, who had been granted a large tract of land surrounding the present site of the city of Albany, on both sides of the Hudson River. Jansen leased the farm known as the "Hooge-Berg," located on an elevation immediately opposite the present city. His latent energy and enterprise were so confined by his work as a farmer that he branched out into fur trading with the Indians, and speedily came into conflict with the parent trust of the hemisphere, the Dutch West India Company.[1] Undismayed, Jansen brought the questions at issue into court and was later sustained on all the counts. Adding to the products of his farm the fish and oysters which were so plentiful in the adjoining waters, he found market in the city opposite and speedily acquired a fortune as fortunes went in those days, which he invested in cattle. When the Dutch colony was settling on the Delaware, Jansen supplied them with part of their cattle. One year after his

coming

[1] "Records of New Amsterdam," Vol. 3, pages 36–41; Vol. 4, page 46.

coming to Communipaw, Governor Peter Stuyvesant took up the reins of government in New Amsterdam, and, being anxious to maintain a representative government, appointed nine advisers, Jansen being made the representative for the west side of the river. He must have proved to be a good adviser, because in 1656 he was offered the Vice-Governorship at Fort Orange, later Albany, but he declined the honor, preferring, evidently, to stay and work for his present constituency. As in Albany, the reputation of the fairness of his dealings with the Indians made him popular in Communipaw; his friendship with the red men acted in his favor during the awful times of 1655, when his family was exempted from capture or death.

VAN WINKEL

JACOB WALIGH, WALINGS, WALINGEN or WALINGSEN and his brother Symon were among the very first farmers to permanently locate in New Netherland. Symon's untimely death[1] cut short this branch of the Walicks family, who were residents of the Village of Winkel in North Holland, located about fifteen miles northwest of Hoorn, as far back as the beginning of the fourteenth century.[2] Jacob, the progenitor of the Van Winkle family in New Netherland, was the occupant of one of the six Company-Bouweries on Manhattan Island started by the Dutch West India Company in 1624[3] and continued by the Company in May, 1630, under new management. An inventory of Jacob's possessions on July 2, 1631, indicates that he had on his farm six saddle horses, two stallions, six cows, two bulls and twenty-two sheep, and that he was successful with his breeding of cattle. He made a trip to Holland for the purpose of further stocking his farm, in 1633, in the ship *De Soutbergh* on its return trip, after bringing the new Governor, Wouter Van Twiller, to

[1] Symon Wallingsen was murdered by an Indian at Paulis Hook, in Pavonia, in the spring of 1649.

[2] See Van Winkle Record, page 21.

[3] A document giving the inventory of the Company's farms on July 2, 1631, showing increase since May, 1630, drawn up by Kiliaen Van Rensselaer, was recently discovered by L. P. de Boer, Historian, among the documents in the Archives at the Hague.

to New Netherland in April, 1633. While at Hoorn he united with the Dutch Church by certificate on December 18, 1633.[1] His stay in Hoorn was short, for in the fall of the next year Jacob Walingsen returned to New Netherland on *De Coninck David* (*King David*) captained by David de Vries, arriving at New Amsterdam in June, 1635, a little over a year prior to the expiration of his lease of the Company's-Bouwerie No. 5.[2] During his absence the bouwerie was managed by Claes Cornelisz Swits.[3] After the expiration of his lease, Jacob Walingsen entered into a contract with Patroon Kiliaen Van Rensselaer, August 15, 1636, and settled on a farm at Rensselaerswyck. On October 1, 1650, he returned to Manhattan, although offered the choice of several farms if he would remain in the colony.

August 29, 1641, Jacob Walingsen was appointed a member of the Board, "The Twelve Men," the first representative official body within the limits of New York and New Jersey. This Board was advisory to Governor Kieft and represented the inhabitants of Manhattan, Brooklyn and Pavonia in the consideration of the general treatment of the Indians.

Prior to 1635, Jacob Walingsen led a movement to establish a settlement on the Connecticut River,[4] but, because of the lack of support of his contemporaries and failure to obtain permission of the West India Company, owing to fear of Indian attack, the project was abandoned. October 23, 1654, he secured a grant of land at Pavonia, now Jersey City, New Jersey, where the family has been continuously represented for eleven generations.

Jacob Walingsen died in the early part of the year 1657, leaving a widow, Trintje Jacobs, and six minor children, three girls and three boys. Michael Jansen

Vreeland

[1] In the records of the Dutch Church at Hoorn appears the following entry, under that date: "Have come over with certificate from other Churches to our congregation—Jacob Walingen of New Netherland."

[2] For a description of the bouwerie No. 5, see "Valentine's Manual" for 1860, pages 557, 558.

[3] Whose murder in 1641 was the chief cause of the first recorded Indian War. HOLLAND SOCIETY YEAR BOOK 1914, page 11.

[4] See HOLLAND SOCIETY YEAR BOOK 1914, page 25.

Vreeland and Burgomaster Van der Grift[1] were appointed guardians of the children.

The Van Winkle line from the first progenitor in New Netherland to the Recording Secretary of The Holland Society is as follows: Jacob Walingsen Van Winkle, one of the Board of Twelve Men, member of the General Court in 1640, and Trintje Jacobs; Jacob Jacobse Van Winkle and Grietje Hendrickse Hellingh; Hendrick Van Winkle and Catrina Waldron; Jacob Van Winkle, 1st Lieutenant in Captain Nicausa Terhune's Company of Militia in the Precinct of New Barbadoes, 1775–1778, deacon of the First Dutch Church in New Jersey chartered by the Crown and incorporated under the name of The Ministry Elders and Deacons, December 20, 1771, and Rachel Cammega; Daniel Van Winkle and Antje Winne; Jacob D. Van Winkle and Antje Vreeland; Jacob Van Winkle, who served in the War of 1812, and Maria Sip, daughter of Colonel Garret Sip; Edward Van Winkle, who served in the Civil War—Company G—37th Regiment of New York, and Mary Jane Wandle; Edward Van Winkle, Recording Secretary of The Holland Society of New York, and Sama Le Roy Batdorf.

STEYNMETS

Caspar Steynmets was born in Holland; it is said at Schiedam, but the exact time or place has not been authenticated. He arrived in New Amsterdam in 1631 and with his brother sailed up the river to Albany, and there became prominent in trading with the Indians. His oldest child, named after him, was baptized in 1650; his wife being Dorothea Arentsen (Van Wagenen). At her death he married again Jennetje Gerritsen (Van Wagenen) of Ahasimus. He therefore became connected by marriage with both of the distinct branches of the Van Wagenen family, that of Esopus and that of Bergen. Steynmets purchase a plot of land on Winkle Street, near Fort Amsterdam. In 1652, he removed to New Jersey and purchased a "Bouwery" in Ahasimus. Here he combined the two businesses of farming and

trading

[1] Burgomaster Van der Grift of Nieuw Amsterdam.

trading and became well-to-do. The Indian troubles forced him back to New Amsterdam but he returned in 1658 and lived within the Bergen Township limits until his death in 1702. All of his children were baptized in the old church at the fort. He was organizer of a company of militia and was commissioned lieutenant and later became captain. He was well educated and his knowledge of the Indian language made him valuable as an interpreter in their dealings with the whites. After the English occupation in 1664, he was continued in office by Governor Philip Carteret, having previously been made a judge by Governor Stuyvesant. In 1671, he was married, for the third time, to the widow of Michael Tades, and moved to her farm in Ahasimus. At her death he gave the home farm to his sons John and Gerrit, but continued to live in the homestead until his death. He was buried in the old Bergen cemetery. John Steynmets willed his portion of the farm to his sister, Joanna Prior, and she in turn gave it to her son, Jacob Prior.

VAN BUSKIRK

The common ancestor of the Van Buskirk family in this country was Laurens Andriessen, who came over in 1655. His name appears as an owner of a lot on Broad Street, New Amsterdam, June 29, 1656. Shortly after he purchased land in Minkakwa, later Greenville. In 1668, he was appointed "Recorder and Marker" for Minkakwa, and in 1676 was appointed "Marker General" for the Town of Bergen. He was commissioned a member of the Court of Bergen in 1677 and was made president of the same in 1681. He married Jannetje Jans, widow of Christian Barentsen in 1658. He died in 1694. His son, Pieter, born in 1666, married Trintje Harmanse of Constable Hook, and went there to live in the house which was torn down only last year. He was the ancestor of the Van Buskirks of Bergen, later Hudson County.

TALLMAN

TALLMAN

The original spelling of this name was *Taelman*, and occasionally *Talma*, which literally translated means a linguist or an interpreter. The early records of the Dutch branch of the family in this country are found under the patronymics of Harmens, Harmense, Hermzen, Harmenszen, Dowsa, Douwens and Douwenszen.

The first known American ancestor of this branch of the family was Douwe Harmense Taelman, who with his wife and children emigrated from the province of Friesland, Netherland, in the ship *Brownfish*, arriving in New Amsterdam on the 19th of June, 1658. While in the "Records of New Amsterdam" he is mentioned as having been in the courts upon different matters in the years 1658 and 1659, we have reason to believe he took up his residence at Bergen, now a part of Jersey City, soon after his arrival in this country. For we also find in the same records that in the description of a plot of land he bought on the east side of "Heere Gracht" (Broad Street), in New Amsterdam, on August 2, 1662, he is mentioned as being a resident of Bergen. And in December of the same year he subscribed six florins a year for the support of a minister at this latter place.[1]

In an official survey of some plots or tracts of land "in the new maize lands," made by Jacques Cortelyou, C.E.,[2] for Douwe Harmense in November, 1660, lying in and about the Town of Bergen, preparatory to making an application for a patent for the same, the name of *Bergen* was first used; and the patent for such plots was granted by Governor Philip Carteret for some five parcels under date of May 12, 1668. This same patentee later secured a further patent for lands embracing the present village of Nyack, N. Y.

Douwe Harmense Taelman died at Bergen and was buried on the nineteenth of June, 1687. A declaration of his will was recorded in the office of the Secretary of

State

[1] See 1913 YEAR BOOK OF THE HOLLAND SOCIETY, page 18.

[2] See 1914 YEAR BOOK OF THE HOLLAND SOCIETY, page 3.

State, at Trenton, N. J.[1] All his property was left to his two sons, Harmen Douwenszen Taelman and Thunis Douwenszen Taelman, who soon after their father's death removed to Nyack, N. Y. The older son, Harmen, died early in life, and previous to April, 8, 1691; as on this date his widow was married to Abraham Blauvelt. The younger son, Thunis, finally came into possession of most of the estate left by his father, and died at Nyack, N. Y., July 17, 1739. From these two sons have descended most of the families bearing the name of Tallman, Talman, or Taulman. And while in their early history they resided in the vicinity of New York City, they may now be found in nearly every section of the United States.

VAN WAGENEN

Wageningen is one of the prominent towns of Holland, located on the banks of the River Rhine, in the Province of Gelderland, and is noted as a summer resort. The family in this country has descended from two distinct pioneers, so far as we know in no way related. The first was Aert Jacobsen, who came over about 1648 and settled in Bethlehem, New York, and later in Esopus. The Van Wagenens of that section are his descendants.

Gerrit Gerritsen, of Bergen fame, arrived in New Amsterdam with his wife Annetje Hermans, December 23, 1660, and settled in Communipaw. He soon took a leading part in public affairs. He brought with him a certificate which reads as follows:

> "We, Burgomasters, schepens, and counsellors of the city of Wageningen, declare by these presents that there appeared before us Hendrick Elissen and Jordiz Speer, citizens of this city, at the request of Gerrit Gerritsen and Annetje Hermans, his wife.
>
> "They have testified and certified as they do by these presents that they have good knowledge of the above-named Gerritsen and Annetje Hermans, his wife, as to their life and conversation, and that they have always

[1] In Liber 3 of Deeds, etc., page 144.

always been considered and esteemed as pious and honest people, and that no complaint of any evil or disorderly conduct has ever reached their ears; on the contrary, they have always led quiet, pious and honest lives as it becomes pious and honest persons. They especially testify, that they govern their family well, and bring up their children in the fear of God and in all modesty and respectability. As the above-named persons have resolved to remove and proceed to New Netherland, in order to find greater convenience, they give this attestation, grounded on their knowledge of them, having known them intimately and having been in continual intercourse with them for many years, living in the same neighborhood.

"In testimony of the truth, we, the burgomasters, of the city, have caused the private seal of the city to be hereto affixed.

"Done at Wageningen, 27th of November, 1660.

"By the ordinance of the same,

J. Aquelin."

NEWKIRK

It is not positively known from which of the many towns in Holland called "Niewekerke" the particular ancestor of this family came, but it is generally believed that he was from Nijkerk, or Nieuwekerke, in Gelderland, from whence also came the Van Rensselaers, Van Twillers, and Van Curlers. As an eloquent writer puts it: "Here, in the midst of tobacco lands, pretty gardens and grain fields, three-fourths of an hour's walk from the Zuyder Zee; from this ancient home came scores of the ancestors of the people of New Netherland. These hardy sons and daughters of the Dutch Republic were true argonauts. They sailed away to cover the soil of New Netherland with a golden fleece."

Guert Cornelissen Van Nieuwkerke came over in the ship *Moesman* from Holland, arriving on April 15, 1659.

Matthew Cornelissen, the common ancestor of the Bergen families of Newkirks was, according to Dr. A. B. Newkirk

A. B. Newkirk, the family historian, a brother of Guert; but Thomas J. Newkirk, a worker in the genealogical field, insists that he was Guert's son. It is reported that in 1659, Guert came with his wife and a son twelve years old and a "nursing child." Matthew marrying in 1670, is supposed to have been the oldest child, rather than the brother. He went first to Flatbush, Long Island, where he bought a farm bordering on Corlear's Flats. In 1665, he sold this and moved to Bergen. Five years later he married Anna, daughter of Jacob Luby, who had served under the West India Company. His wife died in 1685, and the next year he married Catherine, daughter of Paulus Pietersen. His lineal descendants still live on the original house site, the present building having been erected in 1810.

POST

Adrian Post was the pioneer of this family, and he arrived in this country from the Hague, Holland, in 1650, and settled in Communipaw. He was very prominent in public affairs in Staten Island till 1655 and then settled in New Jersey. He was elected ensign of the first militia company, under Captain Caspar Steynmets. His son Adrian married, in 1677,[1] Catrintje Gerrits, daughter of Gerrit Gerritsen (Van Wagenen). The other sons went out to Acquackanonck, and the numerous families of that name in Bergen and Passaic Counties are descended from these. The Post homestead site on the shores of New York Bay is still occupied as a home, in which, until very recent years, resided a lineal descendant of one of Bergen's First Settlers.

VAN HORN

In North Holland the once famous city of Hoorn is situated on the Zuyder Zee, about twenty miles north of Amsterdam. From this place came Jan Cornelissen to New Amsterdam about 1645. He settled in Hackensack and here raised a family, some of his descendants continuing

[1] See Holland Society Year Book 1914, page 59, entry 29.

continuing in the Hackensack section, and others going to Communipaw, where land is still owned by members of the family. Cornelissen's son Joris (George) married Maria Rutgers, and in his turn his oldest son married a granddaughter of Michael Jansen Vreeland.

SIP

This old Dutch family has been continuously located in New Jersey, for two and a half centuries, and seven generations have been born in one house. This house was built in 1664, and is still occupied by a lineal descendant of the founder of the family, Adrian Hendricksen Sip. He came from Breda, Holland, in 1641, and joined the church in Bergen in 1666. The homes of the period were usually one-story structures, built of stone or wood, or both. As in the old country, the gable ends generally were turned to the road. This, in old country custom, was done to conserve the rain water supply for washing purposes, and also that the snow would not fall on the people passing, a consideration not so generally exercised nowadays. Adrian Sip married, first, Countess Gritje Warnants van Schoneveldt and second, Geertruje Aurians. Among the children, Antje married Simon Jacobs Van Winkle. Jan Arianse, the second son, was an important and influential personage in the town of Bergen; he served in the militia, as did his son Ide. Ide's son, Garret, had a son, Peter, who was a prominent jurist, serving as Judge in both Bergen and Hudson Counties. He was one of the earliest supporters of the Republican party, founded in 1856. His son, Richard, followed in his father's footsteps in position and politics, and his son, Richard Garret Sip, now occupies the old homestead. Rumor has it that when Light Horse Harry Lee came from Hackensack to Bergen he stopped at the Sip homestead stables, and, by force of arms, exchanged his wornout horse for a fresher and better one. Three spies were hung on the old willow tree in front of the house.

GARRABRANT

GARRABRANT

Gerbrand Claussen was a man of much influence in Bergen and held many official positions. He married a daughter of Claus Pieterson Cos, whose name will be found on the original petition. About 1657, Cos purchased a part of the farm of Jan Evertson Bout at Communipaw. Claussen's children lived on the original farm for many years, but the original settler in 1689 moved to Dutchess County, New York. Some of his descendants moved to Pequannock. Two of his sons and one daughter married Van Ripens, one a Merselis, one son wed a Prior, one a Van Winkle, and a daughter married a Van Wagenen, thereby linking up a number of the old leading families of that day and generation.

VAN REYPEN

Jurian Tomassen was the common ancestor of the family which now spells its name in the various forms of Van Reypen, Van Ripen, and Van Riper, and also of the Yearance family. He sailed to this country in the ship *De Bonte Coe* (*The Spotted Cow*) from Amsterdam on April 16, 1663.[1] There is a place called Rypend in Friesland and another called De Ryp in North Holland, and Tomassen came from one of these, and most likely the latter. After arriving in this country, Tomassen first went further west and in 1664 he was a member of a syndicate which secured the Acquackanonck patent in what is now Passaic County. He did not settle there permanently, but at least one of his sons, Harman, and other descendants settled there later. Tomassen came to the settlement of Bergen between 1664 and 1667 and acquired the plot which has been continuously occupied by some of his descendants to the present day, viz., lot 161 in the survey of 1660 of Bergen[2] and Buyten Tuyn, and which is now known as 311 Academy Street, at the intersection of Academy and Van Reypen Streets. Tomassen was recorded as a

[1] See Holland Society Year Book 1902, page 25.

[2] See map 1914 Year Book of The Holland Society, page 3.

a member of the Bergen Church in 1667. In addition to the above plot, he acquired other land, both within the stockade and among the Out Gardens, under the will of Guert Coerten, dated 1671. He married Reycke Hermens, May 25, 1667. They had ten children, five sons and five daughters. The sons, following the custom of the time, took as a surname one constructed from the father's given name. Juriaense, Jurjanse and Jurijaense are various forms in which it was spelled in the old church records. With some later descendants this was gradually changed into Jurrianse, then Yereance. The line of descent from Juriaen Tomassen to his descendants who now occupy the old homestead, is through his second son: Gerrit Juriaense, Jurijaense or Jurjanse (1670–1748). The name is spelled in all the three ways in the church records. Cornelis Gerretsen or Jurrianse (1707–1771), fourth son of Gerrit; Daniel Van Reypen (1736-1818), second son of Cornelis; Cornelius Van Reypen (1767–1842), eldest son of Daniel; Cornelius C. Van Reypen (1813–1900), eighth child and youngest son of Cornelius. Surgeon General Wm. K. Van Reypen, U. S. N., retired; only surviving son of C. C. The homestead is now occupied by the youngest daughter of Cornelius C., Mrs. Anna Van Reypen Green. In the old records of the Bergen church the first appearance of this new name is under the date of October, 1761, when the witnesses to a baptism are given as "Daniel Van Rype" and his sister, "Beeletje Van Rype." In February, 1762, Merytye Van Rype is noted as a witness. In December, 1762, was recorded the birth and baptism of Catrientye, the eldest child of Daniel Van Reype and Elisabet Terheun. (Daniel was the second son of Cornelis.) It appears that the only ones to use the spelling Van Reypen were those most closely associated with the Bergen homestead. Other descendants use some of the many other forms. Van Riper seems to be the form used by the greatest number of the present descendants of Juriaen Tomassen, although Van Ripen would seem to have been the most logical form.

WINNE

WINNE

So little is recorded of the early history of this old Bergen family, that we are only permitted to note that the founder, Peter Winne, came from Ghent in Flanders in 1650. His wife's name was Jannetje Adams. His grandson, Martin, went to Albany to live for a while but returned to Bergen, and the family then descended, generation by generation, to Johan, Martin, Martin, Johan, Martin, John and then John again, who now lives on what the march of the city's improvement has left of the old home farm.

BRINKERHOFF

Joris Dircksen Brinkerhoff, the founder of the family, came from Drenthe, Holland, about 1638. He settled in Staten Island, but was driven out by the Indians, and went to Long Island; his oldest son was killed by the red men; his second son, Hendrick, bought land in Bergen in 1667, and his descendants still live there. Hendrick's son, Cornelius, married Aegie Vreeland; the next generation brought Hartman; Hartman's son, Hendrick, married Lea Van Wagenen and their son, Hartman, married Eleanor Clendenny; Hartman's son, John, married Hannah Tise, and from this union came Ex-Senator William Brinkerhoff and Henry, father of Brigadier-General Henry Brinkerhoff, a former Vice-President of The Holland Society.

BURIALS

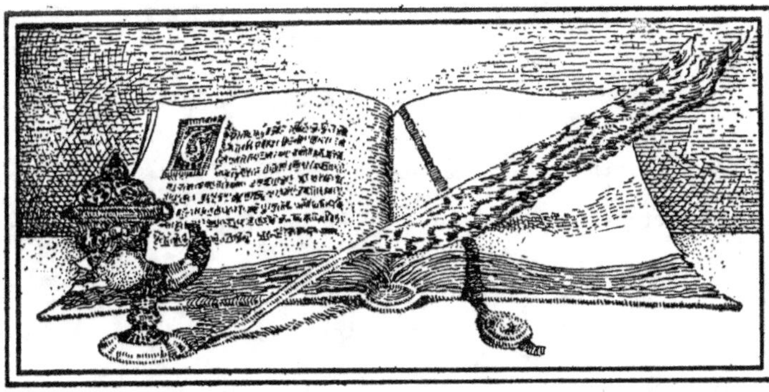

BURIALS IN THE VILLAGE OF BERGEN IN NEW JERSEY BEGINNING 1666

1666

NO. Names of the [Persons] who have died and were buried within the jurisdiction of Bergen and around New York by me R. Van Giesen, in my capacity of Undertaker (Aanspreker).

1 March 4. Bur. Michiel Teunisen at Bergen.

2 May 14. Bur. at Bergen the wife of Jan J——, living at Pemmerepoch.

3 September 20. Bur. the ch. of Beltel Lot, at Bergen.

4 December 26. Bur. the ch. of Douwe Hermensen, at Bergen.

1667

5 October 30. Bur. the ch. of Christiaen Pieters at Bergen.

1668

6 January 16. Bur. Lourus Duyts at Bergen.

7 February 27. Bur. the ch. of Jan Evertse Kerseboom, at Bergen.

8 May 1. Bur. the ch. of Jan Maurits at Bergen.

9 May 5. Bur. Willem Spenser at Bergen.

10 July 29. Bur. the ch. of Hendrick Reycke at Bergen.

11 September 20. Bur. the ch. of Elyas Magiels Vreeland.

1668 NO.

12 October 4. Bur. Lysbet Dircks, wi. of Hermen Smeeman, at Bergen.

13 October 12. Bur. Cristiaen Claesen.

14 October 18. Bur. ch. of Arien Van Laer.

15 December 23. Bur. Echtje Jacobs, wi. of Dirck Claesen Braeck, living at——.

1669

16 April 10. Bur. Merritje ——, wi. of Jan Maurits, at Bergen.

17 September 16. Bur. ch. of Jan Evers ——.

18 October 18. Bur. ch. of Jan Mic ——.

19 November 6. Bur. ch. of Mr. ——.

1670

20 January 12. Bur. Jannetje ——, wi. of Casper Steynmets, at Bergen.

21 March 7. Bur. Is——yse——.

22 April 24. Bur. ch. of ——ich Corne——.

23 May 11. Bur. Getruyt ——, wi. of Jocob Lub, at Bergen.

24 May 14. Bur. ch. of ——.

25 June 28. Bur. ——igge ——eymets.

26 October 17. ——Anna D.

27 October. Bur. da. of Tomas Teckh at Bergen.

1672?

28 March 24. Bur. ch. of English woman, living with Willem Dogelis at Pemmerepoch, at Bergen.

29 June 16. Bur. Roelof Cornelisse at Bergen.

1673

30 May 6. Bur. ch. of R. Van Giesen at Bergen.

31 September 14. Bur. ch. of Jan Lubberts at Bergen.

NO. 1673

32 October 16. Bur. ch. of Mr. Sa. Edsall at Bergen.

33 October 29. Bur. ch. of Hertman Magiels at Bergen.

34 December 19. Bur. ch. of Lourus Arents Toers at Bergen.

35 December 19. Bur. ch. of Poulus Pietersz at Bergen.

1674

36 January 8. Bur. Arent Louersen Toers at Bergen.

37 August 23. Bur. at Bergen Jan Lubberts, son of Lubbert Lubberts, of Hackensack.

38 October 16. Bur. son of Douwen Hermesen Talma, at Bergen.

1675

39 April 7. Bur. ch. of Elias Magiels Vreelant at Bergen.

1677

40 January 3. Bur. Cornelis Abrahams, living at Pemmerepoch, at Bergen.

41 February 18. Bur. Cap. Adriaen Post at Bergen.

42 March 18. Bur. ch. of Matys Mulder at Bergen.

43 May 12. Bur. Treyntje Jacobs, wi. of Casper Steynmets, at New York.

44 October 13. Bur. ch. of Hartman Magiels at Bergen.

1678

45 January 16. Bur. Engelbert Steenhuys, living at Bergen, and bur. there, the first with the pall.

46 July 20. Bur. da. of Hendrick Tonise, the second with the pall, at Bergen.

47 December 9. Bur. newly born infant of Jan Straetmaker, at Bergen.

1679 NO.

48 January 5. Bur. Jannetje Hendricks, wi. of Hermen Eduwaerts, at Bergen, the third with the pall.

49 May 8. Bur. Gerrit Fransen, son of Geertruyt Gerrits, of Pemmerpoch, the fourth with the pall, at Bergen.

50 May 12. Bur. son of Maddaleentje Hansen, wid. of Hendrick Jansen Spier, at Pemmerpoch.

51 June 10. Bur. ch. of Matys Mulder.

1680

52 January 24. Bur. son of Matheus Cornelisz, the sixth with the pall.

53 August 1. Bur. ——, wi. of Pieter Merselisz, seventh with the pall.

54 October 11. Bur. Geertruy Gerrits —— Cornelis Abrahams, having lived at Pemmerepoch, eighth with pall.

55 October 21. Bur. da. of Arien Pietersz Bu——, ninth with pall.

1681

56 March 1. Bur. ch. of Sjarel Mackleeyn.

57 March 30. Bur. Feytje Roelofs, wid. of Joost Van der Linden, has lived at Pemmerepoch, tenth with pall.

58 April 30. Bur. Hermen Eduwaertsz, eleventh with pall.

1682

59 June 28. Bur. da. of Lourens Arense Toers, twelfth with pall.

60 August 1. Bur. da. of Enoch Magielsz Vreeland, the second in the church; thirteenth with pall.

61 September 4. Bur. da. of Hendrick Van Reenen, fourteenth with pall.

62 September 4. Bur. Pieter Mercelisze, third in the church at Bergen, fifteenth with pall.

63 September 8. Bur. son of Claes Janse, the fourth in church, sixteenth with pall.

NO. 1682

64 October 9. Bur. Anna Claes, wid. of Arent Louersen Toers, seventeenth with pall.

65 October 16. Bur. newly born infant of Jurijaan Thomasen, the fifth in the church.

1683

66 March 8. Bur. newly born infant of Johannes Magielsz Vreeland.

67 June 21. Bur. Maeckje Baltusen, da. of Baltus Barentsen, the sixth in church; eighteenth with pall; first with bell ringing.

68 August 6. Bur. wi. of Mr. Willem Dougels, nineteenth with pall.

69 October 1. Bur. son of Gerrit Van Reenen, twentieth with pall.

70 October 17. Bur. son of Jan Adansen, twenty-first with pall.

71 December 28. Bur. Ide Cornelisz Van de Voorst, at New York, with pall, of Bergen; twenty-second with pall.

1684

72 January 5. Bur. Evert Nolde, seventh in church; 23rd with pall.

73 January 11. Bur. Carel Carelsz, Y. M., 24th with pall, at Bergen.

74 May 29. Bur. both newly born infants of Tonis Roelofs.

75 June 7. Bur. ch. of Cornelis Claesz, the eighth in the church.

76 November 16. Bur. two ch. of Sjarel Mackleeyn, 25th with pall.

77 November 29. Bur. ch. of Francoys De Smidt.

78 December 2. Bur. Aertje Gerrits, wi. of Hermen Koerten, 26th with pall; ninth in the church, at Bergen.

1685

79 January 13. Newly born infant of Francoys De Smidt.

80 October 17. The son of Gerbrandt Claesz, tenth in church, 27th with pall.

1685 NO.

81 December 20. Anna Lubi, wi. of Matheus Cornelisz, 28th with pall. (82 deaths.)

1686

82 May 4. Cateleyntje Koetere, wi. of Francoys De Smidt, 29th with pall.

83 June 22. Son of Leysbeth Jacobs, wid. of Wybrant Abrahamse, living at New York, 30th with pall.

84 September 23. Gerrit Dirckse Straetmaker, son of Jan Dirckse Straetmaker, at Bergen; 31st with pall.

85 October 1. Thomas Louwersz, son of Louwerus A Toers, at Bergen, 32nd with pall.

86 October 10. Johannes, son of Lourus Arentse Toers, at Bergen, 33rd with pall.

87 October 20. Francoys De Smidt at Bergen, 34th with pall.

1687

88 June 19. Douwe Hermense Talma, the eleventh in church, 35th with pall.

1688

89 April 26. Son of Jan Ariaansen Sip, twelfth in church, 36th with pall.

90 July 8. Son of Baltus Barents Van Kleeck, named Pieter, at Bergen, 37th with pall.

91 July 30. Sjarel Mackeleyn's son, at Bergen; 38th with pall.

92 August 14. Da. of Gerrit Steynmets, the 13th in the church; 39th with pall.

93 August 15. Jacob Jansen Kleumpje, Y. M., having lived at Gemoenepa, with Andries Preyer; 40th with pall.

94 August 30. Pieter Hessels from Bergen, 41st. with pall.

95 October 5. Dierckje Meyers, wi. of Enoch Michiels Vreelant, the 14th in church; 42nd with pall.

96 November 8. Vroutje Claes, wi. of Gerrit Steynmets, living at Ahasymes, 43rd with pall.

NO.

97 November 9. Son of Jo Michelsz Vreelant, living at Ackquechge. 1688

98 November 24. Da. of Gerrit Steynmets, 16th in the church.

99 November 30. Claes Jansen Kuyper, living at Ahasymus, the 17th in church; 44th with pall.

1689

100 February 2. Da. of Matheus Cornelisen, at Bergen.

101 August 25. Da. of Tonis Roelofs at Tappaen.

102 September 11. Gerritje Cornelis Van Nes, wi. of Jacob Lubi, living at Bergen.

103 October 11. Arien Thomasen, living at Achquechnonk, 46th with pall; 18th in the church, at Bergen.

104 November 9. Lysbeth Cornelis, wid. of Jan Van Rossen, bur. by the deaconry; 47th with pall.

105 November 26. Hermen Koerten, 19th in the church; 48th with pall.

106 December 8. Son of Cornelis Van Voorst, 20th in the church; 49th with pall.

1690

107 March 31. Newly born infant of Hertman Michiels Vreelant.

108 May 6. Newly born infant of Johannes Jansen, at Achquechnonk.

109 May 9. Son of Thomas Cerven, smith at Bergen.

110 May 23. Hans, son of Matys Mulder, 50th with pall.

111 July 22. Mary Karpis, wi. of Michel Diercks, son of Dirck Tonise and Jannitje Michiels Vreelant, 51st with pall.

112 October 29. The ch. of Abraham Ackerman, at Bergen.

113 October 31. Da. of Catryna Gerrits, wid. of Adriaan Post, 52nd with pall.

114 December 13. Willem Hendricks, son of Sophia Van Ackersloot (?) at Bergen, 53rd with pall.

1691 NO.

115 January 17. Son of Matheus Cornelisen at Bergen.

116 March 28. Benjamin Steynmetz, Y. M., at Bergen.

117 April 16. Jan Seylder, having lived with Annetje Cornelis, wid. of Claes Jansen, at Ahasymus; 55th with pall.

118 May 15. Jannetje, da. of Matheus Cornelisse; 56th with pall.

119 May 17. Neeltje Ariaans Sip, wid. 57th with pall.

120 June 7. Cornelis Matheusse, son of Matheus Cornelisse, at Bergen, 58th with pall.
(From now on six guilders for an adult; for a ch. one-half as much.) This refers to the hire for the pall.

121 June 11. Jacob Lubi, living at Bergen, widr. of Gerritje Cornelis; 59th with pall.

122 September 29. The da. of Abraham Mes——.

123 October 25. Dirck Fransz, who has been wrecked with his boat; 60th with pall.

1692

124 January 15. Mr. Gerrit Gerr—— van Gilde, at Bergen; 21st in the church; 61st with pall.

125 January 15. Michiel Hertmans Vreelant, son of Hertman Michielsz Vreelant; 62nd with pall.

126 January 28. Dierck Claesen Kuyper, son of the late Claes Jansen Kuyper, at Bergen; 22nd in church; 63rd with pall.

127 February 5. Joris Hendricks, son of Hendrick Jorisz; 23rd in the church; 64th with the pall.

128 April 21. Newly born infant of Jacob Jacobsz.

129 June 2. Aeltje Daniels, wi. of Jacob Jacobs Van Winckel; 65th with pall.

1693

130 March 26. Dierck Claesz Braeck, has lived at Gemonepa; 24th in church; 66th with pall.

131 May 18. Reynier, son of Isacq Van Giesen.

1694

NO.
132 January 24. Samuel Hendricks; 67th with pall.

133 February 28. Hendrick Jansen Ralewyn, Y. M., at Bergen; 68th with pall.

134 May 26. Claes Arentse Toers' son, named Arend; 69th with pall.

1695

135 April 11. The ch. of Catryn Jans, da. of Jan Lubbertsz, which ch. was born dead in the earlier part of night on Tuesday, April 9th.

136 June 2. The da. of Gerrit Steynmets at Bergen; the 25th in ch.

137 August 7. Gerrit Pietersen, son of the late Pieter Hesselsen at Bergen. The 70th with pall.

138 September 12. Juriaan Tomasen. The 26th in the church; the 71st with pall.

1696

139 January 24. The da. of Abraham Ackerman at Bergen.

140 May 16. Cornelia Jans Ralewyn, wi. of Jan Willemsz Gesscher, at Bergen. 72nd with pall.

141 September 7. Annetje Hermens wi. of Gerrit Gerritsen; 73rd with pall. 27th in the church.

142 September 28. Ysbrand Eldersen, widower of Neeltje, 74th with pall.

143 October 2. Newly born infant of Lourus A. Toers, at Bergen.

1697

144 February 28. Geurt Gerritse, at Bergen, 75th with pall.

145 September 7. Son of Gerbrand Claesen, named Gerbrand. 76th with pall.

146 September 22. Ariaantje Michielse Vreeland, Y. D. at Bergen. 77th with pall.

147 October 17. Feytje Hertmans, wid. of Michiel Jansen Vreeland, at Bergen. 78th with pall.

1697 NO.

148 October 28. Willempje Waernaers at Constable's Hook, wi. of Hans Hermense. 79th with pall.

149 November 20. Grietje Wessels, 2nd wi. of Enoch M. Vreeland, at Bergen. 80th with pall.

1698

150 March 2. Hielitje Aerts, wi. of Berte——aesen, living at Pemmerepog. 28th in church. 81st with pall.

151 June 9. Aeltje Jacobs, wi. of Poulus Douwesen, at Pemmerepoch, bur. at Constable's Hook. 82nd with pall.

152 October. Hans Didericks, who died September 30th, Friday noon, between 12 and 1 o'clock, at Bergen. 83rd with pall.

153 October 17. Dierckje Cornelis, wi. of R. Van Giesen, voorleser, at Bergen. 84th with pall.

154 October 22. Grietje Samuels, wi. of Hendrick Teunisen Hellingh. 85th with pall.

155 November 16. Andries Preyers. 86th with pall.

156 December 20. Annetje Hansen, wi. of Claes Hertmans Vreeland, at Constable's Hook. 87th with pall.

157 December 24. Claes, son of Jan Claesen. 29th in the church. 88th with pall.

158 December 26. Son of William Day. Number of deaths 160.

1699

159 March 30. Jerimes——, bur. at the expense of Jo. Steynmets. 89th with pall.

160 October 12. Cornelis Meyer, son of the late Jo. Meyer and Annetje Van Vorst. 30th in the church. 90th with pall.

161 December 26. Da. of Wander Didericks, named Annetje. 91st with pall.

1700

162 February 11. Geesje Gerrits, wi. of Jan Straetmaker. 92nd with pall.

163 February 12. Newly born infant of Uldrick Brouwer.

NO. 1700

164 April 3. Son of Abel Reddenhars.

165 October 26. Hans Hermensen, at Constable's Hook.

166 November 11. Bertel Claesen. 31st in the church. 93rd with pall.

1701

167 February 18. Mosis Suxbery, who was killed, February 17th, by a tree in the cedar swamp; and bur. by order of Jan Gedi.

168 July 22. Rev. Selyns, at New York in the church, in front of the space set apart for baptism (doophuisje). He was bur. on Tuesday afternoon, and died in the Lord on Saturday afternoon, July 19th.

169 August 17. Guert Koerten; 32nd in church. 94th with pall.

1702

170 March 5. Treyntje Maertens, wi. of Paulus Pietersen. 95th with pall.

171 May 19. Tomas Fredericksen. 96th with pall.

172 May 25. Arien, son of Frederick Tomasen. 97th with pall.

173 June 7. Catheleyntje, da. of Claes A. Toers. 98th with pall.

174 June 28. Anna Claes, da. of Claes Arentse Toers. 99th with pall.

175 September 18. Joanna Steynmets, wid. of Andries Preyers, died at New York. 100th with pall.

176 December 10. Merritje Ariaense, wid. of Tomas Fredricksen. 101st with pall.

177 December 18. Poulus Pietersen, widower of Tryntje Martens. 102nd with pall.

1703

178 March 26. Reynier, son of Isaac Van Giesen. 103rd with pall.

179 April 5. Arien Claesen, Y. M., bro. of Cap. Gerbrant Claesen. 104th with pall.

180 April 6. Gerrit Gerritsen, widower of Annetje Hermens. The 33rd in the church. 105th with pall.

181 June 19. Cap. Gerbrand Claesen, by his life, Captain of a company of foot soldiers, at Bergen. 106th with pall.

1703 NO.

182 October 7. Geertruyt, da. of Robbert Sickels. 107th with pall.

183 October 19. Feytje, da. of Abel Riddenhars. 108th with pall.

184 November 24. Hendrick, son of Abel Riddenhars.

1704

185 January 19. Newly born son of Gerrit Jurijans. The 34th in the church.

186 April 17. Jacob Van Giesen, drowned April 13, and fished up April 15. 109th with pall.

187 August 30. Son of Rutger Van Hooren, living at Pemmerepoch. 110th with pall.

188 September 21. Claes Pietersen Cos, living at Gemonepa. 35th in the church. 111th with pall.

1705

189 January 30. Jacobus Croeger, Y. M. at Constable's Hook, by order of Mr. Andries Boskerck.

190 February 3. Jan Arentse Van de Bilt at Bergen. 112th with pall.

191 May 12. Matheus Cornelisse Van N. Kerck, at Bergen. 113th with pall.

192 July 9. Jan Clasen, from Tappaen, * at Ahasymus in his mother's house. 36th in church. 114th with pall.

193 December 6. Steyntje Jans, wid. of Hendrick Tonisen Hellingh. 115th with pall.

194 December 18. Hilletje Jans, wid. of Ide van de Voors, from Ahasymus. 116th with pall.

1706

195 April 8. Treyntje Brestede, wi. of Thomas Fransen, lived at Monachje Co of Ackinsack, and bur. at Old Ackinsack.

NO. 1706

196 September 25. Da. of Lea Sickels.

197 October 22. Metje Jans, wi. of Jo Janse Van Blerekom, at Bergen. 117th with pall.

1707

198 January 18. Hertman Michielsen Vreelant at Bergen. 118th with pall.

199 January 18. Gysbert Pyper, Plumber, from Amsterdam, at Bergen, by order of Abel Reddenhars. 119th with pall.

200 January 24. Lysbeth Gerrits, wid. of Guert Gerritsen, at Bergen, 120th with pall.

201 May 15. Reynier Bastiaense Van Giesen, Voorlezer of Bergen, after having held the office for near 42 years. 121st with pall.

202 September 4. The son of Claes Arentse Toers, at Bergen.

203 September 7. Cornelia Hendrick, wi. of Isack Van Giesen 122nd with pall.

1708

204 January 24. Son of Jacob Jacobse Van Winkel.

205 March 12. Rachel Straetemaker, wi. of Daniel Van Winkel 124th with pall.

206 March 23. Da. of Cornelis Claesen, * at Ahasymus, in the house of Annetje Stoffels. 125th with pall.

207 August 14. Aagtje Vreeland, wi. of Roelof Helmigsen. 126th with pall.

208 November 16. Ch. of Enog Machielsen Vreland and Aagtje Van Hoorn. 127th (with pall).

1709

209 March 20. * Johannis Stynmets and was bur. March 22, at Bergen on the common burial ground. 128th with pall.

210 October 25. * the son of Abel Riddenhars, and bur. October 27th on the common cemetery. 129th with pall.

1710 NO.

211 January 3. * youngest da. of Gerrit Gerritse by his wi. Niesje Pieters, and was buried in the church (being the 36th that lies bur. in the church) on January 5th. 130th with pall.

212 January 16. * da. of Pieter Van Boskerk, and bur. on his farm. 131st [with pall].

213 January 27. Bur. Machiel and Seitje Vreeland, children of Johannis Michielse Vreeland. 132nd with pall.

214 January 31. Bur. in the church Hillegont, oldest da. of Cornelis Van Vorst and Feytje Gerrits. The 37th in the church. 133rd with pall.

215 May 19. * Esther de Vouw, wi. of Uldrick Brouwer. Bur. May 21st. 134th with pall.

216 August 7. Was drowned and August 11th bur. Andries Claas. Bur. on the Bergen Cemetery. 135th with pall.

217 September 16. Bur. Sofia van Wykensloot, wid. of Jan Nak. 136th with pall.

218 September 30. Bur. in the church Aaltje da. of Gerrit Jurriansen and Beletje Dircks. 137th with pall.

1711

219 January 3. Bur. son of Matheus Demoth and Margrietje Blinkerhoff. 138th [with pall].

220 April 19. Bur. ch. of Harpert Gerrebrantsen and Hillegont Marselis.

221 April 21. Pryntie Machielsen Vreelant, wi. of Andries Claasen. 139th with pall.

222 September 4. * and Sept. 6 bur. Madelena, wi. of Jan Lubbertsen Van Blerkum. 140th with pall.

223 September 20. * and Sept. 22 bur. at Constable's Hook, Jenneken Van Boskerke Y. Woman.

224 December 15. Bur. on the island Sychakes, old man Eduard Earle being in his 84th year. 141st with pall.

NO. 1712

225 January 11. Bur. ch. of Uldrick Brouwer and Adriaantje Pieters.

1713

226 June 26. * and bur. the 29th at Bergen, Johannis Machielsen Vreeland.

1714

227 Bur. Marretje, wid. of Cap. Gerrebrand Claasen.

1716

228 May 8. * and bur. the 11th, Catharina Hopper, wi. of Fredrick Thomassen.

1724

229 October 10. * and bur. the 10th Claas Arentse Toers.

1725

230 July 12. * and bur. the 14th, Annatje Stoffels, wid. of Claas Jansen Kuyper.

1724

231 November 20. * and bur. the 22nd, Jacob Jacobsen Van Winkel.

1727? (May be 1717; much blurred)

232 August. Bur. Enog Machielse Vreeland. In the month of May in the same year, the wife of Cornelis Michielse —— died also.

1728

233 February. Bur. at Bergen Elisabeth Gerrits, wid. of Pieter Hesselsen.

234 Same year. Bur. Joh. Pouwels.

1729

235 August 12. * and August 14 bur. Capt. Jan Sip.

236 August 14. * and —— bur. Jan Arensen Toers.

1729 NO.

237 October 7. * and Oct. 9 bur. Helmig Roelofsen Van Houten.

238 November 13. * and Nov. 15 bur. Nicolaes Arentsen Toers, Y. M.

239 December 27. * and bur. the 29th Robbert Sickels.

1730

240 January 12. * and bur. the 14th, da. of Johannis and Claasje Sickels.

241 April 21. * and bur. the 23rd, son of Casparis Preyer and Saartje Andriessen.

242 October 29. * and bur. November 1st, da. of Pieter Marcelissen and Jenneke Preyer.

243 November 4. * and bur. the 5th, ch. of Hendrick Vander Oef and Eva Slot.

244 November 19. * and bur. the 22nd, Gerrit Stymets, having lived at Ahasymus, and has been bur. on the Bergen Cem^{y}.

245 November 24. * at sunrise, and bur. November 27th, son of Michiel Cornelissen Vreeland and his wife Jen—?

1731

246 October 27. * at midnight and bur. the 29th Geertruy Sikkels, wi. of Hendrik Sikkels; aged 44 years.

247 October 23. bur. newly born infant of Pieter and Jenneken Marcelis.

248 November 3. bur. son of Pieter Post by his wife Catryntje.

249 November 28. bur. newly born infant of Zacharias Sikkels by his wife Adriaantje.

250 December 2. * and bur. the 4th, Arjaantje Hartmanse Vreeland, wi. of Zacharias Sikkels.

1732

251 January 3. Bur. ch. of Jurriaan Gerritsen and Grietje Diederikx.

252 February 7. Bur. ch. of Michiel Hartmansen Vreeland, and Elisabeth Gerrits.

1732

NO.

253 February 13. bur. ch. of Margen Smith and Catlyntje Tades.

254 February 15. bur. ch. of A. Toers and Annetje Spier.

255 March 6. * and bur. the 7th, Jacob Enogsen Vreeland.

256 March 30. bur. son of Pieter Post, named Samuel.

257 July 15. bur. at Constable's Hook, ch. of Pieter Macale, and Marytje Andries.

258 August 13. * and bur. the 15th Wander Diderikx, elder of the Ref. Church at Bergen.

259 September 20. * and bur. the 22nd the wid. of Jacob Jacobsen Van Winkel.

260 October 9. * and bur. the 11th, Gerrit Gerritsen Van Waagening.

261 October 22. * da. of Dirck and Jannetje Fredricksen Cadmus at Pemmerepoch, old about 13 months and named Catryntje. Bur. the 24th at Constables Hook.

262 November 8. * and November 10th bur. at the Bergen Cem^{y}. a son of Mr. Johannes Cavelier by his wife Cathelyntje.

263 December 26. * and bur. the 27th, the 2nd son of Juriaan Gerritsen by his wife Gerretje Diderikx.

1733

264 April 10. bur. at Constables Hook, A. Boskerck.

265 April 29. * and bur. May 2nd, Johannes Pietersen.

266 May 6. bur. Jan Hendriksen, son-in-law of Casper Preyers.

1734

267 February 3. * and bur. the 5th, Catryntje Beekman, wi. of Pieter Post.

268 March 13. bur. Johannis Sikkels. * the 11th.

269 May 19. * Feytje Gerrits Van Wagening, wi. of Cornelis Van Vorst. Bur. the 21st.

1735 NO.

270 March 19. Bur. ch. of P. Stuyvesant and Pryntje Preyer.

271 March 23. Bur. ch. of Morgen Smit and Catje Tades.

272 April 8. Bur. Catharina Andriessen, Y. D.

1736

273 May 10. Bur. son of Lourens Van Boskerk and his wife Feytje Vreeland.

274 June 25. Bur. ch. of Hendrick Sikels and his wife Sara Ackerman.

275 July 17. Bur. ch. of Abraham Dideryck and his wi. Geertruy Bon.

276 August 22. Bur. Geertruy Van Winkel, wi. of Johannis Diederyck.

277 August 26. Bur. Benjamin, son of Enoch Vreelant.

278 November 7. Bur. wi. of Pieter Van Boskerk at Constable's Hook.

1737

279 July 8. Bur. Marte Winnig.

280 July 15. Bur. Antje Pieterse.

1738

281 June 15. * Neeltje Van Vechten, wi. of Rut Van Horn. Bur. the 18th.

282 July 29. * Pieter Van Boskerk. Bur. August 1st at Constable's Hook.

283 August 24. Bur. Gerrit Van Wagenen, son of Johannis Van Wagenen.

284 September 20. Bur. son of Joris Vrelant and wife Annetje Van Wagenen.

285 October 1. The 2nd son of Joris Vreelant and his wife Annetje Van Wagenen.

NO. 1738

286 October 2. Son of Hendrick Vander Hoef and his wife Eva Slot.

287 November 22. Joseph, son of Hendrik Van Winkel, the first on the new Cem^{y}.

1739

288 July 29. Jurjan Gerritz.

1740

289 September 16. Son of Cornelis Juryansen and his wi. Altje Van Winckel.

290 December 10. Johannes, son of Mathys Demoth. * the 8th.

1741

291 May 17. Rut Van Hoorn. * May 15th.

292 July 4. Zara Kuyper, wi. of Johannis Jurrianze. * July 2nd.

293 October 18. Jacob, son of Casparus Preyer. * October 15th.

1742

294 May 10. Barend Spier. * May 8th.

295 December 12. Jacomina Toers. * December 10th.

1743

296 February 21. Katje Tades, wi. of Margon Smith—with pall.

297 March 7. Ch. of Hendrick V. der Hoef.

1744

298 April 11. Gesie, da. of Mathys Demoth, on the old cem^{y}.

299 September. Pietertje Van Vorst, wi. of Marcelis Pieterse.

300 November 13. —— Winckel, wi. of Jacob Diedericks. * November 11.

1745 NO.

301 May 21. Belytje Dircks, wi. of Gerrit Jurrianzen. * May 20th.

302 November 10. Fredrik Cadmus. * November 8th.

1746

303 May 15. Aaltje Jurrianzen. * May 13th.

304 June 16. Jacob Diederikx. * June 14th.

305 July 5. Johannes Spier, at Constable's Hook. * July 2nd.

306 August 8. Annetje, da. of Pieter Marcelusz. * August 6th.

307 September 19. Rutger Kadmus at Tappan. * September 17th.

308 October 1. Johan, son of Derk Kadmus. * September 28th.

309 October 7. Derk, father of Johan Kadmus, aforementioned. * Oct. 5.

310 October 13. (Name obliterated) on the new Cem^{y}. * October 11th.

1747

311 January 18. Catriena Mathewese. * January 16.

312 January 22. Hendrik Vander Hoef. * January 20th.

313 July 20. Helmich Van Wagenen. * July 19th.

314 August 23. David Karmiegel. * August 22nd.

315 October 14. Ch. of Jan De With, on new Cem^{y}.

316 October 26. Marcelis Pieterse, *October 23, aged 91 years

317 November 29. Ch. of Joris Vreland. * November 27th.

1748

318 March 31. Klaasie Vreeland. * March 29th.

319 April 5. Elyas Vreland. * April 2nd.

320 April 9. Rachel Spier. * April 7th.

NO. 1748

321 April 29. Catryna Pier. * April 27th.

322 May 8. Johannes De Logransie at Constable's Hook. * May 6th.

323 August 23. Michiel Andriz. * August 22nd.

324 September 5. Gerrit Jurrianzen. * September 4th.

1749

325 August 12. Catlyntje, da. of Jacob V. Wagenen and his wife Jennetje Van Houte. * August 11th.

326 August 23. Son of Abraham Sickkels.

327 September 9. Catlyna, da. of Geertruy Spier. * September 8th.

328 September 10. Belitje, da. of Margrietje Jurrijanse. * September 8.

329 October 1. Son of Paulus N. Kerck. * September 29th.

330 October 5. Cornelis, son of Helmich Van Wagenen. * October 4th.

331 October 10. Judick, wi. of Gerrit Roos. * October 8th.

332 October 20. Da. of Martje Van Wagenen. * October 19th.

333 November 27. Ch. of Johannis Pryer. * November 26th.

1750

334 January 28. Antje Ziph, wi. of Ide Ziph. * January 25th.

335 May 21. Helena, wi. of Jan Van Hoorn. * May 19th.

1751

336 January 29. Gerrit, son of Joris Vreland. * January 26th.

337 September 14. Catharina, wi. of Gerrit N. Kerk. * September 12—1st with new pall.

1752 NO.

338 March 18. First ch. of Andries Pryer, and wi. Geertruy Sickels. * March 17th.

339 October 10. Son of Joris Kadmus. * October 9th.

340 October 20. Son of Pieter Van Benthuysen, aged 13½ years. The second with the new pall. * October 18th.

341 November 17. Ch. of Johannis Pryer. * November 15th.

342 December 15. Louwrens Van Boskerk, bur. at Constable's Hook. The 3rd with the new pall. * December 13th.

343 December 28. Da. of Thomas Broun, at Constable's Hook. *Dec. 26th.

1753

344 January 13. Frederik Kadmus, Y. M. * January 12th.

345 January 25. Aaltje Diederikx. * January 23rd.

346 January 27. Johannis, son of Johannis Vreland. * January 25th.

347 February 3. Metje, wi. of Johannis De la Grancie. * February 1st.

348 February 5. Cornelis Van Boskerk, at Constable's Hook. * Feb. 4th.

349 February 17. John Schofield, Y. M. from Connecticut. * Feb. 16th.

350 April 28. Ch. of Jan York. * April 27th.

351 May 16. Margrietje, da. of Jan Van Hoorn. * May 14th.

352 May 20. Son of Levinus Winne. * May 19th.

353 July 22. Tryntje, wi. of Myndert Gerbrants. * July 21st.

354 October 22. J.—— da. of Nicolas Van Dam. * October 20th.[1]

355 October 30. Son of Nicolas Van Dam. * October 28th.[1]

356 November 9. Jacob, son of Nicolas Van Dam. * November 7th.[1]

[1] Bur. all at Constable's Hook.

NO. 1754

357 February 15. Geertruy Sickels. * February 13th.

358 May 4. Samuel Van Winkel. * May 2nd.

359 July 29. Klaas Andriese, on the old cem^{y}. * July 27th.

360 September 20. Margrieta Van Winckel, wi. of Johannis Jurijans. * September 18th.

361 September 21. Newly born infant of Joris Vreland. * September 19th.

362 November 25. Johannis, son of Geertruy Spier. * November 24th.

363 December 5. Da. of Hendrick Fielden. * December 4th.

364 December 15. Margrieta Blinkerhoff, wi. of Mathys Demoth. * December 12th.

365 December 24. Aaltje Van Wagenen, wi. of Wander——. * Dec. 22.

1755

366 February 28. Casper Pryer. * February 26th.

367 August 15. Newly born infant of Cornelis Jurrijansen. * Aug. 14.

368 November 27. Newly born infant of Johannis Van Wagenen. * Nov. 25.

1756

369 March 18. Hendrick Cuyper. * March 16th.

370 March 20. Mathys Demoth. * March 18th. Bur. on old cem^{y}.

371 October 2. Antje Waldron. * September 30th.

372 October 8. Johannis Gerritz Van Wagenen. * October 6th.

373 October 21. Sophia Van Boskerck. * October 19th. Bur. at Constable Hook.

1757 NO.

374 January 4. Newly-born infant of Jan Van Horn. * January 3rd.

375 January 12. Daniel Van Winkel, with the pall. * January 10th.

376 March 13. Lea Nieuwkerck, wi. of Cornelis van N. Kerck. *March 11th.

377 June 20. Da. of Jacobus Smith. * June 19th.

378 August 25. Cornelis Kiersted. * August 23rd.

379 October 2. James With? * September 30th.

380 November 24. Ch. of Helmich Van Houten. * November 23rd.

381 December 14. Jan Van Hoorn. * December 12th.

1758

382 January 15. Annetje Jackson, on Sunday in the Church, in the space set apart for baptisms (doophuisje). * January 13th about 8 o'clock A. M. on Friday, aged 49 years.

383 March 17. Ch. of Joris Kadmus. * March 16th.

384 September 14. Newly born infant of Richard Richardson. * Sept. 13.

1759

385 March 13. Rachel Boskerck, wi. of Barent Van Hoorn, at Constable's Hook. * March 11th.

386 April 4. Newly born infant of Marcelis Marcelisse. * April 2nd.

387 April 24. Geertruy Vliereboom, at Constable's Hook. * April 22nd.

388 September 20. Catrina Van Nukerck, Y. D. * September 18th.

389 September 27. Catlyntje Siph, wi. of Claas Vreeland. * Sept. 25th.

1760

390 May 18. Theunis Gerbrantz, Y. M. * May 15th.

391 May 29. Jannetje Kadmus. * May 27th.

392 December 7. Cornelis Van Vorst, with pall. * December 5th.

NO. 1761

393 February 1. Newly born infant of Marcelis Marcelisse. * Jan. 30th.

394 February 4. Jan Rol, at Constable's Hook. * February 2nd.

395 February 23. Aagtje Blinkerhof. * February 20.

396 March 24. Newly born infant of Helmich Van Houten. * March 22nd.

397 October 8. Cornelis Van Vorst, son of Johannis Van Vorst, at Bergen. * October 7th.

398 October 17. Da. of Joseph Walderom. * October 15th.

1762

399 February 28. Ide Sip. * February 26th.

400 August 26. Andries Boskerk, at Constable's Hook. * August 25th.

401 September 13. Jannetje Winne. * September 11th.

1763

402 February 7. Poulus Nieuwkerck. * February 5th.

403 March 1. Newly born infant of Barend Van Hoorn, at Const. Hook. * February 28th.

404 March 7. Johannis, son of Daniel Solder. * March 5th.

405 June 24. Preyntie, wi. of Pieter Stuyvesant. * June 22nd.

406 July 4. Antie, da. of Cornelis Sip. * July 3rd.

407 September 12. Son of Harmanis Veeder, named Cornelis. * Sept. 10th.

408 September 30. Johannis Preyer. * September 28th.

1764 NO.

409 September 3. Son of Willem Haekki. * September 1st.

410 September 4. Son of Cornelis Sip. * September 2nd.

411 September 8. Da. of ——. * September 6th.

1765

412 October 29. Ide, son of Lavynes Winne. * October 27th.

413 November 30. Newly born son of Jacob Van Winkel. * November 28.

1766

414 April 8. Machiel Hartmanse Vreeland. * April 6th.

415 September 15. Wid. of Johannis Evers, named Barbara. * Sept. 13.

416 November 14. Jannetje Vreeland, wi. of Joris Cadmus. * Nov. 12th.

1767

417 January 5. Jakobus Boskerk, at Constable's Hook. * January 3rd.

418 April 26. Son of Dom. Willem Jackson. * April 25th.

419 May 30. Hendrick Van Winckel. * May 28th.

420 June 13. Da. of Joseph Walderon, named Geertruy. * June 11th.

421 July 6. Lourens, son of Tammes Brouyn; at Constable's Hook. * July 4th.

422 July 18. Dirk, son of Joris Cadmus. * July 16th.

423 July 26. Newly born child of Marte Dyell. * July 24th.

424 August 14. Cornelis, son of Cornelis Van Reypen. * August 13th.

425 September 4. Jacob, son of Harmanis Veeder. * September 2nd.

NO. 1767

426 August 6. Eva, da. of Tammes Daden. * August 5th.

427 ? Annatie, da. of Dom. Willem Jackson. * September 30th.

428 November 20. Elisabeth, wi. of Machiel H. Vreeland. * Nov. 18th.

429 December 18. Catlyntje, wi. of Barend Spier, at Constable's Hook. * December 16th aged 91 (?) years.

1768

430 February 14. Newly born infant of Joseph Walderom and Antie Diderix (born February 10th.)

431 December 20. Johannis Van Houte. * December 18th.

1769

432 April 14. Jannetje Van Winkel. * April 12th.

1770

433 January 8. Abraham Callerd. * January 6th.

434 April 3. Pieter Marscelusse. * April 1st.

435 August 11. Pieter Stuyvesant. * August 10th.

436 September 3. Cornelis Blinkerhoff, aged 97 years, 3m. 24 d. * September 1st.

437 September 28. Son of Pieter Boskerk, at Const. Hook. * September 26th.

1771

438 January 10. Son of Cornelis Blinkerhoff, named Hendrik. * Jan. 8th.

439 January 18. Cornelis Van Reype. * January 17th.

440 June 3. Aeltie Diderix, wi. of Johannis Winne. * June 2nd.

441 November 4. Twins (a son and a daughter) of Daniel Van Winkel by his wife Aeltie Van Reype. * both Nov. 3rd; born Oct. 28th.

1771 NO.

442 November 28. Jannetje, wi. of Cornelis Gerbrantse. * November 26th.

443 December 8. Polly Ward, wi. of David Cembel. * December 6th.

1772

444 January 18. Ferdinandus Vrielinghuyse, son of Dom. Willem Jackson. * January 17th.

445 April 3. Jannetje, wid. of Hendrick Kuyper. * April 1st.

446 May 24. Ide, son of Cornelis Sip. * May 23rd.

447 May 26. Marte, son of Robbert Sickels. * May 24th.

448 September 4. Machiel, son of Joris Kadmus. * September 3rd.

449 September 5. Zacharias, son of Andries Pryer. * September 4th.

450 September 17. Newly born infant of Jacob Van Winkel and his wife Rachel Kammegaer. * September 16th.

451 September 19. Rachel, wi. of Jacob Van Winkel. * September 18th.

452 October 30. Jannetje, wi. of Cornelis Gerbrantse. * October 28th.

453 November 2. Poulus, son of Jacob Nieuwkerk. * November 1st.

454 November 5. Johannis Diderix. * November 3rd.

455 December 11. Cornelis, son of Hartman Blinkerhof. * December 9th.

1773

456 July 12. Marregriet, da. of Johannis Diderix. * July 11th.

457 October 11. Claasje, da. of Cornelis Van Vorst. * October 9th.

1774

458 January 8. Maragrietje Lagrancie; wid. of Jacobus Boskerck; at Constable's Hook. * January 6th.

NO.

459 January 11. Geertruy Boskerk; wi. of Pieter Korsen, at Constable's Hook. * January 10th. 1774

460 February 15. Jenneke Stuyvesant, wi. of Hendrick Sickels. * February 13th.

461 February 23. Cornelis Gerbrantse. * February 20th.

462 February 28. Sara, da. of Casparus Stuyvesant. * February 26th.

463 March 17. Helena Vreelant, wid. of Johannis Van Houte. *March 15th.

464 May 24. Maaike, wi. of Abel De Graw. * May 23rd.

465 July 31. Aegje, da. of Johannis Diderix, by his wife Antie Van Wagene. * July 30th.

466 August 27. Sara, wid. of Casparis Pryer. * August 25th.

467 September 28. Eva, da. of Dom. Willem Jackson by his wife Annatie Vrielinghuyse. * September 27th.

1775

468 January 28. Joseph, son of Jacob Van Winkel by his wife Rachel Kammegaer. * January 27th.

469 April 16. Jacob Van Hooren at Constable's Hook. * April 14th.

470 May 7. Daniel Solders ——. * May 6th.

471 May 10. Annatie, oldest da. of Daniel Solders by his wife Jacomyntje Toers. * May 9th.

472 May 11. Sara, 2nd daughter of Daniel Solders by his wife Jacomyntje Toers. * May 10th.

473 May 15. Pryntje, da. of Egbert Post, by his wife Sara Stuyvesant. * May 14th.

474 June 5. At Constable's Hook, Margrietje, wid. of Andries Boskerck. * June 3rd.

475 ——. Zacharyas, son of Robbert Sickels, bur. August 20. * August 18th.

1775 NO.

476 September 25. Jacop Van Wagenen. * September 23rd.

477 October 2. Gerrit Sip. * October 1st.

478 October 19. Ariaantje, da. of Robert Sickels. * October 18.

479 October 28. Catleyntie Van Wagenen, wi. of Gerret Van Reype. * October 27th.

480 December 8. Cornelis Diderix. * December 6th.

481 December 20. Lea, wid. of Jacob Van Wagene. * December 19th.

1776

482 January 1. Daniel, son of Johannis Buys. * December 31, 1775.

483 May 4. Lea Slot, wi. of Jacob Brouwer. * May 3rd.

484 July 26. Lena, da. of Jacob Nieuwkerk. * July 25th.

485 July 27. Margrietje, da. of Gerrit Van Reype. * July 26th.

486 July 28. Cornelis, son of John Van Hoorn. * July 27th.

487 August 3. Lea, da. of Jacob Van Winkel. * August 2nd.

488 August 4. Neeltie, da. of Cornelis Gerbrantse. * August 3rd.

489 August 4. Zacharias, son of Daniel Sickels. * August 3rd.

490 August 1. Marytje, da. of Jacob Nieuker. * August 1st.

491 August 12. Aeltie, da. of Seel Marcelus. * August 10th.

492 August 14. Zacharias Sickels. * August 13th.

493 August 16. John, son of Jacob Vander Bilt. * August 15th.

494 August 18. Joris, son of Jannetje Jansen. * August 17th.

495 August 25. Johannes Van Reype. * August 24th.

496 August 4. Newly-born infant of Jacob Van Wagenen, and his wife Aegje Blinkerhof. * August 3rd.

497 August 27. Poulus, son of Jacob Nieukerk. * August 27th.

NO. 1776

498 August 30. Betsie, da. of Abraham Van Waert. * August 29th.

1777

499 January 12. Albert, son of Dirk Lesier. * January 10.

500 January 13. Dirk Van Reype. * January 11th.

501 January 22. Hendrik Sickels. * January 20th.

502 March 7. John, son of Pieter Stuyvesant. * March 6th.

503 September 4. Hendrik, son of Gerrit Vanderhoef. * September 3rd.

504 June 8. Geertruy Bon, wi. of Abraham Diderix. * June 7th.

505 June 14. Tim Luwis. * June 13th.

506 March 14. Marretje, wi. of Abraham Preyer. * March 12th.

507 June 11. Hester, wid. of Johannes Diderix. * June 9th.

508 August 7. Rachel, da. of Jacob Van Hooren. * August 6th.

509 September 8. Catlyntie, wid. of Johannes Van Wagenen. *September 6th.

510 December 4. Jannetje, da. of John Van Hoorn, by his wi. Beletje Van Reype. * December 3rd.

1778

511 February 9. Helmig, son of Hendrik Dreemus. * February 7th.

512 March 21. Annatie, da. of Jacob Van Wagene, by his wi. Aegje Vreeland. * March 20th.

513 June 26. Elisabeth, da. of Walter Kleyndinni. * June 25th.

514 October 28. Willem Broeks. * October 27th.

515 November 8. Lea, da. of Jacobus Brouwer. * November 7th.

516 December 4. John, son of Tomis Swoords. * December 3rd.

517 December 23. Kobis Smith. * December 21st.

1778 NO.

518 October 3. Rachel, wi. of Zacharias Sickels. * October 1st.

519 October 8. Hester Van Duesen. * October 7th.

1779

520 January 12. Antie, da. of Hendrik Luttye. * January 10th.

521 February 9. Aeltie, da. of Johannis Diderix. * February 7th.

522 May 2. Robbert, son of Dom. Willem Jackson. * May 1st.

523 September 12. Gerrit Roos. * September 10th.

524 September 15. Annatie, wid. of Patrick Jackson. * September 13th.

525 September 19. Arent Toers. * September 17th.

526 September 19. Catrintie, da. of Gerrit Nieukerk. * Sept. 17th.

527 September 21. Ned, son of Casparus Stuyvesant. * September 20th.

528 September 30. Keetje Bokkenove. * September 29th.

529 October 5. Henri Fielden. * October 3rd.

530 October 5. Jenneke, wid. of Pieter Marselus. * October 3rd.

531 October 6. Jannitje, da. of Gerrit Nieukerk. * October 4th.

532 October 15. Joseph Walderon. * October 14th.

533 October 24. Barend Van Hoorn, at Constable's Hook. * October 22nd.

534 November 9. Jacobus Brouer. * November 7th.

535 November 12. Ch. of Barend Nieukerk, named Jannetje. * November 10th.

536 December 5. James, son of James Berret. * December 3rd.

537 November 17. Machiel Demot. * November 16th.

1780

NO.

538 June 23. Catrientie Stuyvesant, wi. of Jacob Van Hooren. * June 21st.

539 September 20. Antje Diderix, wi. of Johannis Vreeland. * September 19th.

540 October 2. Johannes, son of Gerrit Roos. * September 30th.

541 October 27. Johannis, son of Johannis Everse. * October 26th.

542 November 9. Cornelis, son of Egbert Post. * November 8th.

1781

543 March 27. Eva, wid. of Barend Van Hooren. * March 25th. Bur. at the Hook.

544 March 29. Jennie, wi. of Hendrik Sickels at the Hook. * March 28.

545 April 4. Joris Kadmus. * April 2nd.

546 May 6. Meyndert Gerbrantse. * May 5th.

547 May 9. Newly born infant of Johannes Vreeland, by his wife Keetje Hoogland. * May 8th.

548 June 1. Margrietje, da. of Gerrit Van Reype, by his wife Catrientje. * May 31st.

549 July 20. Styntie Eyselstyn, wi. of Johannis Everse. * July 19th.

550 September 7. John Bon. * September 6th.

551 September 8. Annatie, wid. of Arend Toers. * September 7th.

552 September 11. Cornelis Nieukerk. * September 10th.

553 October 3. Antje, da. of Daniel Diderix. * October 2nd.

554 November 21. Fredrick Sickels. * November 19th.

1782

555 March 2. Annatie Van Wagenen, wi. of Joris Vreeland. * Feb. 28th.

1782 NO.

556 June 30. Antie Roos, wid. of Cornelis Diderix. * June 29th.

557 November 2. Tammes Brouyn, at N. York. * October 31st.

1783

558 January 20. Sara Van Woert. * January 18th.

559 January 29. Jacob Van Wagene. * January 27th.

560 February 13. Johannis Vreeland. * February 11th.

561 April 8. Barend, son of Barend Everse. * April 7th.

562 April 23. Sara, 2nd. wi. of Hendrick Sickels. * April 22nd.

563 July 22. Jannetje, wid. of Johannis Van Reype. * July 21st.

564 December 15th. Geertruy, wi. of Andries Preyer. * December 14th.

1784

565 February 10. Gerrit Vreeland. * February 8th.

566 June 2. Billy Jackson. * May 31st.

567 September 28. Johannes Sickels. * September 26th.

568 October 15. Jannetje, wi. of Gerrit Van Reype. * October 13th.

1785

569 April 25. Gerrit Nieukerk. * April 23rd.

570 December 27, 1783 (?) Petrus Vander Hoef. * December 25th.

1786

571 May 28. Da. of Johannes Everse. * May 26th.

572 February 5. Da. of Abraham Preyer, named Arriaentie. * Feb. 3rd.

573 October 11. John Van Hoorn. * October 10th.

574 June 24. Elisabeth da. of John Marcelus. * June 23rd.

1786

NO.

575 November 8. Joris, son of Gerrit Vreeland. * November 7th.

576 November 15. Annatie, da. of Gerrit Vreeland. * November 14th.

577 November 7. Aeltie, da. of Walter Klyndinni. * November 6th.

578 September 19. Walter, son of Abraham Van Winkel. * September 18th.

579 December 21. Katy Baelden, wi. of John Sippe. * December 19th.

580 December 30. Gerrebrand, son of Cornelis Gerbrants. * Dec. 29th.

1783 (?)

581 May 6. —— Blinkerhof, wi. of Koobus Boogert. * May 3rd.

1787

582 March 23. Klaasje Blinkerhof, wid. of Gerrit Kroese. * March 21st.

583 April 25. Susanna Westervelt, wi. of Jacob Van Winkel. * April 23.

584 June 27. Pieter Roos. * June 26th.

1788

585 March 9. Barend, son of Barend Evers. * March 7th.

586 March 6. Klaasje Demot, wid. of Cornelis Van Vorst. * March 4th.

587 April 10. Elisabeth Vreeland, wi. of Cornelis Van Reype. * April 8.

588 October 29. Claesje Winne, wid. of Machiel Demot. * October 27th.

589 September 23. Adriaen Post. * September 22nd.

590 September 9. Andries, son of Hartman Preyer. * *December* 8th.

591 July 28. Abraham Spier. * July 27th.

592 December 6. Jenneke Sip, wi. of Cornelis Vreeland. * December 5th.

593 December 18. Jacob Van Winkel. * December 17th.

Register der Ledematen

Behoorende tot de Kercke van Bergen.

A. 1664.

Mans-persoonen.

Nicolaes Verleth. Overleden.
Tieleman van Vleck. Overleden.
Adolf Hardenbroeck. Vertrocken.
Reynier van Giesen.
Douwen Hermansen.
Engelbert Steenhuysen. Overleden
Barent Leth. Vertrocken
Wiggert Reyniersen. Overleden.
Hans Diedenbergh.

Vrouws-Persoonen

Anna Stuyvesants. Vertrocken.
Magdaleen van Vleck. Vertrocken.
Marritie Hardenbroeck. Vertrocken.
Dirckje Cornelis.
Dirckje Theunis.
Jannetje Stoynis. Overleden.
Anna Claes. Overleden.
Ariaentje Walings. Overleden.
Egbertje Dircx. Overleden.
Geertie Hendricx.
Marritie Adriaens, h. v. Thomas Fredricksen.

Vertr.

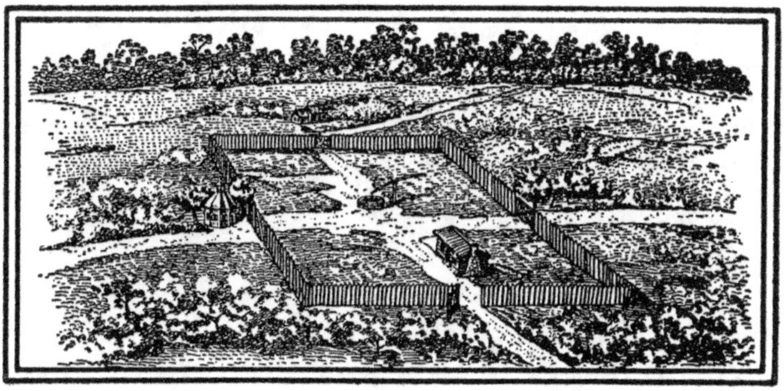

REGISTER OF THE MEMBERS

BELONGING TO THE CHURCH OF BERGEN

A. D. 1664

MALE PERSONS

NO.			1664
594	Nicolaes Verleth	Deceased	
595	Tieleman van Vleck	"	
596	Adolf Hardenbroeck	Dismissed	
597	Reynier van Giesen		
598	Douwen Hermanszen		
599	Engelberth Steenhuyse	Deceased	
600	Bartel Loth	Dismissed	
601	Wiggert Reynierszen	Deceased	
602	Hans Diedericksze		

FEMALE PERSONS

603	Anna Stuyvesants	Dismissed
604	Magdaleen van Vleck	"
605	Marritje Hardenbroeck	"
606	Dirckje Cornelis	
607	Dirckje Theunis	
608	Jannetje Steymits	Deceased
609	Anna Claes	"
610	Ariaentje Walings	"
611	Lysbeth Dircx	"
612	Geertie Hendricx	
613	Marritie Adriaens, wife of	
614	Thomas Fredrickszen	
615	Grietje Jacobs	

1664 NO.		
616	Tryntie Cornelis	Dimissed
617	Lysbeth Cornelis	"
618	Feytie Hertmans	
619	Tryntie Jacobs	Deceased
620	Annetje Cornelis	
621	Hilletie Jans	

A. D. 1665
The 1st of April

622	Pieter Janszen	Dismissed
623	Grietie Jacobs	

The 1st of May

624	Jan Schouten }	"
625	Sara Schouten }	

The 30th of December

626	Jan Dirckszen Straetmaecker	
627	Geurt Dirckszen	"
628	Elias Michielszen	
629	Jan Evertszen Kersenboom	"
630	Annetje Hermans	
631	Tryntie Michiels	"
632	Geesje Gerrits	

A. D. 1666
The 24th of April

633	Carel Carelszen	Deceased
634	Gerrit Corneliszen	Dismissed
635	Geertruydt Luby	Deceased
636	Marritje Jacobs	
637	Chieltje Cornelis	Dismissed

The 8th of May

638	Balthazar Bayard	"
639	Marritje Loockermans	"

The 13th of November

640	Received by D° S. Megapolensis	
641	Thomas Fredrickszen	
642	Isaac van Vleck	"
643	Claes Ariaenszen Sip	"
644	Maria Stammer	

NO.		
	A. D. 1667 The 12th of April	
645	Received by D° John Megapolensis	
646	Jan Willemszen Loosdrecht	Deceased
647	Joost Van der Linden	Dismissed
648	Annetje Hendricks	"
	The 20th of May	
649	Hendrick Van der Water }	"
650	Grietie Vermeulen }	
651	By certificate from D° John Polhemius	
652	Jan Elting }	"
653	Tryntie Jans }	
	The 29th of same	
654	Ide Corn Van der Vorst	Deceased
	The 31st of July	
655	Received by D° John Megapolensis	
656	Claes Arentszen Toers	
657	Catharina Bayard	Dismissed
	The 3rd of November	
658	Isaac Matthyszen	Deceased
659	Ryckje Hermans	
	A. D. 1668 The 8th of July	
660	Arie Andrieszen	Dismissed
661	Elizabeth Gerrits	
662	Belitie Hendricks	"
	The 21st of November	
663	Anna Luby	Deceased
	A. D. 1669	
	None	
	A. D. 1670 The 10th of July	
664	Dirckje Meyers	Deceased
	A. D. 1671 The 24th of April	
665	With certificate from D° Gid. Schaets	
666	Jan Timmer	Dismissed
667	Petronella Timmers	"

1672 NO.

A. D. 1672
The 19th of February

668	Received by D° Wilh. Nieuwenhuysen	
669	Gerrit Gerritszen	

The 29th of May

670	Geurt Coerten	
671	Annetje Idens Van de Vorst	Dismissed
672	Jan Lubbertszen	
673	Enoch Michielszen	
674	Ariaentje Michiels	
675	Marritje Claes	
676	Catryntje Michiels	
677	Hendrickje Aerts	

The 27th of September

678	Evert Nolden	Deceased
679	Arent Laurenszen Toers	"
680	Teeuwis Corneliszen	
681	Geertruyd Gerrits	"
682	Gerritje Cornelis	"
683	Lysbeth Cornelis	"
684	Magdaleentje Jans, wife of	
685	Jan Lubbertszen	
686	Pieter Marceliszen	"
687	Lysbeth Aerts	"

A. D. 1673
The 24th of March

688	Received by D° Wilh. Nieuwenhuysen	
689	Pieter Hessels	"
690	Harmtje Hermans	
691	Jeuriaen Thomaszen	
692	Walyn Jacobszen	
693	Cathryn Andries	

A. D. 1674
The 27th of March

694	Received by D° Wilh. Nieuwenhuysen	
695	Annetje Etsal	Deceased
696	Gerrit Van Rhenen	

1674

NO.

697 Laurens Aertszen—Dismissed the 8th of July 1699 to Acquecqe-nonk

698 Hendrick Joriszen

699 Helmich Roelofzen

A. D. 1675

None

A. D. 1676
The 2nd of October

700 Received by D° Wilh Nieuwenhuysen.

701 Tryntie Pieters, wife of Adriaen Pieters

702 Annetje Jacobs Van Winckel

703 Tryntie Claes

704 Lubbert Lubbertszen Deceased

705 Geesje Roelofs

706 Cornelis Janszen Bogard "

707 Geesje Jans "

708 Jan Corneliszen Bogard

709 Agnietje Jans

A. D. 1677, June 25th.

710 Received by D° Wilhelm Nieuwenhuysen

711 Adriaen Post "

712 Catryntje Gerrits

713 Jacob Jacobszen Van Winckel

714 Aeltie Daniels

715 Johannis Van Gyssen

716 Francyntie Thomas, wife of

717 Laurens Arentz Toers

Later by the same

718 Margrietie Warnarts, wife of

719 Hans Diederickszen

720 Jannetie Pieters, wife of Helmich Roelofszen

721 Johannes Steymits

722 Simon Jacobszen Van Winckel

723 Annetje Ariaens

724 Cornelis Roelofsze

725 Magdaleentie Reyniers Van Gyssen

1677 NO.

726 Metje Dircks
727 Marritje Adriaens
728 Cornelis Lubbertszen

A. D. 1678
The 2nd of April

729 Received by D° Wilh. Nieuwenhuysen
730 Hessel Wiggertszen
731 Ariaen Thomaszen — Deceased
732 Laurens Ackerman
733 Marritje Lubberts

The 21st of June

734 Pietertje Van de Vorst

The 7th of October

735 Johannis Michielszen—young man
736 Susanna Hendriks—young woman
737 Neesie Pieters—young woman
738 Claesje Dircks Braet—young woman
739 Annetje Stymmets—young woman

These by certificate

740 David De Mareets — Dismissed
741 Marie Joorier — Deceased
742 Jean De Mareets
743 Jacomyntie Drywen — "
744 David De Mareets—the younger
745 Rachel Creisson
746 Samuel De Mareets
747 Jacob Lareu

A. D. 1679, April 7th

748 Received by D Wilh. Nieuwenhuysen
749 Johannes Thomaszen and his wife — Dismissed
750 Aechtje Jacobs
751 Nicolaes De Vouw
752 Maria Du Cie
753 Jochem Anthony, Negro — Deceased

NO. 1679

754 Maria Petilions—young woman Dismissed
755 Jannetie Gerrits, young woman
756 Marritje Jans—young woman

The 23rd of June

757 Dirck Claeszen Braeck
758 Geertie Egberts, wife of
759 Laurens Ackermans

The 20th of October

760 Lubbert Lubbertszen, Jr.

A. D. 1680
The 29th of March

761 Received by D° Wilh. Nieuwenhuysen
762 Hendrick Epcese

The 11th of June

763 Maria Druwyn, wife of
764 Samuel De Mareets Dismissed

The 11th of October

765 Hilletie Paulus, wife of
766 Lubbert Lubbertszen, Jr.
767 Machtelt Van de Linden, wife of
768 Albert Saburasky, but left us after having only once communed, and returned to the Lutherans, whose faith she had formerly forsaken—which has been put down as a cliff in the sea, that others seeing this might not be wrecked in their faith.
769 Dirckje Egberts Dismissed

A. D. 1681
The 21st of June

770 Received by D° Casparus Van Zuure
771 Cornelis Verwy
772 Abraham Du Tout
773 Jannetje Bocquet Deceased
774 Nicolaes Duprie

1681 NO.

775 Gerbrant Claeszen
776 Jan Hendrickszen Van Ostrum, Jr.
777 Jan Joosten Van Linden—young man

The 3rd of October

778 Maria Frans, wife of Johannes Spier
779 Hendrickje Jans, wife of Corn Verwey.

A. D. 1682
The 18th of April

780 Received by D° Casperus Van Zuuren
781 Barteld Claeszen
782 Hilletje Arents
783 Jan Aertszen Van de Bilt
784 Annetje Gysberts—young woman
785 Aeltje Theunis Bogard, wife of
786 Corn Claesze
787 Fredrick Thomaszen
788 Gerrit Gerritszen—the younger
789 Marcelis Pieterszen
790 Tades Michielszen
781 Jan Arentszen Toers—young man
792 Gerrit Stynmets—young man
793 Johanna Eerle, wife of Eduard Eerle
794 Vrouwtje Claes—young woman
795 Johanna Idens Van de Vorst—young woman
796 Catharina Thomas—young woman
797 Fytie Gerrits—young woman

The 26th of June

798 Roelof Van de Linden—young man

The 2nd of October

799 Received by Henricus Selyns
800 Jan Roelofszen Seubering and his wife
801 Adriana Polhemy by certificate from Midwout
802 Herman Michielszen

A. D. 1683
The 2nd of April

803 Received by Henricus Selyns
804 Lucas Seubering by certificate from Midwout Dismissed
805 Cornelia Hendricks—young woman
806 Aeltje Hendricks—young woman
807 Pieter Janszen, by certificate from the Esopus

The 2nd of July

808 Maertie Jacobs, wife of Pieter Janszen
809 Pieter Janszen
810 Baltes Barents and his wife
811 Tryntie Jans

The 1st of October

812 Machtelt Roelofs, wife of Jan Van
813 Oostrum, by certificate from Midwout

A. D. 1684
The 1st of April

814 Abraham Bockque and his wife
815 Tanneken Andries by certificate from St. Anna
816 Aeltje Van Laren, wife of
817 Abraham Ackerman, with certificate from Midwout. Dismissed October 3-1696 to Hackensack.

The 18th of June

818 Menno Johannis and his wife
819 Rensje Feddens, with certificate from Midwout Deceased
820 Sebastian Van Giesen—young man
821 Elizabeth Claes—young woman
822 Urzelina Steenmets

The 6th of October

823 Guilliamme Bartholf and his wife
824 Martyntje Hendricx with certificate from Sluis in Flanders
825 Jacomina Van Neste, wife of Claes
826 Arentsze Tours

1685 NO.

A. D. 1685
The 6th of April

827 Harmen Douwenszen Talma

The 22nd of June

828 Janneken Stratemaecker—young woman

A. D. 1686
The 6th of April

829 Willem Hoppen with certificate from New York
830 Mayken Jacobs with certificate from New Albany
831 Cornelis Claeszen on confession
832 Christoffel Steymets "
833 Cornelis Van Vorst "

A. D. 1687
The 3rd of October

834 Johannes Hendricxsen On the confession of faith
835 Theunis Janszen "
836 Frans Post—young man "

A. D. 1688
The 2nd of April

837 Abraham Du Toit and his wife
838 Jenne Bocke by certificate from Hackensacq Deceased
839 Adam Carlier and his wife
840 Mary Dorsuson, by certificate from the French Church of N. Y. Dismissed

A. D. 1689
The 30th of September

841 Hessel Pieterszen
842 Anna Du Toit
843 Abraham Van Giesen—dismissed with certificate to Hackensacq

The 27th of March 1697

844 Isaacq Van Giesen

NO. 1690

A. D. 1690

The 10th of July, with certificate from N. Albany

845 Thomas Greeven, Smith and his wife
846 Emmetje Isbrants. Dismissed to Gravesend on the Long Island the 4th of September 1701
847 Sander Egbertszen and his wife
848 Elsje Pieters with certificate from Staten Island
849 Janneken Thomas—young woman of Bergen
850 Catalyntje Pieters "

The 6th of October

851 Ysbrant Elderszen with certificate from New Albanien
852 Jannetje Jacobus, with certificate from New Albanien
853 Pieter Pauluszen and his wife
854 Tryntie Hans Jacobs
855 Thomas Jeuriaenszen—young man
856 Jacob Van Giesen—young man
857 Aeltie Gerrits—young woman
858 Fytie Andries—young woman, with certificate to Hackensacq the 27th of March, 1697
859 Christina Paulus—young woman
860 Pietertje Claes—young woman, dismissed with certificate to Acequeggenon, September 16–1700
861 Maryken Joris—young woman

A. D. 1697

The 28th of June

862 David Daniels and his wife
863 Annetje Stratenmaecler, dismissed with certificate to Hakkinsak the 6th of October 1700
864 Gerrit Jeuriaenszen and his wife
865 Belitje Dircx
866 Christyne Jeuriaens
867 Sara Van Nest. Dismissed the 8th of July 1699 to Acqueckenonc
868 Tryntie Buys, wife of
869 Dirck Stratenmaecker Dismissed to Tappan the 21st of June 1699
870 Metje Pieters

The .th of October

871 Gerrit Jeuriaenszen

1698 NO.

A. D. 1698
The 4th of April

872 Jannetje Andries—young woman
Here follow now the names of the members who, since the year
873 1700, at which time the services of D° Du Bois took their beginning, were received into the society either on confession of their faith or by certificate.

A. D. 1700
The 3rd of September

874 Hendrick Claasz
875 Jan Adriaansz
876 Grietje Straat. Dismissed to Acquiggenonk the 29th of April 1701
877 Rachel Straat
878 Claarthe Post
879 Aagje Paulusz
880 With certificate, Johannes Mischilsz and his wife
881 Klaasje Dircksz, from Hackkinsack

A. D. 1701
The 2nd of October

882	Barent Rynders	Dismissed with certificate to New York
883	Catharina Walters	"
884	Hester Rynders	"
885	Maria Smith	"
886	Fransyna Luwes	"

The 7th of April 1702

887 Tryntje Vreelandt, with certificate from Akkinsak

A. D. 1703

Is there no one received

A. D. 1704
The 11th of April

888 Abel Ridden Hars
889 Grietje Hendriksz, wife of

1704

NO.
890 Jacob Jacobsz Van Winkel
891–892 Annetje Jacobs, wife of Willem Dey
893 Catharina Jans, wife of
894 Abel Ridden Hars
895 Marytje Jurriaans
896 Sara Cornelisz
897 Christyntje Vrederyks
898 Judikje Claasz Tours

A. D. 1707
The 6th of October

899 Margritje Hendriks Blinkerhof, with certificate from Hakkensak

A. D. 1709
The 4th of April

900 Cornelis Hendricksz Blinkerhof, with certificate from Hakkinsak
901 Andries Hoppe and "
902 Abigael Akkermans "

A. D. 1710
The 31st of March

903 Thomas Frederiksz
904 Haremen Jurriaasz
905 Dirk Helmigsz
906 Aaltje Jurriaansz
907 Marytje Frederiksz
908 Metje Gerbrandz
909 Fytje Siggelsz
910 Geertruy Frederyks
911 Gerritje Helmigsz
912 Saartje Andries
913 Margrietje Sip

A. D. 1712
The 5th of April

914 Antje Thadus, wife of
915 Joh Pietersse, with certificate from Akkingsak.
On the confession of their faith:
916 Gysbert Jansse
917 Dirk Philipse

1712 NO.	
918–919	Adriaantje Pieters, wife of Olrig Brouwer
920–921	Aagje Hartmans, wife of Cornelis Blinkerhof
922–923	Rachel Andries, wife of Dirk Philipsze
924–925	Helena La Comba, wife of Gysbert Jansse
926	Marritje Pieters

1718
The 15th of April
On confession of faith

927	Claas Andriesse
928	Daniel Van Winkel
929	Pieter Marcelisse
930	Casper Pryer
931	Hendrik Sikkels
932	Neeltje Van Vegten, wife of
933	Rutgert Van Hoorn
934	Saartje Vanderbeek, wife of
935	Claes Andriesse
936	Jannetje Vreeland, wife of Daniel [or
937	David] Van Winkel
938–939	Elizabeth Gerritze, wife of Michl Vreelandt
940–941	Janneke Pryers, wife of Pieter Marcellisse
942–943	Geesje Borton, wife of Robbert Berri
944	Jannetje Mattheusse
945	Pietertje Toers
946	Marrytje Sikkelssze
947	Catharina Marcelisse
948	Rutgert Van Horne

1726
The 11th of April
On confession of faith

949	Johs Van Houwten
950	Helena Vreelant, wife of Johs Van Houten
951	Jenneke Van Houwten, wife of
952	Michl Vreelant

The 14th of June

953	Zachs Schiggelsse
954	Michiel Cornelisse Vreelandt
955	Dirk Frederikse Kadmis

1726

NO.
956 Ide Sippe
957 Jacob Van Wageninge
958 Henderik Van Winkel
959 Catelyntje Spier
960 Jannetje Cadmis
961 Adriaantje Siggelsse
962 Lea Van Wageninge
963 Antje Sippe
964–965 Helena Sippe, wife of Jan Van Hoorn
966 Helena Marcelisse
967 Catharina Waldron
968 Elizabeth Siggelsse
969 Claasje De Mott

1730
The 15th of March
On confession of faith

970 Marte Winnen
971 Michiel Hartmansche Vrelant
972 Hermanus Stynmets
973 Pieter Nederman
974 Hendrik Van der Hoef
975 Jurrie Gerritze
976 Jan Van Hoorn
977 Johannes Siggelse
978 Johannes Johannesse Vrelant
979 Cornelis Gerritze
980 Jannetie Johannesse Vreelant, wife of
981 Marte Wennen
982 Antje Dideriks, wife of
983 Johannes Johannesse Vrelant
984 Grietie Didericks, wife of
985 Jurrian Gerritze
986 Elsje Heriman, wife of
987 Hermanus Stymets
988 Evertie Slot, wife of Hendrik Van der Hoeven
990 Claasje Brinkerhof, wife of
991 Johannes Siggelsche
992 Aaltje Van Winkel, wife of
993 Cornelis Gerritse
994 Marrytie Brinkerhof—995 Annatie Spier
996 Antje De Mot

1731 NO.

1731
The 20th of September
With certificate

997–998 John Dideriks and Geertruy Van Winkeles, from Akquegenonk

1737
The 25th of April
On confession of faith

999 Helmig Van Wagenen
1000 Joris Vreland
1001 Abraham Sikkels
1002 Abraham Dideriks
1003–1004 Marytje Van Vorst, wife of Gerrit Hennion
1005–1006 Rachel Van Winkel, wife of Zacharias Sikkels
1007–1008 Geertruy Con [or Bon], wife of Abraham Dideriks
1009–1010 Annaatje Van Wagenen, wife of Joris Vreland
1011 Annaatje Van Winkele
1012 Saartje Kuyper
1013 Geertruy Kuiper
1014 Janneke Kuiper

1740
The 1st of April
On confession of faith

1015 Hartman Vreland
1016 Marytje Gerbrants, wife of
1017 Hartman Vreland
1018–1019 Aage Brinkerhof, wife of Abraham Siggels
1020 Elizabeth Van Namen

1743
The 28th of March
On confession of faith

1021 Hendrik Brinkerhof
1022 Jacob Van Wagenen
1023 Robert Siggelsse
1024 Jannetje Van Houwten, wife of
1025 Jacob Van Wagenen
1026 Catharina Siggels, wife of
1027 Cornelis Van Wagenen

NO. 1750 1750

The 2nd of April
On confession of faith

1028 Robert Siggelsse
1029–1030 Antje Winne, wife of Roberd Siggelsse
1031 Claasje Winne
1032 Marritje De Mot
1033 Geertruy Siggelsse

1751
The 6th of May
With certificate

1034 Pieter Adolf and
1035 Marritje Aalsze, married people of Akqueggenonck
1036 Here follow now the names of the members who by me, Pieter De Wint, are received, beginning in the year 1751 also, too, of those who are received with certificate.

A. D. 1751
September 5th

1037 Henricus Kuyper
1038–1039 Catharina Gerrebransen, wife of H. Kuyper
Here follow now the names of the members who, since the year 1757, at which time the services of the Reverend Mr. William Jackson took their beginning, are received into the congregation of Bergen either on confession of their faith or with certificate.

A. D. 1758
The 18th of June, with certificate from Tappan

1041 Elizabeth Fliereboom, wife of
1042 Marselus Marselus

A. D. 1758
The 18th of June

Are received to membership of the congregation on confession
1043 of faith Anna Frielinghuysen, wife of the Reverend Mr. William Jackson V. D. M. (Minister of the Word of God)
1044 Abraham Pryer and his wife
1045 Marritye Siggelse
1046 Johannes Pryer and his wife
1047 Geertje Siggelse

1758 NO.

The 30th of June

1048 Joris Cadmus and his wife
1049 Jannetje Vreeland

The 1st of December

1050 Jenneke Pryer and
1051 Catleyntje Toers

The 29th of December

1052 Pieter Steuversandt and
1053 Jan Roel

1759

The 2nd of June

1054 Cornelus Van Vorst Jun'r and his wife
1055 Anatje Van Hoorn
1056 Marytje Winne
1057 Lavinus Winne and his wife
1058 Anatje Sipp
1059 Machiel De Mot
1060 Nicholas Pryer
1061 Hermanus Veeder and his wife
1062 Antje Hennion
1063 Catharina Nieuwkerck
1064 Jennetje Nieuwkerck
1065 Jacob Van Winkel and his wife
1066 Rachel Camegar
1067–1068 Sytje Spier, wife of Johannes Evers
1069 Paulus Nieuwkerk and his wife
1070 Helena Spier
1071 Helmic Van Houten and his wife
1072 Effitje Vreelandt
1073 Johannes Van Wagenen and his wife
1074 Neestje Van Wagenen

The holy sacrament of the Lord's Supper has been administered in our congregation at Bergen by its Reverend Pastor and teacher first on the second day of rest of December 1759 being the 9th of the month.

Was received to membership in our congregation at Bergen on June the 6th

NO. 1760

A. D. 1760

1075 Cornelus Van Vorst—the elder

1761
The 6th of June

The holy sacrament of the Lord's Supper was administered here
in our church on the first Sabbath in June by our Pastor and
1076 guardian Wilhelmus Jackson
Is received to our congregation with certificate from New York
1077 Anna Van der Spiegel, widow of
1078 Mr. Patrick Jackson.

1762—May 21st

1079 Received to church membership Henoch Vreeland

A. D. 1763
The 11th of July

1080 Johannes Van Houwten, Jr. and his wife
1081 Aeltje Siggilse

The 24th of July

1082 Cornelius Gerribrans Jun'r and his wife
1083 Jannetje Van Horne

1764
The 10th of October

1084 Daniel Van Rypenen and his wife
1085 Elizabeth Terhunen

1765
The 14th of May

1086 Cornelius Gerribransen and his wife
1087 Jannetje Pier
1088 Cornelius Sipp and his wife
1089 Beeltje Vreeland
1090 Catharina Stuyversandt
1091 Daniel Van Winkel and his wife
1092 Aaltje Van Rype

1769 NO. 1769

The first Sabbath in April—the 2nd

1093–1094 Garrit Sip and his wife Jenneke Mercelius

It is determined by an ecclesiastical resolution to celebrate the Lord's Supper three times a year—the service being held four times a year on Staten Island.

Done in our consistory the first Sabbath in March 1769—Colleagues agreeing.

1095 Wilhelmus Jackson
Pastor.

1751

May 6th. Elected as consistory

1096 Elder—Michiel Vreland

1097–1098 Deacons: Joris Vreland; Robbert Siggelse Zachariaszoon

1099–1100 Churchmasters: Hendrik Van Winkel; Hendrik Brinkerhof

1785 March 28th.

1101–1102 Elders: Joannes Van Wagenen; Helmich Van Houte

Deacons:

1103 John Winne

1104 Daniel Diedricks

1105 Nicolas Toers

1106 Matheus —— Nieuwkerck

1786 April 16th

1107–1108 Elders: Helmich Van Houten; Joannes Van Wagenen

1109–1110 Deacons: Daniel Diedericks; Nicolas Toers

1111–1112 Churchmasters: Cornelis Van Vorst; Matheus Gerritse Nieuwkerck

1788 March

1113–1114 Elders: James Collerd; Gerrebrand Gerbrands

1115–1116 Deacons: Joannes Winne; —— Sickels

1117–1118 Churchmasters: Joseph Waldron; Hendrick Sickels

1119 Elders and deacons who signed the call to Rev. W. Jackson (done in the year 1753)

Elders:

1120 Zacharias Sickels

1121 Michiel Vreeland

1122 Johannes Diedericks

1123 Hendrik Van Winkel

1788

NO.

Elders—*Continued*

1124 Zacharias Sickels
1125 Joris Vrelandt
1126 Jacob Van Wagenen
1127 Abraham Sickels
1128 Machiel C. Vreeland
1129 Hendrik Van Winkel
1130 Hendrick Siggelse
1131 Jacob Van Wagenen
1132 Abraham Diedericks
1133 Zacharias Sickels
1134 Gerrit Van Nieuwkerk
1135 Lavinus Winne, and
1136 Robert Siggelse

Deacons:

1137 Joris Vrelandt
1138 John Van Horn
1139 Robbert Sickels
1140 Ide Sip
1141 Jacob Van Wagenen
1142 Gerrit Nieuwkerk
1143 Abraham Sickels
1144 Abraham Diedericks
1145 Hendericus Kuyper
1146 Joris Cadmus
1147 Helmigh Vanhoute
1148 Johannis Van Wagenen
1149 Pieter Stuyvesandt
1150 Lavinus Winne
1151 Hendricus Kuyper
1152 Abraham Preyer
1153 Joris Cadmus
1154 Johannis Van Wagenen
1155 Nicolaes Pryer
1156 Daniel Van Winckel

RECORDING SECRETARY 1914

OF

THE HOLLAND SOCIETY OF NEW YORK

MINUTES OF THE CONSISTORY,

BURIALS AND LIST OF MEMBERS

of the

REFORMED PROTESTANT DUTCH CHURCH

OF BERGEN IN NEW JERSEY,

Founded in 1660.

BERGEN, May 14–1716

Meeting of the consistory and resolved after calling upon the Lord's Name:

to remove some inconveniences in regard to the seatings. And it was further resolved; in order to prevent dissensions in the future, and that the church-masters may know how to deal without any (fear of) opposition, in several cases; to lay before the male members of the church certain salutary (heilzame) propositions made by the consistory, in order to decide upon them by a majority of votes. (For that purpose the congregation will be requested from the pulpit, in the forenoon, to come together in the barn belonging to Helmig Roelofse.)

This having been done, on the date and at the place aforesaid, all male members of the congregation who met

met there with the churchmasters and the consistory, resolved that in the future the following five articles shall be observed by the churchmasters and that everybody, whom they concern, shall have to submit to them, without opposition. Viz.:

I Members of the Church, who are in the possession of seats, by purchase, or by other lawful manner, shall remain in the peaceful possession of them, either till their death or until their departure or leave-taking from the congregation.

II All those who do not belong to the village of Bergen, or to this church and who do not contribute for the church, the school or the religious services, shall pay for every seat (either for man or woman) six shillings current money per annum, to the churchmasters or to one, authorized by them.

III The seats of those who die, shall revert to the church; but under condition that the churchmasters shall sell those seats for two shillings to the next heir of the deceased, if that individual applies for them, within one year, and if he or she belongs to the church, as described in the IInd Art. and under condition that such seat be one come down from the original builders of the church.

IV Those, possessing no seats in the church, and desiring to have one, shall apply to the churchmasters for the purchase of one and shall make arrangements with them.

V Those belonging to the congregation, as mentioned in Art. II, and having no seats, shall apply to the churchmasters,* who will, for this first time, in a very reasonable manner, make arrangements about their seatings.

* die met haar over hare zit plaatsen by deze eerste reize op eene zeer civile wyze wel zullen accordeeren.

EXPLANATION

EXPLANATION OF ABBREVIATIONS

ch.	means	child
wi.	"	wife
wid.	"	widow
da.	"	daughter
*	"	died
Bur.	"	buried
Y. M.	"	young man
Y. D.	"	maiden

(The *pall* was owned by the Church, and those able to pay for its use could have their relatives or friends carried to the grave with it on the coffin.)

CORRESPONDING SECRETARY 1914

OF

THE HOLLAND SOCIETY OF NEW YORK

INDEX OF BURIAL REGISTER AND LIST OF MEMBERS

of the

REFORMED PROTESTANT DUTCH CHURCH OF BERGEN

Prepared and Arranged by

DINGMAN VERSTEEG

Aalsze, Marritje, 1035.
Abrahams, Abrahamse, Cornelis, 40, 54.
Wybrant, 83.
Ackerman, Ackermans, Akkermans, Abigael, 902.
Abraham, 112, 139, 817.
Laurens, 732, 759.
Sara, 274.
Adansen, Jan, 70.
Adolf, Pieter, 1034.
Adriaens, Adriaansz, Ariaense, Ariaens, Annetje, 723.
Jan, 875.
Merritje, Marritie, Marritje, 176, 613, 727.
Aerts, Arents, Aertszen, Hendrickje, 677.
Hielitje, Hilletje, 150, 782.
Laurens, 697.
Lysbeth, 687.
Andrieszen, Andriessen, Andries, Andriese, Andriesse, Andriz, Arie, 660.
Catharina, Cathryn, 272, 693.
Fytie, 858.
Jannetje, 872.
Klaas, Claas, Claes, 359, 927, 935.
Marytje, 257.
Michiel, 323.
Rachel, 922.
Saartje, 241, 912.
Tanneken, 815.
Anthony, Jochem, 753.
Baelden, Katy, 579.
Baltusen, Macckje, 67.
Barentsen, Barents, Baltus, Baltes, 67, 810.
Bartholf, Guilliamme, 823.
Bayard, Balthazar, 638.
Catharina, 657.
Beekman, Catryntje, 267.
Berret, James, 536.
Berri, Robbert, 943.
Bockque, Bocquet, Bocke, Abraham, 814.
Jannetje, Jenne, 773, 838.
Bogard, Boogert, Aeltje Theunis, 785.
Cornelis Janszen, 706.
Jan Corneliszen, 708.
Koobus, 581.
Bokkenove, Keetje, 528.
Bon, Geertruy, 275, 504, 1007.
John, 550.
Borton, Geesje, 942.
Braeck, Braet, Claesje Dircks, 738.
Dirck Claesen, Dierck Claesz, Dirck Claeszen, 15, 130, 757.
Brestede, Treyntje, 195.
Brinkerhof, Blinkerhoff, Blinkerhof, 581.
Aagtje, Aegje, Aage, 395, 496, 1018.
Cornelis, 436, 438, 455, 900, 921.
Hartman, 455.
Hendrik, 438, 1021, 1100.
Klaasje, Claasje, 582, 990.
Margrietje, Margrieta, Margritje, 219, 364, 899.
Marrytie, 994.
Broeks, Willem, 514.
Brown, Brouyn, Lourens, 421.
Thomas, Tammes, 343, 421, 557.
Brouwer, Brouer, Jacob, 483.
Jacobus, 515, 534.
Lea, 515.
Uldrick, Olrig, 163, 215, 225, 919.
Bu——, Arien Pietersz, 55.
Buys, Daniel, 482.
Johannis, 482.
Tryntie, 868.
Cadmus, Kadmus, Kadmis, Cadmis, Catryntje, 261.
Dirck, Derk, Dirk, 261, 308, 309, 422, 955.
Fredrik, Frederik, 302, 344.
Jannetje, 261, 391, 960.
Johan, 308, 309.
Joris, 339, 383, 416, 422, 448, 545, 1048, 1146, 1153.
Machiel, 448.
Rutger, 307.

Camegar, Kammegaer, Rachel, 450, 468, 1066.
Carelsz, Carelszen, Carel, 73, 633.
Carlier, Adam, 839.
Cavelier, Cathelyntje, 262.
Johannes, 262.
Cembel, David, 443.
Cerven, Thomas, 109.
Claas, Claasen, Claes, Claesen, Claeszen, Claesz, Claesze, Clasen, Claasen, Andries, 216, 221.
Anna, 64, 609.
Arien, 179.
Bertel, Barteld, 166, 781.
Claes, 157.
Cornelis, Corn, 75, 206, 786, 831.
Cristiaen, 13.
Elizabeth, 821.
Gerbrandt, Gerbrand, Gerbrant, 80, 145, 179, 181, 227, 775.
Hendrick, 874.
Jan, 157, 192.
Marietje, Marritje, 227, 675.
Pietertje, 860.
Tryntie, 703.
Vroutje, Vrouwtje, 96, 794.
Coerten, Koerten, Guert, 169, 670.
Hermen, 78, 105.
Collerd, Callerd, Abraham, 433.
James, 1113.
Con, Geertruy, 1007.
Corne—, —ich, 22.
Cornelis, Corneliszen, Cornelisse, Cornelisz, Cornelissen, Cornelisen, Annetje, 117, 620.
Chieltje, 637.
Dierckje, Dirckje, 153, 606.
Gerrit, 634.
Gerritje, 121, 682.
Jannetje, 118.
Lysbeth, 104, 617, 683.
Matheus, Teeuwis, 52, 81, 100, 115, 118, 120, 680.
Roelof, 29.
Sara, 896.
Tryntie, 616.
Cos, Claes Pietersen, 188.
Creisson, Rachel, 745.
Croeger, Jacobus, 189.
Daden, Eva, 426.
Tammes, 426.
Daniels, Aeltje, Aeltjie, 129, 714.
David, 862.
De Grau, Abel, 464.
Maaike, 464.
De la Grancie, De Logransie, Lagrancie, Johannes, 322, 347.
Maragrietje, 458.
Metje, 347.
De Mareets, David, 740, 744.
Jean, 742.
Samuel, 746, 764.
De Mot, De Mott, Demoth, Demot, Antje, 996.
Claasje, Klaasje, 586, 969.
Gesie, 298.
Johannes, 290.
Machiel, 537, 588, 1059.
Marritje, 1032.
Matheus, Mathys, 219, 290, 298, 364, 370.
De Smidt, Françoys, 77, 79, 82, 87.
De Vouw, Esther, 215.
Nicolaes, 751.
De Wint, Pieter, 1036.
De With, Jan, 315.
Dey, Day, Willem, William, 158, 892.
Diederikx, Diederix, Dideryck, Diderix, Dideriks, Diedericks, Didericks, Diedricks, Diderikx, Diederyck, Diedericksze, Diedericksz en, Aaltje, Aeltie, 345, 440, 521.
Abraham, 275, 504, 1002, 1008, 1132, 1144.
Aegje, 465.
Annetje, Antie, Antje, 161, 430, 539, 553, 982.
Cornelis, 480, 556.
Daniel, 553, 1104, 1109.
Gerretje, 263.
Grietje, Grietie, 251, 984.
Hester, 507.
Jacob, 300, 304.
Johannis, Hans, John, 152, 276, 454, 456, 465, 507, 521, 602, 719, 997, 1122.
Marregriet, 456.
Wander, 161, 258.
Dircks, Dircx, Dirckszen, Dircksz, Diercks, Beletje, Belytje, Belitje, 218, 301, 865.
Geurt, 627.
Klaasje, 881.
Lysbet, Lysbeth, 12, 611.
Metje, 726.
Michel, 111.
Dorsuson, Mary, 840.
Dougels, Dogelis, Willem, 28, 68.
Douwesen, Poulus, 151.
Dreemus, Helmig, 511.
Hendrik, 511.
Druwyn, Maria, 763.
Drywen, Jacomyntie, 743.
Du Bois, Do, 873.
Du Cie, Maria, 752.
Duprie, Nicolaes, 774.
Du Tout, Du Toit, Abraham, 772, 837.
Anna, 842.
Duyts, Lourus, 6.
Dyell, Marte, 423.
Earle, Eerle, Eduard, 224, 793.
Johanna, 793.

Edsall, Etsal, Annetje, 695.
Sa, 32.
Eduwaerts, Eduwaertsz, Hermen, 48, 58.
Egberts, Egbertszen, Dirckje, 769.
Geertie, 758.
Sander, 847.
Eldersen, Elderszen, Ysbrand, 142, 851.
Elting, Jan, 652.
Epcese, Hendrick, 762.
Evers, Everse, Barbara, 415.
Barend, 561, 585.
Jan, Johannes, Johannis, 17, 415, 541, 549, 571, 1068.
Eyselstyn, Styntie, 549.
Feddens, Rensje, 819.
Fielden, Hendrick, Henri, 363, 529.
Fliereboom, Elizabeth, 1041.
Fransz, Fransen, Frans, Dirck, 123.
Gerrit, 49.
Maria, 778.
Thomas, 105.
Frederyks, Frederiksz, Fredericksen, Fredricksen, Fredrickszen, Geertruy, 910.
Marytje, 907.
Tomas, Thomas, 171, 176, 614, 641, 903.
Gedi, Jan, 167.
Gerbrants, Gerrebransen, Gerbrantse, Gerribrans, Gerribransen, Gerbrands, Gerrebrantsen, Gerbrandz, Gerbrantz, Catharina, Tryntje, 353, 1038.
Cornelis, Cornelius, 442, 452, 461, 488, 580, 1082, 1086.
Gerrebrand, 580, 1114.
Harpert, 220.
Jannetje, 442, 452.
Marytje, 1016.
Metje, 908.
Myndert, Meyndert, 353, 546.
Neeltie, 488.
Theunis, 390.
Gerrits, Gerritse, Gerritze, Gerritsen, Geritszen, Gerrritz, Aeltie, 857.
Aertje, 78.
Catryna, Catryntje, 113, 712.
Cornelis, 979, 993.
Elisabeth, Elizabeth, 233, 252, 661, 938.
Feytje, Fytie, 214, 797.
Geertruyt, Geertruy, Geertruyd, 49, 54, 681.
Geesje, 162, 632.
Gerrit, 141, 180, 211, 669, 788.
Geurt, 144, 200.
Jannetie, 755.
Jurrian, Jurjan, Juriaan, Jurrie, Jurriaan, 251, 263, 288, 975, 985.
Lysbeth, 200.
Gesscher, Jan Willemsz, 140.
Greeven, Thomas, 845.
Gysberts, Annetje, 784.
Haekki, Willem, 409.
Hansen, Annetje, 156.
Maddaleentje, 50.
Hardenbroeck, Adolf, 596.
Marritje, 605.
Hartmans, Hertmans, Aagje, 920.
Feytje, Feytie, 147, 618.
Hellingh, Hendrick Tonisen, (Teunissen), 154, 193.
Helmigsz, Helmigsen, Dirk, 905.
Gerritje, 911.
Roelof, 207.
Hendricks, Hendrick, Hendricx, Hendriksz, Hendriksen, Hendricxsen, Aeltje, 806.
Annetje, 648.
Belitie, 662.
Cornelia, 203, 805.
Geertie, 612.
Grietje, 889.
Jan, Johannes, 266, 834.
Jannetje, 48.
Joris, 127.
Martyntje, 824.
Samuel, 132.
Susanna, 736.
Willem, 114.
Hennion, Antje, 1062.
Gerrit, 1004.
Heriman, Elsje, 986.
Hermens, Hermans, Hermensen, Hermanszen, Annetje, 141, 180, 630.
Douwe, Douwen, 4, 88, 598.
Hans, 148, 165.
Harmtje, 690.
Ryckje, 659.
Hessels, Hesselsen, Pieter, 94, 137, 233, 689.
Hoogland, Keetje, 547.
Hoppe, Hoppen, Hopper, Andries, 901.
Catharina, 228.
Willem, 829.
Isbrants, Emmetje, 846.
J——, Jan, 2.
Jackson, Annetje, Annatie, 382, 427, 524.
Eva, 467.
Patrick, 524, 1078.
Robbert, 522.
Willem, Wilhelmus, William, W., Billy, 418, 427, 444, 467, 522, 566, 1040, 1043, 1076, 1095, 1119.
Jacobs, Jacobsz, Aechtje, Echtje, 15, 750.

Aeltje, 151.
Annetje, 891.
Grietje, Grietie, 615, 623.
Jacob, 128.
Leysbeth, 83.
Marritje, Maertie, 636, 808.
Mayken, 830.
Treyntje, Tryntie, 43, 619, 854.
Walyn, 692.
Jacobus, Jannetje, 852.
Jans, Janse, Jansen, Jansse, Janszen, Agnietje, 709.
Catryn, Tryntie, Catharina, 135, 653, 811, 893.
Claes, 63, 117.
Geesje, 707.
Gysbert, 916, 925.
Hendrickje, 779.
Hilletje, Hilletie, 194, 621.
Jannetje, 494.
Johannes, 108.
Joris, 494.
Magdaleentje, 684.
Marritje, 750.
Metje, 197.
Pieter, 622, 807, 808, 809.
Steyntje, 193.
Theunis, 835.
Johannis, Menno, 818.
Joorier, Marie, 741.
Jorisz, Joriszen, Joris, Hendrick, 127, 698.
Maryken, 861.
Juriansen, Jurrianzen, Jurriaansz, Jurryanse, Juryansen, Jurryansen, Jeuriaens, Juryans, Jurriansen, Jeuriaenszen, Jurriaasz, Jurrianze, Jurriaans, Aaltje, 218, 303, 906.
Belitje, 328.
Christyne, 866.
Cornelis, 289, 367.
Gerrit, 185, 218, 301, 324, 864, 871.
Haremen, 904.
Johannis, 292, 360.
Margrietje, 328.
Marytje, 895.
Thomas, 855.
Karmiegel, David, 314.
Karpis, Mary, 111.
Kerseboom, Kersenboom, Jan Evertse, (Evertssen), 7, 629.
Kiersted, Cornelis, 378.
Kleumpje, Jacob Jansen, 93.
Klyndland, Kleyndland, Aeltie, 577.
Elisabeth, 513.
Walter, 513, 577.
Koetere, Cateleyntje, 82.
Korsen, Pieter, 459.
Kroese, Gerrit, 582.
Kuyper, Kuiper, Cuyper, Claes Jansen, 99, 126, 230.
Dierck Claesen, 126.
Geertruy, 1013.
H., 1039.
Hendrick, Henricus, Hendericus, Hendricus, 369, 445, 1037, 1145, 1151.
Jannetje, Janneke, 445, 1014.
Zara, Saartje, 292, 1012.
La Comba, Helena, 924.
Lareu, Jacob, 747.
Lesier, Albert, 499.
Dirk, 499.
Loockermans, Marritje, 639.
Loosdrecht, Jan Willemszen, 646.
Lot, Loth, Beltel, Bartel, 3, 600.
Louwersz, Thomas, 85.
Lub, Jocob, 23.
Lubbertszen, Lubberts, Lubbertsz, Cornelis, 728.
Jan, 31, 37, 135, 672, 685.
Lubbert, 37, 704, 760, 766.
Marritje, 733.
Lubi, Luby, Anna, 81, 663.
Geertruydt, 635.
Jacob, 102, 121.
Luttye, Antie, 520.
Hendrik, 520.
Luwes, Luwis, Fransyna, 886.
Tim, 505.
Macale, Pieter, 257.
Mackleeyn, Mackeleyn, Sjarel, 56, 76, 91.
Martens, Maertens, Treyntje, Tryntje, 170, 177.
Mathewese, Matheuse, Matthysen, Mattheusse, Catriena, 311.
Cornelis, 120.
Isaac, 658.
Jannetje, 944.
Maurits, Jan, 8, 16.
Megapolensis, John, 645, 655.
S., 640.
Mercelis, Marcelus, Marcelusz, Marcelisse, Marselis, Marselus, Mercelius, Merseliz, Mercelisze, Marcelissen, Marcelis, Marscelusse, Marceliszen, Marcellisse, Aeltie, 491.
Annetje, 306.
Catharina, 947.
Elisabeth, 574.
Helena, 966.
Hillegont, 220.
Jenneken, Jenneke, 247, 530, 1004.
John, 574.
Marcelis, Marselus, 380, 393, 1042.
Pieter, 53, 62, 242, 247, 306, 434, 530, 686, 929, 941.
Seel, 491.

Mes, Abraham, 122.
Meyer, Meyers, Cornelis, 160.
Dierckje, Dirckje, 95, 664.
Jo., 160.
Mic—, Jan, 18.
Michiels, Michielsz, Michielse, Michielszen, Magiels, Mischilsz, Ariaentje, 674.
Catryntje, Tryntie, 631, 676.
Cornelis, 232.
Elias, 628.
Enoch, 673.
Hertman, Hartman, Herman, 33, 44, 802.
Johannis, Johannes, 735, 880.
Tades, 790.
Mulder, Hans, 110.
Matys, 42, 51, 110.
Nak, Jan, 217.
Nederman, Pieter, 973.
Nieuwenhuyzen, Nieuwenhuysen, Wilh, 668, 688, 694, 700, 710, 729, 748, 761.
Nieuwkerk, N. Kerk, Van Nukerck, Nieuwkerck, Van N. Kerck, Nieukerk, Van Nieuwkerk, Nieuker, Barend, 535.
Catharina, Catrina, Catrintie, 337, 388, 526, 1063.
Cornelis, 376, 552.
Gerrit, 337, 526, 531, 569, 1134, 1142.
Jacob, 453, 484, 490, 497.
Jannitje, Jannetje, 531, 535, 1064.
Lea, 376.
Lena, 484.
Marytje, 490.
Matheus, 191, 1106, 1112.
Paulus, Poulus, 329, 402, 453, 497, 1069.
Nolde, Nolden, Evert, 72, 678.
Paulus, Paulusz, Pauluszen, Pouwels, Aagje, 879.
Christina, 859.
Hilletie, 765.
Joh, 234.
Pieter, 853.
Petilions, Maria, 754.
Philipse, Philipsze, Dirk, 917, 923.
Pier, Catrina, 321.
Jannetje, 1087.
Pieters, Pieterse, Pietersen, Pieterszen, Pietersse, Pietersz, Adriaantje, 225, 918.
Adriaen, 701.
Antje, 280.
Catalyntje, 850.
Christiaen, 5.
Klaje, 848.
Gerrit, 137.
Hessel, 841.
Jannetie, 720.
Johannes, 265, 915.
Marcelis, 299, 316, 789.
Marritje, 926.
Metje, 870.
Niesje, Neesie, 211, 737.
Poulus, 35, 170, 177.
Tryntie, 701.
Polhemy, Polhemius, Adriana, 801.
John, 651.
Post, Adriaen, 41, 113, 589, 711.
Catryntje, 248.
Claartje, 878.
Cornelis, 542.
Egbert, 473, 542.
Frans, 836.
Pieter, 248, 256, 267.
Pryntje, 473.
Samuel, 256.
Preyer, Pryer, Preyers, Pryers, Abraham, 506, 572, 1044, 1152.
Andries, 93, 155, 175, 338, 449, 564, 590.
Arriaentie, 572.
Casparis, Casparus, Casper, 241, 290, 293, 300, 400, 930.
Geertruy, 564.
Hartman, 590.
Jacob, 293.
Jenneke, Janneke, 242, 940, 1050.
Johannis, Johannes, 333, 341, 408, 1046.
Marretje, 506.
Nicholas, Nicolaes, 1060, 1155.
Pryntje, 270.
Sara, 466.
Zacharias, 449.
Pyper, Gysbert, 199.
Ralewyn, Cornelia Jans, 140.
Hendrick Jansen, 133.
Reycke, Hendrick, 10.
Reynierszen, Wiggert, 601.
Richardson, Richard, 384.
Riddenhars, Reddenhars, Ridden Hars, Abel, 164, 183, 184, 199, 210, 888, 894.
Feytje, 183.
Hendrick, 184.
Roelofsze, Roelofs, Roelofzen, Roelofszen, Cornelis, 724.
Feytje, 57.
Geesje, 705.
Helmich, 699, 720.
Machtelt, 812.
Tonis, 74, 101.
Rol, Roel, Jan, 394, 1053.
Roos, Antie, 556.
Gerrit, 331, 523, 540.
Johannes, 540.
Judick, 331.
Pieter, 584.
Rynders, Barent, 882.
Hester, 884.
Saburasky, Albert, 768.
Samuels, Grietje, 154.

Schaets, Gid., 665.
Schofield, John, 349.
Schouten, Jan, 624.
  Sara, 625.
Selyns, Henricus, 799, 803.
  Rev., 168.
Seubering, Jan Roelofszen, 800.
  Lucas, 804.
Seylder, Jan, 117.
Sickels, Sickkels, Sikkels, Siggels, Siggilse, Siggelsse, Siggelsz, Siggelse, Sikels, Siggelsche, Sikkelssze, Schiggelsse, ——, 1116.
  Abraham, 326, 1001, 1019, 1127, 1143.
  Adriaantje, Ariaantje, 249, 478, 961.
  Aeltje, 1081.
  Catharina, 1026.
  Claasje, 240.
  Daniel, 489.
  Elizabeth, 968.
  Fredrick, 554.
  Fytje, 900.
  Geertruyt, Geertruy, Geertje, 182, 246, 338, 357, 1033, 1047.
  Hendrik, Hendrick, 246, 274, 460, 501, 544, 562, 931, 1118, 1130.
  Jennie, 544.
  Johannis, Johannes, 240, 268, 567, 977, 991.
  Lea, 196.
  Marrytje, Marritye, 946, 1045.
  Marte, 447.
  Rachel, 518.
  Robbert, Robert, 182, 239, 447, 475, 478, 1023, 1028, 1030, 1098, 1136, 1139.
  Sara, 562.
  Zacharias, Zacharyas, Zachs, 249, 250, 475, 489, 492, 518, 953, 1006, 1120, 1124, 1133.
Sip, Ziph, Sippe, Sipp, Siph, Antje, Antie, Anatje, 334, 406, 963, 1058.
  Catlyntje, 389.
  Claes Ariaenszen, 643.
  Cornelis, Cornelius, 406, 410, 446, 1088.
  Gerrit, Garrit, 477, 1093.
  Helena, 964.
  Ide, 334, 399, 446, 956, 1140.
  Jan, John, 89, 235, 579.
  Jenneke, 592.
  Margrietje, 913.
  Neeltje Ariaans, 110.
Slot, Eva, Evertie, 243, 280, 988.
  Lea, 483.
Smeeman, Hermen, 12.
Smith, Smit, Jacobus, Kobis, 377, 517.
  Maria, 885.
  Margen, Margon, Morgen, 253, 271, 296.
Solders, Solder, Annatie, 471.
  Daniel, 404, 470, 471, 472.
  Johannis, 404.
  Sara, 472.
Spenser, Willem, 9.
Spier, Abraham, 591.
  Annatie, Annetje, 254, 995.
  Barend, 294, 429.
  Catlyna, Catlyntie, Catelyntje, 327, 429, 959.
  Geertruy, 327, 362.
  Helena, 1070.
  Hendrick Jansen, 50.
  Johannes, Johannis, 305, 362, 778.
  Rachel, 320.
  Sytje, 1067.
Stammer, Maria, 644.
Steenhuys, Steenhuyse, Engelbert, Engelberth, 45, 599.
Stoffels, Annetje, Annatje, 206, 230.
Straat, Grietje, 870.
  Rachel, 877.
Stratenmaecker, Straetmaker, Straetmaecker, Stratemaeccker, Straetemaker, Annetje, 863.
  Dirck, 869.
  Gerrit Dirckse, 84.
  Jan, 47, 84, 162, 626.
  Janneken, 828.
  Rachel, 205.
Stuyvesant, Stuyvesants, Stuyversandt, Steuversandt, Stuyvesandt, Anna, 603.
  Casparus, 462, 527.
  Catharina, Catrientie, 538, 1090.
  Jenneke, 460.
  John, 502.
  Ned, 527.
  P., 270.
  Pieter, 405, 435, 502, 1052, 1149.
  Preyntie, 405.
  Sara, 462, 473.
Stymmets, Steynmetz, Steynmets, Steymets, Stymets, Stynmets, Steymits, Steenmets, Annetje, 739.
  Benjamin, 116.
  Casper, 20, 43.
  Christoffel, 832.
  Gerrit, 92, 96, 98, 136, 244, 792.
  Hermanus, 972, 987.
  Jannetje, 20, 608.
  Jo., 150.
  Joanna, 175.
  Johannis, Johannes, 200, 721.
  Urzelina, 822.
Suxbery, Mosis, 167.
Swoords, John, 516.
  Tomis, 516.

Tades, Thadus, Antje, 914.
Catlyntje, Catje, Katje, 253, 271, 296.
Talma, Douwen Hermesen, Douwe Hermense, 4, 38, 88, 598.
Harmen Douwenszen, 827.
Teckh, Tomas, 27.
Terhunen, Elizabeth, 1085.
Theunis, Tonise, Teunisen, Dirck, 111.
Dirckje, 607.
Hendrick, 46.
Michiel, 1.
Thomas, Thomassen, Tomasen, Thomaszen, Thomasen, Tomassen, Arien, Ariaen, 103, 172, 731.
Catharina, 796.
Francyntie, 716.
Frederick, Fredrick, 172, 228, 787.
Janneken, 849.
Johannes, 749.
Juryaan, Juriaan, Jeurinen, 65, 138, 601.
Timmer, Timmers, Jan, 606.
Petronella, 607.
Toers, Tours, A., 254.
Anna, Annatie, 174, 551.
Arent, Arend, 36, 64, 134, 525, 551, 679.
Catheleyntje, Catleyntje, 173, 1051.
Claes, Claas, Nicolaes, Nicolas, 134, 173, 174, 202, 229, 238, 656, 826, 1105, 1110.
Jacomina, Jacomyntje, 295, 471, 472.
Jan, 236, 791.
Johannes, 86.
Judikje Claasz, 898.
Lourus, Lourens, Louwerus, Laurens, 34, 59, 85, 86, 143, 717.
Pietertje, 945.
Van Ackersloot, Sophia, 114.
Van Benthuysen, Pieter, 340.
Van Blerkum, Van Blerekom, Jan Lubbertsen, 222.
Jo., Janse, 197.
Madelena, 222.
Van Boskerck, Boskerk, Van Boskerk, Van Boskerke, Boskerck, A., 264.
Andries, 189, 400, 474.
Cornelis, 348.
Geertruy, 459.
Jakobus, Jacobus, 417, 458.
Jenneken, 223.
Lourens, 273, 342.
Margrietje, 474.
Pieter, 212, 278, 282, 437.
Rachel, 385.
Sophia, 373.
Van Dam, Jacob, 356.
Nicolas, 354, 355, 356.
Vanderbeek, Saartje, 934.
Van der Bilt, Van de Bilt, Jacob, 493.
Jan Arentse, Jan Aertssen, John, 190, 493, 783.
Vanderhoef, Van der Oef, Van der Hoef, V. der Hoef, Van der Hoeven, Gerrit, 503.
Hendrick, Hendrik, 243, 286, 297, 312, 503, 974, 989.
Petrus, 570.
Vander Linden, Van de Linden, Van Linden, Jan Joosten, 777.
Joost, 57, 647.
Machtelt, 767.
Roelof, 798.
Van der Spiegel, Anna, 1077.
Van der Water, Hendrick, 649.
Van Duesen, Hester, 519.
Van Giesen, Van Gyssen, Abraham, 843.
Isack, Isacq, Isaac, Isaacq, 131, 178, 203, 844.
Jacob, 186, 856.
Johannis, 715.
Magdaleentie Reyniers, 725.
R., 30, 153.
Reynier, 131, 178, 201, 597.
Sebastian, 820.
Van Gilde, Gerrit Gerr., 124.
Van Hoorn, Van Hooren, Van Horn, Van Horne, Aagtje, 208.
Anatje, 1055.
Barent, Barend, 385, 403, 533, 543.
Cornelis, 486.
Eva, 543.
Helena, 335.
Jacob, 469, 508, 538.
Jan, John, 335, 351, 374, 381, 486, 510, 573, 965, 976, 1138.
Jannetje, 510, 1083.
Margrietje, 351.
Rachel, 508.
Rutger, Rutgert, Rut, 187, 281, 291, 933, 948.
Van Houten, Van Houte, Vanhoute, Van Houwten, Helmig, Helmich, Helmic, Helmigh, 237, 380, 396, 1071, 1102, 1107, 1147.
Jannetje, Jenneke, 325, 951, 1024.
Johannis, Johannes, Johs, 431, 463, 949, 950, 1080.
Van Kleeck, Baltus Barents, 90.
Pieter, 90.
Van Laer, Van Laren, Aeltje, 816.
Arien, 14.
Van Namen, Elizabeth, 1020.

Van Nes, Van Nest, Van Neste, Gerritje Cornelis, 102.
Jacomina, 825.
Sara, 867.
Van Oostrum, Van Ostrum, Jan, 776, 813.
Van Reype, Van Rype, Van Reypen, Van Rypenen, Aeltie, Aaltje, 441, 1092.
Beletje, 510.
Catrientje, 548.
Cornelis, 424, 439, 587.
Daniel, 1084.
Dirk, 500.
Gerret, Gerrit, 479, 485, 548, 568.
Jannetje, 563, 568.
Johannes, Johannis, 495, 563.
Margrietje, 548, 485.
Van Rhenen, Van Reenen, Gerrit, 69, 696.
Hendrick, 61.
Van Rossen, Jan, 104.
Van Vechten, Van Vegten, Neeltje, 281, 932.
Van Vleck, Isaac, 642.
Magdaleen, 604.
Tieleman, 595.
Van Vorst, Van de Vorst, Van Voorst, Van de Voorst, Van de Voors, Van der Vorst, Annetje, 160, 671.
Claasje, 457.
Cornelis, Cornelus, 106, 214, 269, 392, 397, 457, 586, 833, 1054, 1075, 1111.
Hillegont, 214.
Ide, 71, 194, 654.
Johanna Idens, 795.
Johannis, 397.
Marytje, 1003.
Pietertje, 299, 734.
Van Waert, Abraham, 498.
Betsie, 498.
Van Wagenen, Van Wagene, V. Wagenen, Van Wagening, Van Waagening, Van Wageninge, Aaltje, 365.
Antie, Annatie, Annaatje, Annetje, 284, 285, 465, 512, 555, 1009.
Catlyntje, Catleyntie, Catlyntie, 325, 479, 509.
Cornelis, 330, 1027.
Feytje Gerrits 269.
Gerrit, 260, 283.
Helmich, Helmig, 313, 330, 909.
Jacob, Jacop, 325, 470, 481, 490, 512, 550, 957, 1022, 1025, 1126, 1131, 1141.
Johannis, Johannes, 283, 368, 372, 509, 1073, 1101, 1108, 1148, 1154.
Lea, 481, 962.
Martje, 332.
Neestje, 1074.
Van Winckel, Van Winkel, Van Winkele, Van Winkeles, Aaltje, Altje, 289, 992.
Abraham, 578.
Annetje, Annatje, 702, 1011.
Daniel, 205, 375, 441, 928, 937, 1091, 1156.
Geertruy, 276, 998.
Hendrik, Hendrick, Henderik, 287, 419, 958, 1099, 1123, 1129.
Jacob, 129, 204, 231, 259, 413, 450, 451, 468, 487, 583, 593, 713, 890, 1065.
Jannetje, 432.
Joseph, 287, 468.
Lea, 487.
Margrieta, 360.
Rachel, 451, 1005.
Samuel, 358.
Simon Jacobszen, 722.
Walter, 578.
Van Woert, Sara, 558.
Van Wykensloot, Sofia, 217.
Van Zuure, Van Zuuren, Casparus, Casperus, 770, 780.
Veeder, Cornelis, 407.
Harmanis, Hermanus, 407, 425, 1061.
Jacob, 425.
Verleth, Nicolaes, 594.
Vermeulen, Grietie, 650.
Verwey, Verwy, Cornelis, Corn, 771, 779.
Vliereboom, Geertruy, 387.
Vrederyks, Christyntje, 897.
Vreeland, Vrelant, Vreelant, Vreelandt, Vreland, Aagtje, Aegje, 207, 512.
Annatie, 576.
Ariaantje, Arjaantje, 146, 250.
Beeltje, 1089.
Benjamin, 277.
Claes, 156, 389.
Cornelis, 592.
Effitje, 1072.
Elisabeth, 428, 587.
Elyas, Elias, 11, 39, 319.
Enoch, Enog, Henoch, 60, 95, 149, 208, 232, 277, 1079.
Gerrit, 336, 565, 575, 576.
Helena, 463, 950.
Hertman, Hartman, 107, 125, 198, 1015, 1017.
Jacob Enogsen, 255.
Jannitje, Jannetje, 111, 416, 936, 980, 1049.
Johannes, Johannis, Jo., 66, 97, 213, 226, 346, 539, 547, 560, 978, 983.

Joris, 284, 285, 317, 336, 361, 555, 575, 1000, 1010, 1097, 1125, 1137.
Klaasie, 318.
Michiel, Machiel, Michl., 125, 147, 213, 245, 252, 414, 428, 939, 952, 954, 971, 1096, 1121, 1128.
Pryntie Machielsen, 221.
Seitje, Feytje, (both a modification of Sophia), 213, 273.
Tryntje, 887.
Vrielinghuyse, Annatie, 467.
Ferdinandus, 444.
Waldron, Walderon, Walderom, Antje, 371.
Catharina, 967.
Geertruy, 420.
Joseph, 398, 420, 430, 532, 1117.
Walings, Ariaentje, 610.
Walters, Catharina, 883.
Ward, Polly, 443.
Warnarts, Waernaers, Margrietie, 718.
Willempje, 148.
Wessels, Grietje, 149.
Westervelt, Susanna, 583.
Wiggertszen, Hessel, 730.
Winckel, ——, 300.
Winne, Winnig, Winnen, Wennen, Antje, 1029.
Claesje, Claasje, 588, 1031.
Ide, 412.
Jannetje, 401.
Johannis, Joannes, John, 440, 1103, 1115.
Levinus, Lavynus, Lavinus, 352, 412, 1057, 1135, 1150.
Marte, 279, 970, 981.
Marytje, 1056.
With, James, 379.
York, Jan, 350.

ED:—The page proof of these records was read and compared by Dr. William B. Van Alstyne, a member of our Society, and the Society hereby acknowledges it indebtedness to him.

G

TREASURER 1914

THE HOLLAND SOCIETY OF NEW YORK

www.ingramcontent.com/pod-product-compliance
Lightning Source LLC
Chambersburg PA
CBHW071957220426
43662CB00009B/1169
* 9 7 8 0 7 8 8 4 0 6 3 5 5 *